REFORMING PUBLIC WELFARE

Reforming Public Welfare

A Critique of the Negative Income Tax Experiment

PETER H. ROSSI
KATHARINE C. LYALL

Russell Sage Foundation New York

PUBLICATIONS OF RUSSELL SAGE FOUNDATION

Russell Sage Foundation was established in 1907 by Mrs. Russell Sage for the improvement of social and living conditions in the United States. In carrying out its purpose the Foundation conducts research under the direction of members of the staff or in close collaboration with other institutions, and supports programs designed to develop and demonstrate productive working relations between social scientists and other professional groups. As an integral part of its operation, the Foundation from time to time publishes books or pamphlets resulting from these activities. Publication under the imprint of the Foundation does not necessarily imply agreement by the Foundation, its Trustees, or its staff with the interpretations or conclusions of the authors.

Russell Sage Foundation
230 Park Avenue, New York, N.Y. 10017

Library of Congress Catalog Card Number: 75-41509
Standard Book Number: 87154-754-6
Printed in the United States of America

To

Bettina Porcelli Rossi
Eleanor Guillan Lyall

CONTENTS

Preface *ix*

Chapter **1** Introduction: Background to the NIT Experiment *3*

Chapter **2** Designing the NIT Experiment *13*

Chapter **3** Fielding and Administering the NIT Experiment *45*

Chapter **4** Defining the Experimental Treatments *63*

Chapter **5** Measurement of the Dependent Variables in Analyses of the Labor Supply Response *87*

Chapter **6** Findings: Labor Supply Response *107*

Chapter **7** Non-Labor Supply Experimental Responses *133*

Chapter **8** The External and Internal "Politics" of the Experiment *157*

Chapter **9** An Overview Evaluation of the NIT Experiment *175*

Index *193*

PREFACE

This volume is a description and critique of one of the more important happenings in empirical social science research, the New Jersey–Pennsylvania Negative Income Tax Experiment. Its importance lies in several dimensions: It is a field experiment conducted according to the requirements of randomized controlled experimental design. It is also a research that is designed to yield information that is policy relevant in a direct way: The issue to which it was addressed was the detection and measurement of the work response of poor families to a set of policies that would provide them with guaranteed annual incomes and various graduated incentives to maintain, seek, and increase employment.

The research that went into the preparation of this volume was supported by Russell Sage Foundation as part of its program to support evaluations of policy related research. The senior author spent part of his time for a period of several years on the project although most of the effort was expended during 1973 and 1974 after the *Final Report* of the experiment was issued. In addition to a careful analysis of the *Final Report,* we also interviewed many of the principal researchers who contributed to the *Final Report*.

Margaret E. Boeckmann served for a year as a research assistant on the project, conducting interviews with researchers and policymakers on the influence of the experiment on welfare legislation, particularly the Family Assistance Plan introduced by the Nixon administration into Congress in 1969 and 1970.

This volume is the collaborative effort of the two authors, one a sociologist and the other an economist. The division of labor between the two of us was expressed in each taking primary responsibility for chapters that most closely fitted the individual's interests and skills. The senior author wrote drafts of Chapters 1, 3, 4, 7, 8, and 9. The junior author wrote Chapters 2, 5, and 6. The final chapter, 9, may be regarded as truly a joint product since it rests so heavily on the chapters that preceded it.

There are many persons who contributed to whatever success this volume may represent. We are especially grateful to the staffs of Mathematica and the Institute for Research on Poverty (IRP) for being generous with their time and for the open frankness with which they discussed their work and the research project. We are also indebted to the Writers of the Russell Sage, an informal group of persons working on evaluation research periodically brought together by Russell Sage Foundation staff. Members of the group, Hugh F. Cline, Howard Freeman, Arnold Shore, Henry Levin, Thomas Cook, Richard Snow, and Richard Berk patiently read early drafts of the manuscript and made many helpful comments as well as providing some of the more delightfully funny moments of the past three years.

The final version of this manuscript was materially improved by the comments on an earlier version provided by David Kershaw and the staff at Mathematica and by Harold W. Watts and his colleagues at the Institute for Research on Poverty. We have considered seriously every one of their comments, modifying the manuscript where that seemed to us to be appropriate. In the end there undoubtedly remain some—hopefully not too many—points of disagreement over interpretation and evaluation, as is probably inevitable.

Several versions of this manuscript were typed with skill, patience, and good humor by Laura Martin and Marcia Alves.

We are grateful for the help provided by all of the preceding: Obviously we are the only ones to be held responsible for the defects of the manuscript.

Peter H. Rossi
Amherst, Massachusetts

Katharine C. Lyall
Baltimore, Maryland

REFORMING PUBLIC WELFARE

Chapter 1

Introduction: Background to the NIT Experiment

INTRODUCTION

Although both are officially over, the two wars pursued by the administration of President Lyndon Johnson linger on. The scars of the Vietnam war will mark that country for some time to come, and poverty persists even though the headquarters of the War on Poverty, the Office of Economic Opportunity (OEO), has been closed. Our country will never quite be the same for its participation in these wars: The heritage of Vietnam has been a demystification of our institutions and that of the War on Poverty, a greatly expanded welfare sector in our federal, state, and local governments.

The War on Poverty had a special impact on the social sciences fostering the growth of applied social research far beyond what might have been extrapolated trends. A new high growth industry, consisting of firms and research centers specializing in evaluation research, is a direct outgrowth of the participation of social scientists close to the policymaking circles. Applied social research has become more and more respectable to social scientists aided, of course, by the shrinking of employment opportunities in higher education.

The immediate stimulus to the growth of applied social research arose out of the information needs of the poverty warriors. At the outset of the War on Poverty, it became almost immediately apparent that very little was known about the enemy. How many poor were there? How permanent was their condition? What were the special characteristics of the poor?

Where were they located? What role did discrimination in employment and in educational opportunities play in the maintenance of the poor in their condition? All these were questions for which only fragmentary answers existed in 1964. Social scientists were called upon to provide the answers.

As the war wore on, it also became abundantly obvious that we did not know what was an effective anti-poverty strategy. The very name, "Office of Economic *Opportunity,*" stressed that differential access to employment and other opportunities may well be the roots of poverty and that root causes lay in some maldistribution of opportunities. Part of the stress of poverty programs was on making institutions more responsive, as in the Community Action Programs (CAP). Some of the emphasis went into changing the characteristics of the poor: Noting that IQ's, and hence academic learning abilities, seem to be fixed at an early age, Project Head Start was almost immediately set in motion to aid disadvantaged preschool children to come into par with the more advantaged sector. A similar goal was set for the manpower retraining programs and for such youth oriented programs as the Job Corps and Neighborhood Youth Corps.

It did not take very long for everyone to begin to raise questions about the effectiveness of such programs. They certainly did not fulfill the highest aspirations of their advocates, but were they doing anything at all? Out of such questions arose the interest in evaluation research, the art of assessing the effectiveness of social programs through systematic research on outcomes.

To fill in the gaps of information on poverty and the poor, the Office of Economic Opportunity set under way a series of researches. Greatest in volume were the evaluation studies ranging from narrative accounts of what had transpired in a local manifestation of a program (e.g., a local CAP agency) to national assessments of a broad program, such as Head Start. Basic research that stood apart from the evaluation of any specific program was also undertaken. An inventory was taken of the size and distribution of the poverty population through the Survey of Economic Opportunity conducted by the Bureau of the Census. A longitudinal study of household income dynamics was launched by OEO and conducted by the Survey Research Center at the University of Michigan. Other studies looked at the characteristics of families on Aid to Families with Dependent Children (AFDC) programs, poor youths, and so on. Taken together, the studies of poverty launched by OEO provide us with quite detailed information on the poor, their distribution, and social characteristics.

Toward the end of the Johnson era, OEO launched what must be considered the most innovative of its applied social research projects. It undertook to apply experimental methods in settling of certain critical policy issues in a social program that had yet to be enacted. The New Jersey-

Pennsylvania Negative Income Tax Experiment stands out as an important departure from all previous researches conducted on social programs. First, it was a genuine experiment, involving the use of a social program as an experimental "treatment" given to certain subjects and withheld from a statistically equivalent control group.[1] Experiments with human subjects had been undertaken within a laboratory or within closed institutions, but a field experiment in which treatments were given to persons and families living *in situ* had not been undertaken before on such a large scale. One cannot stress too much *the importance of this experiment as setting a precedent,* one which was almost immediately taken up in a number of additional experiments sponsored by OEO, the Department of Health, Education, and Welfare (HEW), and the Department of Housing and Urban Development (HUD). Field experiments have become established as an acceptable and, even more important, especially desirable social science research technique in the study of social policy and its effects.

The second distinguishing feature of the experiment was that it dealt with *prospective* social policy. The negative income tax, which it was designed to evaluate, was a policy that at the time of the design of the experiment was seemingly far from appearing on the political agenda of either the White House or the Congress. Although negative income tax programs had been proposed for some years prior to the experiment, no one expected that any such proposals would be set before Congress within a decade or so. The purpose of the experiment was to contribute to the *formation of future policy* by providing information on several critical political issues, the most important being the labor supply responses of families receiving cash benefits.

An important theoretical issue was at stake for economists, namely the shape of the tradeoff relationships between work and leisure as affected by wage rate changes. Existing empirical data did not permit the unraveling of the relationships involved while the experiment promised an unparalleled opportunity to do so. It is clear that for economists the use of a "true experiment" would help to fix the form of a relationship about which only speculation existed. Empirically oriented economists were also interested in the possibilities of the experimental method as a new addition to their research arsenal.

In addition one of the more attractive features of the experiment to social scientists was that it seemingly provided a way in which the social scientist could play a more active role in the formation of social policy. There is

[1] This is not to say that large-scale field experiments had not been carried out before—the evaluation of the effectiveness of the Salk vaccine must be regarded as perhaps the largest scale field experiment yet conducted. The point is that the New Jersey-Pennsylvania Experiment used a social program as a "treatment."

more than a bit of the philosopher-king fantasy among social scientists to which the idea of social experimentation plays up.

"The New Jersey Graduated Work Incentive Experiment" is the official[2] name of the negative income tax experiment conducted under the sponsorship of OEO. Its importance as a precedent technically and politically was the rationale for this volume. There are important lessons that can be learned, we believe, from a careful examination of the Negative Income Tax Experiment (or NIT, as we will term it here).

Although the purpose of the experiment as seen by the experimenters at the outset was a relatively narrow one, the importance of the experiment was such that it had implications for matters that went far beyond the original purpose of testing out the work responses to a limited range of negative income tax plans among the poor with intact families living in urban areas of the Northeast. Correspondingly, there are a variety of ways to examine and evaluate the experiment.

Although we could stay within the narrow framework of the designers' intentions, to do so would not be responsive to the many ways in which NIT has been used. Hence, we will consider NIT from a variety of perspectives:

as a limited objective field experiment;

as part of the political decision-making process;

as a contribution to the advancement of social experimentation in the field.

There are many lessons to be learned from the experiences of NIT in each of the enumerated respects. It is the purpose of this volume to draw out these lessons as clearly as possible.

The central tone of this book is critical by definition of its purpose. It is by probing around and uncovering mistakes as well as good judgments that one can derive lessons for the future. It is all too easy to be hypercritical, for no research lives up to the standards any novice can set for high quality research. It is much more difficult to judge whether a research is fulfilling its purpose, given the constraints of time, money, and previous knowledge. We are sure that we have often fallen into the trap of being more critical than charitable. Hence, it may be easy for a reader to misapprehend the critical nature of this study as a negative judgment on the experiment as a whole. Since that would be far from our actual judgment, we want to state firmly at the outset our overall assessments of the NIT Experiment.

> First, the NIT Experiment is a remarkable achievement in design, data collection, and analysis.

---

[2] The understandable sensitivity of OEO to possible political flak for its sponsorship of the experiment is well expressed by this official title. The purpose of the experiment was to ascertain whether there was any work *disincentive:* Hence the title turns everything around and concentrates on the happy rather than unhappy outcome.

Second, it is difficult to imagine a set of social scientists doing much better in those respects given the state of prior knowledge concerning the substantive area and the state of the art concerning field experiments.

Third, ranked in relation to other larger scale researches of the contemporary period, the NIT must be considered, if not first, at least among the best two or three.

In short, we are unabashed admirers of the researchers and of their accomplishments. Our critical comments are designed not to detract from these accomplishments but to capitalize upon them.

BACKGROUND TO NIT

The idea of a negative income tax as a substitute for existing welfare programs had been circulating since the rediscovery of the poor in the early 1960s. The essential features are appealingly simple: A floor under income is to be set to which all persons or families would be entitled if they had no earnings or other income. Families or persons with positive incomes would receive subsidies until their total income (including subsidies) reached a break-even point. Subsidies for persons with positive incomes would be reduced by a "tax rate" such that for every dollar earned the subsidy would be reduced by a rate less than one. Hence, the essential features of a negative income tax plan are a set of guarantees (g) setting the income floors below which persons or families would not be allowed to sink and tax rates (r) applicable to earned income. A break-even point would be defined by income reaching g/r, the point at which subsidies would be reduced to zero.

There are several attractive features to the negative income tax proposal: First, as a substitute for existing welfare programs, it defined the problem of poverty as primarily a matter of income. Second, it appeared to simplify the administration of welfare. As the title of the proposal implies, the negative income tax could be administered by the Internal Revenue Service with persons or families receiving subsidies based on year-end rebates (if eligible) or prospectively on the basis of estimated income. Third, the line between the poor and the non-poor would be less clearly drawn with subsidies going to the working poor as well as those with no income at all. Fourth, there would be a positive incentive for work effort since, unlike then existing welfare programs, subsidies would not be reduced dollar for dollar if there were earnings.[3]

[3] A change in the Social Security Act in 1967 imposed a tax rate of .67 on welfare, meaning that welfare benefits would be reduced by two-thirds of a dollar for each dollar of other income. Certain forgiveness features actually reduce the tax rate even more. (See Chapter 4.)

Very early in the life of the Office of Economic Opportunity, the research staff, consisting mainly of economists, had discussed a negative income tax as a proposal that might be put forward as an anti-poverty program. There was little optimism in that early period, however, concerning its political viability. The objections to a negative income tax program were strong ones: First, it would undoubtedly cost more than the existing welfare programs, since coverage would be extended to the working poor, the amount of extension being a function of what set of *g*'s would be proposed. Second, although there were incentives for working, there were also incentives for decreasing work effort. A person could cut back on his work effort entirely and subsist on *g* or cut back proportionately and have an increment to his leisure subsidized by the government. These objections, it was felt by the staff, would be especially strongly held among the more conservative members of Congress.

As the War on Poverty wore on and poverty seemed obstinately resistant to the main programs of OEO, staff members became more interested in negative income tax plans. In addition, in 1967 President Johnson set up a White House task force to investigate income maintenance plans and to report to him on their feasibility. It was into this atmosphere of increasing interest in the negative income tax idea that a proposal came into OEO suggesting that the negative income tax be tried out in an experiment to be conducted in Washington, D.C.

The proposal had been submitted to OEO by Heather Ross, a graduate student in economics at MIT, who had been serving as a fellow at Brookings Institution. Her proposal, submitted under the sponsorship of a Washington, D.C., CAP agency, called for an experiment in which a group of 1,000 D.C. families would be enrolled, some to be given payments under an NIT plan and others to serve as a control group. The purpose of the experiment was to measure the labor supply response of the families.

Heather Ross' proposal was circulated among the staff and to others outside OEO. Although the particular proposal was turned down, the idea of an experiment did take hold. OEO research staff began to look for someone to undertake the experiment and found a congenial organization in Mathematica, a research firm started in Princeton, New Jersey, by academics at Princeton University. A proposal submitted by Mathematica in 1967 with Albert Rees and William Baumol (both at Princeton) as principal investigators was seen as representing a reasonable approach.

Because OEO officials were concerned that the direct financing of a negative income tax experiment might be viewed by Congress as encroaching on its policymaking role, it was decided to fund the Mathematica proposal through the University of Wisconsin Institute for Research on Poverty. IRP had been established by OEO as its basic research arm and "think tank": Funding NIT through IRP, it was thought, would emphasize the research as opposed to the policy aspects of the experiment. Hence, the final arrangement was for the prime contractor to be the Institute for Research on Poverty with Mathematica as subcontractor.

The final proposal was very strongly supported by OEO's research staff, presented to OEO head Sargent Shriver, and approved in early 1967. By fall, 1968, a tentative design had been agreed upon and recruitment of families to participate started in Trenton, New Jersey.

As finally decided upon, the experiment's main purpose was to estimate the labor supply responses of families to a range of negative income tax plans. Subsidiary interests included other possible effects as, for example, purchase patterns, family stability, and health. The target population was to be intact families whose male heads fell within the age range of 18 to 58, who were below 150 percent of the then current poverty level as determined by the Bureau of Labor Statistics (BLS), a group selected because the labor supply response of these families were most critical politically.

A number of specific decisions had to be made before the experiment could be sent into the field. Some of these decisions, as we will show in later chapters, had profound effects on the conduct of the experiment and the generalizability of results. To begin with, a decision was made to field the experiment as a small number of "test bores" rather than as a national effort. Initially three sites within New Jersey were selected, later to be augmented with a fourth site in Pennsylvania. New Jersey was selected for a number of reasons besides convenience, including a sympathetic state welfare administrator and the absence of an AFDC plan that would cover families with unemployed fathers (AFDC-UP) in New Jersey.[4]

A second critical decision involved the range of NIT plans that would be tested: Guarantee levels were set to range over the following values: 50 percent, 75 percent, and 100 percent of the poverty level[5] (as defined by BLS standards), and tax rates were to range from 30 percent through 50 percent to 70 percent. These levels were picked to center around what were thought to be the levels of *g* and *r* that were politically acceptable.

Fieldwork started in the summer of 1968 with the first families enrolled in Trenton in the fall of 1968. Enrollment efforts continued through the fall of 1969 with families being enrolled in Paterson-Passaic, Jersey City, and finally in Scranton, Pennsylvania. By the end of 1969, more than 1,000 families had been enrolled in the experiment, assigned either the

[4] New Jersey's welfare plans provided for welfare payments to father-absent poverty families but barred payments to families in which an adult employable male was present. Initially this meant that the experiment would not be competing with an existing welfare plan since eligibility for participation in the experiment was restricted to precisely those families that were excluded from New Jersey's existing (1968) welfare plan.

[5] After New Jersey enacted a very generous AFDC-UP welfare plan, an additional guarantee level, 125 percent of poverty level, was added.

experimental or control condition, and within experimental conditions to one of eight different NIT plans, as described in greater detail in Chapter 2.

As planned, the experiment ended in 1972 after three years of fieldwork.

THE ORGANIZATION OF THE EXPERIMENT

The original division of labor between Mathematica and the Institute for Research on Poverty called for the former to bear the operational responsibilities and both to share the design and analytical responsibilities. The staff at Mathematica included David Kershaw, who managed the operations side, and Albert Rees and William Baumol, faculty members at Princeton University, who served as principal investigators. Additional faculty members and graduate students from Princeton participated from time to time.

The Wisconsin group included the director of IRP, Harold Watts, and staff members of the IRP. The list of participants on one or another stage of the experiment is relatively large. The *Final Report* has almost a score of authors.

Economists played dominant roles in all phases of the experiment. The principal investigators at Princeton and Mathematica were well-known economists. The major staff members at IRP, for example, Harold Watts, Glen Cain, Robinson Hollister and Charles Metcalf, were also economists. Sociologists and social psychologists were to play minor roles in both the design and the analysis.

The dominance of the economists is quite in line with the major purpose of the experiment. After all, as we will see in Chapter 2, it was economic theory that predicated a labor supply response although theory was quiet about its magnitude. Yet, in another sense, the dominance of economists in an *experiment* is not in line with disciplinary use of experimentation as a technique. The experimental tradition is very strong in many of the life sciences and strongest among the social sciences in psychology. Sociologists —particularly social psychologists—also have used experiments primarily in laboratories or small scale field settings. But economists have very little experience with the technique.

In addition, most of the experiment's operations were similar to those involved in sample surveys. Disciplinary traditions were stronger in the use of sample surveys among sociologists and social psychologists than among economists.

The intellectual dominance of the economists shows throughout the design of the experiment and in the *Final Report*. The design controversy, discussed in detail in Chapter 2, was essentially an issue over the efficient allocation of resources given a theoretically expected model of labor supply response. The modes of analysis are those favored by persons trained in econometrics. Not only are the strengths of economists reflected in the experiment, but also some of the mistakes and omissions of the experiment show the mark of the dominant economists.

THE SCOPE OF THE NIT EXPERIMENT

The experiment ran for three years and involved about 1,300 families, approximately equally divided between the experimental and control groups. Families in the experimental group were placed in one of eight NIT plans, defined by a combination of g and r. When an experimental family's income fell below the break-even point for its plan, as revealed in its monthly income report to Mathematica, it received a payment. Payments were adjusted monthly to reflect the income of the family.

Families allocated to the control group were interviewed quarterly and annually as were members of the experimental group. The quarterly and annual interviews were concerned mainly with detecting family responses to the experiment: A core section was devoted to ascertaining earnings, hours of work, and other sources of income for members of each of the families, and a variable supplement measured other types of response, e.g., expenditures, stocks of durables, attitudes, and so on. The thirteen quarterly interviews obtained from the participating families serve as the basic data series that were analyzed.

More than $7.5 million was expended in the conduct of the experiment, as shown in Table 1.1. The expenditures were a considerable overrun on

Table 1.1
Overall Cost of the NIT Experiment

A. *Administration and Research*		
Mathematica	$4,426,858	
IRP-University of Wisconsin	812,648	
Subtotal		$5,239,506
B. *Transfer Payments*		2,375,189
Grand Total		7,614,695

the initial estimates of approximately $3 million. Most of the unanticipated expenses occurred on the research side. The handling of large and complicated data sets was simply much more costly than anyone had anticipated. In addition, the extra costs incurred by a heavy attrition rate also sent the expenditures higher on the operations side. Kershaw[6] estimates that

[6] David Kershaw, *Final Report*, vol. III.

the administrative costs of handling transfer payments amounted to about $90 per family per year, or about $350,000 for the three-year duration of the experiment. The remainder of administrative and research costs (approximately $4.6 million) was expended in the collection of research data (quarterly and annual interviews), data preparation, and analysis. Since most of the analysis staff costs are represented by the funds expended by IRP at Wisconsin, it is apparent that data handling was the most expensive part of this very expensive experiment.

THE ORGANIZATION OF THIS STUDY

The purpose of this study is to provide an overview of the NIT Experiment and an evaluation of its conduct and outcome. It is based primarily on the *Final Report* issued by Mathematica and IRP.[7] In addition, we visited both Mathematica and the Institute for Research on Poverty and interviewed many of the principals involved.

The *Final Report* contains about 1,500 typed manuscript pages. It consists of chapters contributed by those who worked on the analysis of the resultant data. Some of the chapters appear to be interim reports; others are more finished in content and style. Nothing will replace reading the *Final Report* itself. However, since the *Final Report* is some months from printing and is by no means an easily accessible volume, we have taken the liberty of summarizing some of the major findings here.

Our plan is as follows: Chapter 2 considers the design of the experiment and examines the reasoning that lies behind the particular forms taken by the experiment. Chapter 3 looks at the fielding and administration of the experiment. Chapter 4 is concerned with what were the treatments that were administered to families participating in the experimental group and contrasting that treatment with what was available to families in the existing welfare systems of New Jersey and Pennsylvania. Chapters 5 and 6 are concerned with the central purpose of the experiment, measuring and evaluating the labor supply responses of the families. Chapter 7 covers nonlabor force measures and results. Chapter 8 provides a view of the external politics of the experiment. Finally, Chapter 9 contains an overall assessment of the experiment.

Throughout the chapters that follow, references are given to volumes of the *Final Report* in its current (1974) form.

---

[7] Institute for Research on Poverty and Mathematica, *Final Report of the New Jersey Graduated Work Incentive Experiment,* vols. I–IV, mimeographed (Madison, Wis. and Princeton, N.J., 1974). These volumes are scheduled to be published by Academic Press, New York, N.Y. in 1976.

Chapter 2

Designing the NIT Experiment

INTRODUCTION

Since the design of an experiment is so critical to the interpretation of its findings, we will devote this chapter to laying out the considerations that went into the design of the NIT Experiment. We will pay a great deal of attention to the controversy (briefly described in the previous chapter) that arose within the research group over several crucial design issues. The design controversy is a particularly valuable focus since so many of the issues in question lie at the heart of a much larger issue, namely, the generalizability of the empirical findings of NIT.

The particular resolutions of the design controversy that were adopted turned out to constrain interpretation of the experimental results in ways not always sufficiently anticipated or appreciated at the time. This issue has greater import than it might at first appear since subsequent experiments (Seattle, Denver, Gary, and the rural experiments) faced many of the same design decisions and have drawn heavily on the New Jersey experience in resolving them. Since all experiments are necessarily limited in time and budget, design choices embody certain unavoidable tradeoffs between precision and the scope of questions that can be posed. In the course of identifying and analyzing these choices the NIT Experiment has made a number of important contributions to the experimental design literature.

Most of the information on the content of the controversy lies in memoranda exchanged internally among the members of the project at the University of Wisconsin and Mathematica; so far as can be ascertained, only the final "resolution" of the controversy in the form of the Watts-Conlisk model[1] and the Tobin solution,[2] reported as the final sample allocation in the *Final Report* documents, are readily available in published form.

In analyzing the impact of experimental design decisions on the interpretation of results, it is useful to think of the experimental design process as a series of design decisions, both exclusionary and enabling, ranging from the formulation of the major experimental hypothesis to structuring of simple administrative and field procedures.

In the NIT[3] these included decisions to

1. structure the experiment as a *single treatment* design (i.e., as a test of NIT plans alone) thereby ruling out the possibility of discovering interactions between NIT and other programs, such as manpower training and day care. (Such composite programs were incorporated in later income maintenance experiments in Seattle, Denver, and Gary.)
2. define the *target population* as work-eligible, male-headed families thereby precluding tests of the responses of a large percentage of the poor located in female-headed families and unemployables.
3. reject a *national probability sample* in favor of test bores in a few sample sites thereby reducing the ability to generalize to a national population.
4. specify *urban sites* thereby introducing the possibility of site bias from special features of those particular labor markets and eliminating generalizations of results to the *rural* poor.[4]
5. define a *particular policy space* in *g* and *r* as "relevant" and specify eight points within it as the plans to be tested thereby eliminating the detection of direct response outside this range and to other parameters.
6. select a *particular regression model* embodying certain assumptions about the probable shape of the response surface and the values of its parameters as the *method by which the sample was allocated* across the eight experimental plans and the control group thereby introducing misspecification error as the price of minimizing inefficiency in use of the experimental budget.

To identify these discriminations in the experimental design is *not* to

[1] John Conlisk and Harold Watts, "A Model for Optimizing Experimental Designs for Estimating Response Surfaces" (1969 Proceedings of Social Statistics Section, American Statistical Association), pp. 150–156.

[2] James Tobin, "Sample Design for NIT Experiment" (internal memo to Harold Watts and William Baumol), May 1969.

[3] See Margaret Boeckman, "The Contribution of Social Research to Social Policy Formulation: A Study of the New Jersey Income Maintenance Experiment and the Family Assistance Plan" (Ph.D. diss., The Johns Hopkins University, 1973), p. 66.

[4] A complementary rural NIT experiment was mounted shortly after the urban experiment was designed to complete the evidence on the range of potential labor response.

imply that all or any of these design decisions were wrong—although we argue later that some *were* indeed unfortunate in terms of limiting the interpretation that could later be made of the experiment's results—but rather to sketch out the reasoning that lay behind the choice to limit and focus their design. Since in an NIT, the cost of the treatments themselves vary with the experimental parameters, the problem of experimental design was centered on an optimal efficient allocation design. The bulk of the following discussion is concerned with the contributions of NIT to the efficient allocation of a fixed budget over alternative treatments. Internal debate on this became known as the "design controversy." As will be seen, an important outcome of this debate was a strong contribution to the literature on the design of field experiments.

ANALYTICAL STRUCTURE OF THE NIT EXPERIMENT—A BRIEF SUMMARY

To understand the technical design problems that are the main subject of this section, it is necessary first to have a rather specific notion of the theory that the experiment was expected to test. The negative income tax was proposed by economists to meet the income needs of poor families. The major negative attribute of NIT was seen to be the work disincentive it might set up in a sizable proportion of the population. Accordingly it was determined to focus the experiment on estimating the direction and magnitude of the labor supply response over the feasible range of two crucial negative income tax characteristics: the minimum income guarantee level (g) and the marginal tax rate (r) on earnings up to the break-even income level.

A concise way of viewing the analytics of the labor supply problem is represented graphically by a standard consumer choice diagram (Figure 2.1) showing the relation between cash income (earned by working) and leisure.[5] The indifference curves (1, 2) represent the preferences of an individual or family unit for division of their available time resources between work (i.e., the income earned) and leisure. By definition, the slope of line AB represents the rate at which leisure can be exchanged for income, that is, the relevant wage rate (w) for that household. (Note that increasing work time on this diagram is measured from point B, representing twenty-four hours/day of leisure, left towards the origin.) The equilibrium combination of income and leisure for such a consuming unit is found at the point of

[5] A standard exposition is Christopher Green, "Negative Taxes and Monetary Incentives to Work: The Static Theory," *Journal of Human Resources* 3 (1968): 280–288.

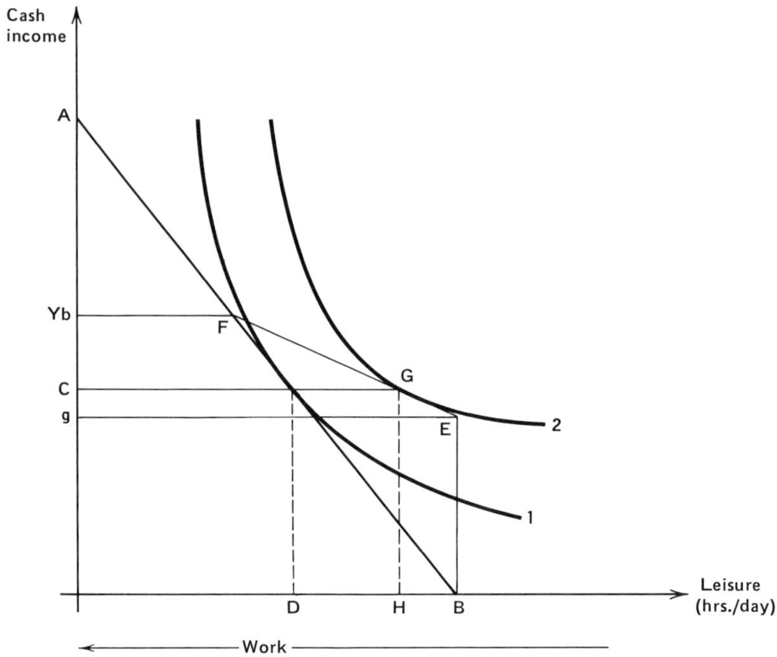

Figure 2.1
Theoretical Model of Work Response

tangency between *AB* and indifference curve 1, corresponding to *C* dollars of cash income and *D* hours of leisure; that is, *DB* hours of work yield *$C* of income.

The effect of an NIT program is twofold: 1) It sets a floor or minimum cash income (g) that can be received even at full leisure (B); 2) it changes the relevant wage rate faced by the respondent since he is permitted to keep, on income earned over the minimum, only a fraction ($l - r$) that is translated into cash income, the difference being used to offset the NIT payment.[6] At earned income levels above the break-even point (Y_b), no payments are received and the market wage (w) is effective.

Clearly, this "broken" wage line (AFE) is tangent to a higher indifference curve (2) at point *G* corresponding to more leisure (H), i.e., less

[6] Existing categorical welfare programs until recently taxed earnings at 100 percent; that is, earnings were deducted dollar for dollar from welfare entitlements. Recent changes in this much criticized feature have produced some reduction in the implied tax on earnings by exempting the first so many dollars and including certain work-related expenses as deductions from earned income. (See Chapter 4 for computations of empirical tax rates applicable to NIT sites' welfare plans.)

work, and, as drawn here, about the same cash income level (C). This is not the *only* possible result, however, since the positioning of the particular respondent's indifference map, steeper or flatter, governs the position of G relative to F. Should the second tangency occur at E, the recipient ceases work altogether and accepts the minimum income (g)—the apparent fear of many conservative congressmen. It follows that the higher the tax rate (r) is set—and so the flatter the wage segment (FE)—the greater the probability that the corner solution "quit option" will occur. The same effect would be produced by increasing the marginal tax rate (r) on earnings above the minimum.[7]

Thus the functional relation of the policy parameters to the work-leisure choice is defined: The higher g and/or r are set, the greater the reduction in work and the more likely are large numbers to find the "quit option" optimal. By the same token varying combinations of g and r alter the "gap" between the minimum income and the "break-even" level, that is, the range over which one is eligible for NIT payments—the larger this gap, the more people become eligible recipients and, of course, the more costly is the total program. The feasible combinations of these policy parameters, then, are constrained by

1. some maximum limit on the size of the gap;
2. some political-social minimum (or maximum?!) limit on g;
3. some behavioral or psychological maximum (based on feelings of equity) on r.

It is the income (or work) response over this feasible policy space that the NIT Experiment was designed to estimate.

How best to design the experiment to address these issues engaged the IRP staff and the staff at Mathematica in a heated intellectual debate. This controversy is of interest here because of the considerable body of theoretical literature[8] generated on optimal experimental design and because of the adoption of the same or a similar design model for subsequent large-scale social policy experiments, such as SIME, DIME, and the RAND Health Insurance Experiment.

---

[7] Further theoretical investigations have been made of schemes incorporating both progressive and regressive marginal tax rates. These were eliminated in the experiment as being too complex to be understood by participants and too difficult to administer. See Perlman, *Journal of Human Resources*.

[8] Much of this literature is in the form of mimeographed memos exchanged between members of the Institute for Research on Poverty at the University of Wisconsin and Mathematica in Princeton, New Jersey, which are relatively inaccessible. The major published documents on the design problem are Watts and Conlisk, "A Model for Optimizing Experimental Designs for Estimating Response Surfaces," and a more recent, generalized contribution by Conlisk, "Choice of Response Functional Form in Designing Subsidy Experiments," *Econometrica* 41 (1973): 643–656.

The substance of the design controversy can be characterized as a choice between testing more experimental alternatives with greater sampling variance in the results versus coverage of fewer experimental treatments with a smaller sampling variance in results. The essence of the dispute sprang from the fact that an experimental design that covered only a few points with greater accuracy would, as it turned out, allocate a large part of the observations to inexpensive "no-payment" families composed of the non-poor and control groups and provide little coverage of interior design points. While statistically and economically efficient, it was argued that an attempt to estimate the national reaction to a poverty program from observations drawn largely from the non-poor and nonpayment recipients is counterintuitive. Furthermore, because the experiment was expensive and lengthy, both groups were anxious that its results be as conclusive as possible. In this sense, the design controversy concerned critical issues in the attempt to establish experimentation as a useful and effective technique for social policy analysis.

CONSTRUCTION OF THE POLICY SPACE

One simple way to comprehend the substance of the allocation problem in social policy experimentation is to envisage the relevant policy space to be investigated. A policy space is defined by the range of one or more policy parameters deemed of interest to decisionmakers. In the case of the NIT Experiment the relevant policy space was defined over the following ranges of the minimum income guarantee level (g) and the marginal tax rate (r) on income received above level g.

Graphically, the policy space for each of the three income strata may be represented as in Figure 2.2 where $g =$ the minimum income guarantee expressed as a percentage of the officially defined poverty level for a family of four (taken to be \$3,300 in 1968 when the experiment was begun), and $r =$ the constant marginal negative tax rate to be applied to earnings above g. $Y =$ the response surface measured in earned income (or alternatively, in hours worked).

While any point in this space is *possible,* only a subset of points represent *relevant*[9] policy alternatives. In the case of the NIT the relevant ranges of alternatives were thought to lie between $r = 30$ percent to 70 percent and

[9] "Relevant" had several specific meanings in the design process: it sometimes meant what was possible within the budget constraints of the project; sometimes what was within the range of politically possible future NIT enacted programs; and at other times, what would be politically acceptable in a social experiment started in 1968.

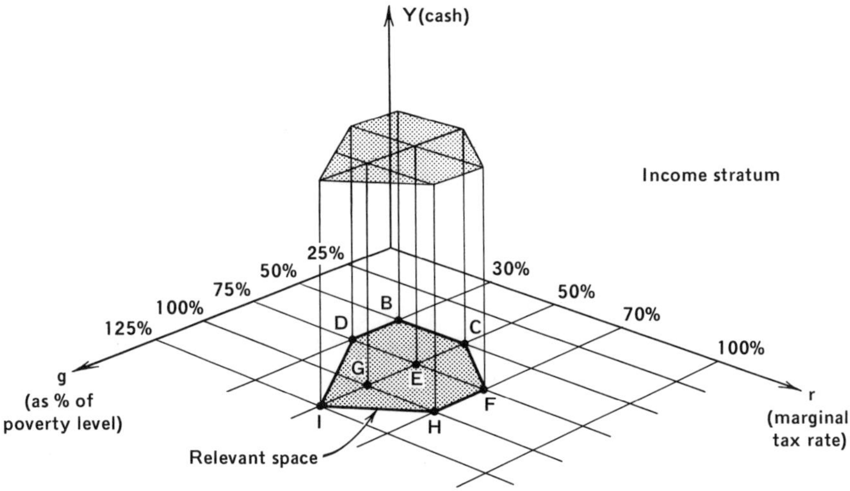

Figure 2.2
Diagrammatic Representation of Policy-Outcome Space

$g = 50$ percent to 125 percent of poverty level, the space outlined in the *gr* plane in the diagram. Theoretically, with unlimited budget and resources virtually the entire policy space could be estimated. In practice, however, this is both undesirable and unnecessary—a discrete number of design points or experimental treatments can be used for estimation. The general objective is to estimate the height of the response surface (Y) at each design point in the relevant policy space. (In the NIT case a policy space was selected for each of three income strata covering the four city sites.) As will be seen, this estimation process is easier under some sets of assumptions about the shape of Y than under others. The design controversy centered on the question of how a limited budget can be distributed across a given number of design points most efficiently, that is, to provide the greatest amount of information about Y with the smallest variance.

Efficient Allocation of a Given Budget over Specified Design Points

A traditional approach to statistical design regards each design point as an independent treatment, the measured response to which is independent of the response to any other treatment; that is, the expected income change at any given point is viewed as independent of its proximity to any other point in the policy space. Since the variance of the error in estimation of each response point is the sum of the variance for that design point (σ_x^2) and the variance of the estimated income response for its control group ($\sigma_{y_0}^2$), total sample variance is:

$$\sum_{i=1}^{m} (\sigma^2_{y_o} + \sigma^2_x)_i$$

where i = a design point in the treatment/outcome space and m = the number of such points.

As in the case of the NIT, where differential responses are expected by income class (or some other sample dimension), the sample must be stratified, and some weights assigned to reflect the relative importance of each stratum in the total response.

For the simplest case of a single treatment group and a control group (or multiple treatment groups where one is equally interested in comparisons among all pairs of groups), minimizing this sum subject to the relevant constraints on sample size ($N = n_1 + n_2$) and/or total budget ($B = c_1n_1 + c_2n_2$) where n_2 and n_1 are the sizes of the experimental and control groups and c is the cost per observation, produces the following distribution rules:

1) under a sample size constraint, distribute N such that:

$$\frac{n_1}{n_2} = \frac{\sigma_{x_1}}{\sigma_{x_2}}$$

sample sizes are proportional to their standard deviations. If it is assumed that $\sigma_{x_1} = \sigma_{x_2}$ then $n_1 = n_2$ and an equal distribution, including the control group, is optimal.

2) Under a budget constraint, distribute N such that:

$$\frac{n_1}{n_2} = \frac{\sigma_{x_1}}{\sigma_{x_2}} \sqrt{\frac{c_2}{c_1}}$$

sample sizes are proportional to their standard deviations weighted inversely by the treatment (variable) cost of observations at each point.

The allocation model used in determining the NIT design also weighted the variance in each treatment cell by a "policy weight" reflecting the importance attached to that particular policy package by decisionmakers. A list of the policy weights and a discussion of the manner in which they were selected follow in a later section.

However, where interest attaches primarily to experimental-control comparisons across the policy-outcome space, a single control group properly allocated by stratum can serve for all experimental groups, the optimal total sample allocation does not follow any simple proportional rule-of-thumb, and a more complex model is required to determine an optimal design. That an optimal design under these conditions is significantly more efficient than one constructed under traditional forms is made evident by the following discussion of the NIT design model.

Digression on the Assumption of Equal Variances

While, in the absence of prior knowledge one would assume $\sigma_{x_1} = \sigma_{x_2}$, there is some reason to expect in the NIT case that the variance in some cells (or points in the policy space) may be greater than that in others. The reasons for this belief are drawn from external observations of work response under existing welfare and tax schemes and fall into at least two groups.

> 1. Individuals for whom the guaranteed income (g) exceeds their initial earned income. The possibility here is that a large proportion of these people may reduce their regular work effort to zero and live on the guaranteed income.
> 2. Families whose initial earned incomes exceed the break-even level (g/r) by virtue of the fact that they have multiple earners in the work force. The expectation here is that such families will withdraw one member from the labor force bringing family income below the break-even level and making the unit eligible for some NIT payments.

Graphically, these variance responses may be represented on the standard work/leisure choice diagram by two sets of indifference curves marked (1, 1′) and (2, 2′) in Figure 2.3.

> (1, 1′) These individuals expand their leisure time from C to B and enjoy an increase in cash income from l to g.
> (2, 2′) These families expand their leisure from D to C by withdrawing a worker from the labor force and accept a reduction in cash income from n to m.

In his May 1969 memo,[10] Tobin identifies these high-variance groups with design points *G, H, I* for Income Stratum I, points *C, F, I* for Income Stratum II, and points *C, F, H* for Income Stratum III (see Table 2.1).

It follows from the preceding allocation formula that the number of observations assigned to these points should be increased proportional to their standard deviation (estimated by Tobin to be twice the variance in the remaining cell in each income stratum).

Some Objections to the Traditional Approach

Objections to applying the traditional approach to the NIT design were raised by the Wisconsin economists on the grounds that:

1. The assumption of complete independence of response at each treatment point is unnecessarily naive since, on the basis of observations from existing welfare and tax programs, there is evidence of some continuity in

[10] Tobin, "Sample Design for NIT Experiment."

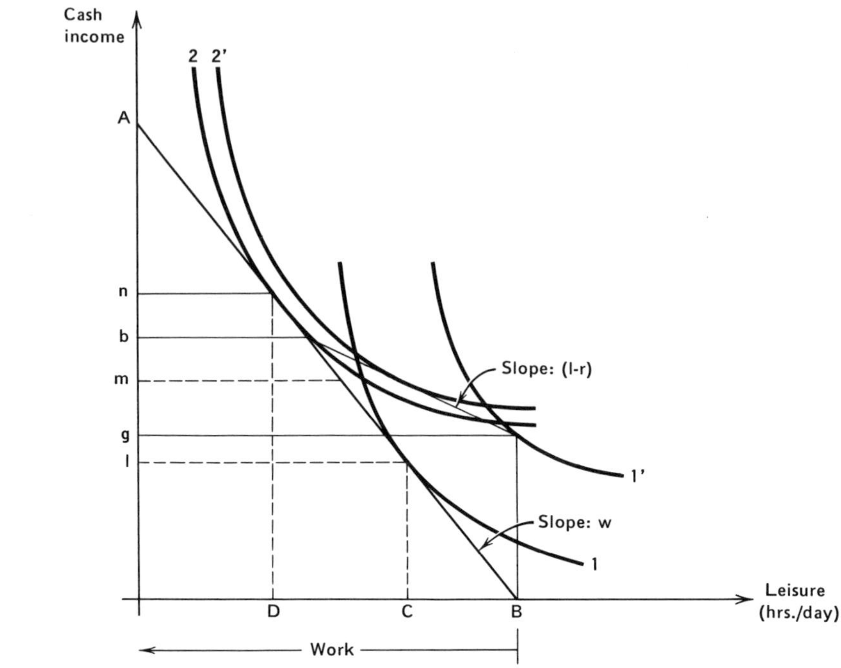

Figure 2.3
Some Theoretically Expected Work Responses

the behavioral adjustments individuals make to income changes. The conventional approach amounts to estimating the *points* (Y_i) above the design points *A* through *I* in Figure 2.2, not the whole *surface;* this leads to the second objection.

2. With the resulting *point* estimates of Y_i produced by traditional methods, it becomes necessary to make some interpolations for policies that may fall between the tested design points. But the traditional approach has specifically eschewed any assumptions that would link such responses in a continuous function, so that the translation from eight separate response points to an objective function that can project a nationwide response across many more points and income strata than included in the experiment involves the adoption of some external assumptions of continuity anyway. This being so, it is more efficient to begin with some explicit assumption about the shape of the response *surface* which, in turn as shown below, permits a more efficient distribution of sample observations and control groups.

3. Finally, Tobin notes that the conventional approach treats expensive observations (i.e., high-payment points, such as *H* and *I*) as equal in in-

Table 2.1
Final Allocation of Households
by Income Strata and Sites Among Experimental Treatments

	Design Points			*Income Stratum I.*		
	g	*r*	*Trenton*	*Paterson/Passaic*	*Jersey City*	*Scranton*
A	0	0	22	76	78	62
B	.5	.3	5	0	0	0
C	.5	.5	3	21	3	2
D	.75	.3	7	18	3	2
E	.75	.5	5	0	0	0
F	.75	.7	4	9	0	0
G	1.0	.5	5	17	0	0
H	1.0	.7	4	7	0	0
I	1.25	.5	0	9	23	18
	Total		55	157	107	84
				Income Stratum II.		
A	0	0	25	55	47	38
B	.5	.3	6	0	14	11
C	.5	.5	6	16	8	7
D	.75	.3	4	0	6	4
E	.75	.5	7	20	17	13
F	.75	.7	4	22	14	11
G	1.0	.5	2	7	14	11
H	1.0	.7	4	7	8	7
I	1.25	.5	0	8	0	0
	Total		58	135	128	102
				Income Stratum III.		
A	0	0	27	90	72	58
B	.5	.3	2	10	0	0
C	.5	.5	5	0	0	0
D	.75	.3	3	17	17	13
E	.75	.5	2	34	0	0
F	.75	.7	0	0	0	0
G	1.0	.5	6	9	3	2
H	1.0	.7	2	31	0	0
I	1.25	.5	0	14	36	30
	Total		47	205	128	103

SOURCE: Heather Ross, "An Experimental Study of the Negative Income Tax" (Ph.D. diss., MIT, 1970), Ch. 5.

Table 2.2
Consolidated Final Sample Allocation by Site and Treatment

	Design Points		*All Three Income Strata*				
	g	*r*	*Trenton*	*Paterson/ Passaic*	*Jersey City*	*Scranton*	*Total*
A	0	0	74	221	197	158	650
B	.5	.3	13	10	14	11	48
C	.5	.5	14	37	11	9	71
D	.75	.3	14	35	26	19	94
E	.75	.5	14	54	17	13	98
F	.75	.7	8	31	14	11	64
G	1.0	.5	13	33	17	13	76
H	1.0	.7	10	45	8	7	70
I	1.25	.5	0	31	59	48	138
	Total		160	497	363	289	1309

SOURCE: Heather Ross, "An Experimental Study of the Negative Income Tax" (Ph.D. diss., MIT, 1970), p. 223.

formation value to all other points and so provides a smaller assignment of observations to such cells in contrast to the optimization approach, which concentrates observations at the extremes (high-payment and no-payment [control] cells) where they serve to position the response surface with greater accuracy.

THE OPTIMIZATION APPROACH

The optimization approach views the experimental design problem as the proper specification of a response *surface* assuming a functional link between adjacent design points. Thus, when the form of the response function is known, or estimated, the value at any point on the response surface can be calculated. The problem then becomes a matter of determining the form of the function from which estimates of the partial regression coefficients for g, r, and Y_0 can be derived.

In a three-dimensional policy-outcome space only three design points at the extreme edges of the relevant policy space are necessary to estimate a linear response surface. (As it happens in the NIT case, it is extremely efficient to have one of these three be the control group at the origin since control observations are relatively cheap, requiring the payment of only a small reporting fee.) Further, it is optimal to select these points at extremes on the edge of the relevant policy space since this will minimize the variance of estimates from the surface. Middle-income, middle-treatment options are by this criterion inefficient test points. In this instance, interior points need not be covered at all; they can be estimated from the general response function by interpolation.

If, however, the surface is assumed to have some nonlinear form, then interior points must also be observed to get an estimate of the degree of curvature in the surface. The higher the degree of the assumed polynomial function, the greater the number of inflection points and the more interior design points must be covered to pick these out.

The specific response function worked out for the experiment by Watts and Conlisk[11] was a quadratic (described in detail in the next section) capable of detecting simple convexity in work responses. The objective of the design was to allocate observations over plans so as to maximize the precision of the estimated cost attributable to labor supply response across the policy space. The general approach is to minimize the error variance around a response (transfer) cost function subject to an experimental budget constraint.

BRIEF DESCRIPTION OF THE WATTS-CONLISK MODEL APPLIED TO THE NIT

The Watts-Conlisk sample allocation model as applied to the New Jersey Experiment consisted of four elements embodying rather specific assumptions about behavioral responses of experimental families.[12]

1) *Response Function: Z, a basic quadratic response function* specifying that the ratio of post-treatment to "normal" earnings (Z) is a complex function of responses to g, r, g^2, r^2 and the interaction of gr:

$$\begin{aligned} Z = \beta_1 &+ D(\beta_2 U + \beta_3 U^2)g + D(\beta_4 U + \beta_5 U^2)r \\ &+ D(\beta_6 U + \beta_7 U^2)g^2 + D(\beta_8 U + \beta_9 U^2)r^2 \\ &+ D(\beta_{10} U + \beta_{11} U^2)gr + u \end{aligned}$$

where the D's are dummies $= \begin{cases} 1, U > 0 \\ 0, U < 0 \end{cases}$ and U = index of how close the observed earnings are to the upper bound (M) for a negative tax response calculated as: $U = (M - w)/M$, where

[11] Conlisk and Watts, "A Model for Optimizing Experimental Designs for Estimating Response Surfaces."

[12] For the details of this section, we have drawn heavily on Heather Ross, "An Experimental Study of the Negative Income Tax" (Ph.D. diss., MIT, 1970), Harold Watts and John Conlisk, ibid., internal memoranda made available to us by the staffs of IRP and Mathematica (see Appendix to this chapter), and personal communications from Watts.

$$M = \frac{(1.3 + r)g}{(.1 + r)}$$ calculated for the *g* and *r* values of each of the eight plans

$w = .7, 1.15 \text{ and } 1.4$ for each of the three income strata in the sample; *w* equals the ratio of "normal" earnings to the poverty level.

The upper bound was imposed to reflect an assumption that families with normal earnings substantially above the poverty level are expected to be unresponsive to the tax and guarantee parameters in any case. *M* was set at levels ranging up to 1.75 Y_b in order to examine the behavior of families just above Y_b who, some had argued, might respond by reducing their earnings enough to drop into eligibility for payments. It happened also that families between Y_b and *M* became cheap observations since they received no payments so that the positioning of *M* assisted the final result of allocating large numbers of observations to "nonrecipient" cells (see detailed discussion, next section).

The quadratic form for *Z* was selected as the function that could best allow for the estimation of a nonlinear response surface. While this choice raised considerable debate, since it required acceptance of some assumptions about the maximum probable degree of curvature in the response surface and the continuity of response, cubic forms were tried and rejected as being computationally cumbersome (IM 8) and implying a more complex response than anyone really expected. The income strata proportions were scaled to distribute the sample in proportion to the national income distribution.

Since labor supply response is inherently costly to an NIT and the objective of the experiment was to generate as precise estimates of this response-induced transfer cost as possible within the specified budget constraint, it was necessary to define both the response cost of an allocation over all families and plans and an objective function to be optimized subject to constraints.

2) *Response-cost due to reduced work effort* (i.e., the transfer cost of a specified allocation) was specified for a family at each point in the treatment-stratum space as a linear function of the β's in the *Z* function:

$$C_i = rY(1 - Z)$$

and across all points as:

$$\sum_{i=1}^{27} C_i = u_i[rY(1-Z)(f)(h)] + (1+u_i)[rY(1-Z)(f)(h)]/3$$

where C_i is the average transfer cost for families in cell i attributable to reduced work effort weighted by the United States' national population frequency for male-headed families (f), the proportion of response taking place below Y_b, (h), where h converts work response into transfer cost, and the probability of attrition $(1 - u_i)$ on the assumption that attrited observations cost only one-third as much as a family that "survives" the full three-year experiment.

The proportion of response occurring below the break-even level (h) and therefore entailing a transfer cost to eligible units was specified judgmentally to equal 1.0 for incomes up to 90 percent of break-even and to decline linearly with incomes between 90 percent Y_b and M, the maximum at which there is any experimental effect. The proportion of families in cell i expected to remain in the sample for the full three years of the experiment (u_i) was taken to rise linearly from a minimum of 80 percent for families receiving no payments to 100 percent for those whose expected annual tax payment is greater than 18 percent of the poverty standard.[13]

Substituting the response function (Z) into the total response-cost function (ΣC_i) yields an expression for the total cost of response over all nine plans (including the controls) and three income strata in terms of the β coefficients of the basic response function.

3) *Objective Function:* Q(x), *a weighted total variance* of the response-cost estimates for each design point calculated from a sample of families allocated to plans according to a vector (x) and weighted by a set of policy weights. The vector x represents the assignment of families to each of the 27 cells in the design space and is to be chosen to minimize this total variance subject to a series of constraints. Since the variance of the β's in the response function can be predicted from the sample, the variances of the response-cost estimates can be calculated as a transform of the β variances. Then Q is minimized subject to a set of linear constraints on minimum and maximum cell sizes, budget shares, and an overall experimental budget constraint.

---

[13] The estimated attrition rate turned out to be on the low side. The overall attrition rate was close to 20 percent with the rate for controls close to 25 percent. (See Chapter 3.)

4) The overall *experimental budget constraint* for the NIT was set in dollars at:

$$\sum_{i=1}^{27} K_i n_i \leq \$1,450,000$$

where K_i is the total (transfer plus administrative) cost of an observation assigned to cell i and n_i is the number of families allocated to that cell by the model.
For purposes of setting the overall budget constraint, it was necessary to make some prior *assumption* of the response cost for the sample—precisely the magnitude the NIT was designed to estimate—as well as the administrative cost of collecting and analyzing the experimental data. It was generally agreed that some average of the transfer costs to be anticipated under the extremes of zero work response (all benefits taken in income) and zero income response (all benefits taken in leisure) should be used although some experimenting was done with alternative weights to be used for the two effects (see Table 2.4). Watts found that the allocation assignments were not very sensitive to alternative weightings of the two extreme responses and the final sample allocation assumed weights of $(1 - .5r)$ and $(.5r)$ on the work- and income-responses respectively. Part-way through the experiment filing fees (an administrative cost) were increased to reduce attrition from the sample.

This general design model was used to generate a number of alternative sample allocations for the NIT, some with additional constraints on minimum cell assignments, maximum budget shares permissible for certain plans, and maximum shares of controls in the total sample.

THE RESULTING SAMPLE DESIGN ALLOCATION

Initial runs of the Watts-Conlisk model produced very "unbalanced" distributions of the sample, concentrating as much as 95 percent of all observations in a very few "cheap" cells at the extreme edges of the policy space—specifically in the control group (which received no transfer payments) and at treatment cells in which large numbers of families were above Y_b (and so ineligible for payments). In such allocations, only 10 percent of NIT payment recipients would have been drawn from poverty level income strata.

This resulted in part from the differential costs of various treatments and in part from the original specification of the cost function itself that substantially underestimated the cost of attrited observations (substantial expenditures were made later in the experiment to stem high rates of attrition from precisely those cells—controls and high-income families—that were favored in the initial allocations).

Objections were raised to such unbalanced allocations that left a large number of interior points in the policy space unobserved on the grounds that

1. It is counterintuitive to draw inferences about the feasibility of a national anti-poverty program from an experiment that draws only a minority of its observations from a poverty population.
2. The purpose of learning something about the administrative costs of such a program is thwarted by a design that actually makes payments to such a small number of participants.
3. The "threshold effects" of a number of sociological hypotheses can only be tested with observations at all treatments.
4. The traditional design allocation is more robust with respect to misspecification of the initial response function.
5. The continuity-of-response assumption implicit in the optimization approach is unfounded.

The Watts-Conlisk model allocation was defended with the arguments that

1. There surely *is* some continuity of response to tax conditions over the specified range of incomes in the policy space, and it is senseless to make a more naive assumption especially where it leads to a more costly (less efficient) design.
2. The quadratic form of the Watts-Conlisk function allows for the most variation in response that we can reasonably hope to detect with so crude an experimental process. The quadratic is much less restrictive than a simpler linear (planar) form would have been.
3. The minimization of the national cost per family due to reduced work effort alone is the relevant objective function since out-of-pocket costs of experimentation are merely transfers from experimenters to participants—important to Mathematica, perhaps, but not to the implied cost of instituting a nationwide program.

These objections to the initial model allocation plus higher-than-anticipated attrition rates in Trenton in the first half-year and the discovery that additional observations from another site would have to be added to the total sample in order to enroll the desired number of white families produced a series of efforts to modify the design model and shift some observations to interior plans.

DEBATE ON CHANGES IN THE OBJECTIVE FUNCTION

In the early stages of the development of the Watts-Conlisk model, casual agreement had been gained to express the objective of the experiment as the estimation of the *national transfer cost due to work response* of an NIT program. This focus turned out to have ramifications that some of the staff, particularly at Mathematica, were unwilling to live with as the resultant "unbalanced" allocations generated by the model were revealed.

In particular, it was protested that 1) this left no room for incorporation of some important secondary objectives of the experiment (e.g., the testing of certain hypotheses about the effects of payments on family stability, fertility, political and social integration, and consumption patterns). This argument asserted that these goals were at least as important to resolving pragmatic political opposition to NIT as the labor supply issue. As Albert Rees (IM 17) expressed it,

> The negative income tax proposal will have brighter prospects if our results should show that experimental families spend their payments on children's shoes more than on beer, or that experimental families participate more in elections than control families, or if experimental families stay together more than controls. Observations on families above the break-even point are of no use in answering such questions.

The counter argument was that a limited three-year experiment could not reasonably expect to produce differences in these long-term life style patterns in any case and that the cost of accommodating this objective would be unacceptable in terms of weakening the evidence for the labor supply tests.

2) While the reduction in work effort results in a transfer cost attributable to the NIT, this is not the *only* cost of a national program; lost output is equally important and is not reflected in the Watts-Conlisk model of cash (out-of-pocket) costs alone.

To accommodate this opportunity cost in the experimental design would have required vastly expanding the orientation of the experiment.

The emphasis on the national transfer cost of response focused attention on the work response of non-poor families above Y_b and made the particular specification of h, the weight attached to observations approaching the "vanishing point" (M), and the positioning of M itself of crucial importance to the allocation results.

DEBATE ON THE FORM OF h AND POSITIONING OF M

The precise specification of h as a calculation of the weight to be assigned to the responses of households at varying distances from the "vanishing point" (M) and the positioning of M itself became the subjects of some controversy, since together with the attrition probabilities these were the only parameters in C_i with discretionary value and hence the only points of entry for an argument that the costs of observation in high-income cells had been understated.

Graphically, the h function was determined as shown in Figure 2.4 embodying the judgment that all households within 90 percent of Y_b or lower would show some work response while some declining fraction of those with "normal" Y_o's between $.9Y_b$ and M would exhibit a response entailing a transfer cost; families above M were considered "immune" to influence on work behavior from the potential option of NIT payments. Sensitivity tests of the model made by Conlisk (IM 7, IM 8, IM 9) suggested that the resulting allocations were rather sensitive to the positioning of M for the reason that in the national population there are a much larger number of families clustered just above Y_b (in the range $Y_b - M$) so that even a declining fraction of this denser population yields a substantial transfer cost.

The suggestion was made by Mathematica (IM 15) that M be set closer or equal to Y_b in order to limit the range of observations drawn from above-break-even (nonpayment) households—a range that was attractive to the Wisconsin staff precisely because of their cheapness (in transfer terms) and their ability to supply information on potential "threshold effects" that could have a sizable impact on total program costs. Sensitivity tests were run for alternative positions of M (IM 19 and IM 22) including

$M = Y_b$, $M = \frac{1}{2}(M_o - Y_b)$, $M = M_o$, and $M = 2M_o$ (where M_o = the original Watts-Conlisk value of $\frac{(1.3 + r)g}{(.1 + r)}$).

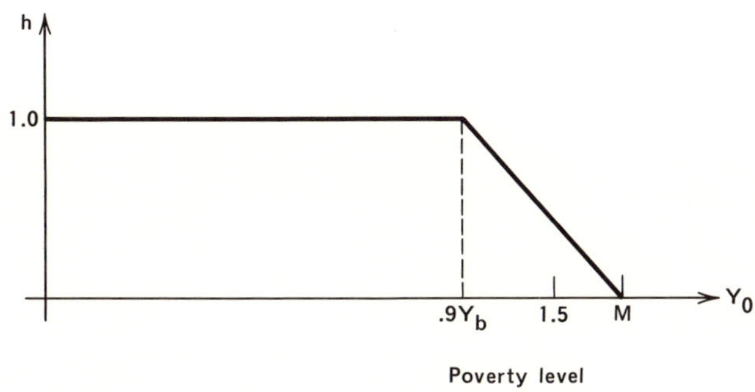

Figure 2.4
Graphic Presentation of *h* Function: Labor Response in Areas Below the Break-Even Point

The result was that as M was moved closer to Y_b with constraints on the total N permitted in each of the three income strata, the overall allocation by stratum was affected very little for the lowest income stratum. Moving M closer to Y_b tended to shift observations in the middle income stratum out of the control group into the .5/.5 and the 1.0/.5 plans and in the highest income group from the 1.0/.5 to the .5/.5 plan. (That is, observations were moved from the edges to interior points of the policy space.)

But it was primarily on the argument that the work response of families located some distance above Y_b was 1) unobservable from any other source and 2) potentially important to estimating total program costs that Wisconsin retained its original positioning of M at M_o.

ADJUSTMENT OF ATTRITION FUNCTION

The "survival rate" (u_i), or proportion of families originally enrolled in plan i expected to remain in the experiment for the full three years, was set as a function of their expected relative payments level such that households with expected annual payments of 18 percent or more of their guaranteed income level were anticipated to "survive" the whole experimental period ($u_i = 1.0$) while units with smaller anticipated payments would drop out at rates ranging up to 33 percent for zero expected payments—the case of controls and a large number of families with incomes above Y_b.

As the researchers gained experience in the field with the Trenton sample, it became evident that attrition rates were running much higher for some experimentals and for the controls so that several new model runs were made assuming a 50 percent attrition rate for controls and attaching higher administrative costs to observations with a higher probability of attrition as a reflection of the cost of attempting to keep them in the sample.[14]

In the final allocation Tobin specified additional fixed costs of $240 and $100 respectively for experimentals and controls as the cost of reducing the maximum attrition rate to 20 percent for zero payment families (see Figure 2.5).

THE POLICY WEIGHTS

The question of what policy (or "interest") weights should be attached to each of the eight treatment points is particularly interesting because these weights, together with the definition of the policy space itself, are

---

[14] Final attrition rates were lower than those initially experienced in Trenton partially in response to countermeasures taken in 1969 (see Chapter 3).

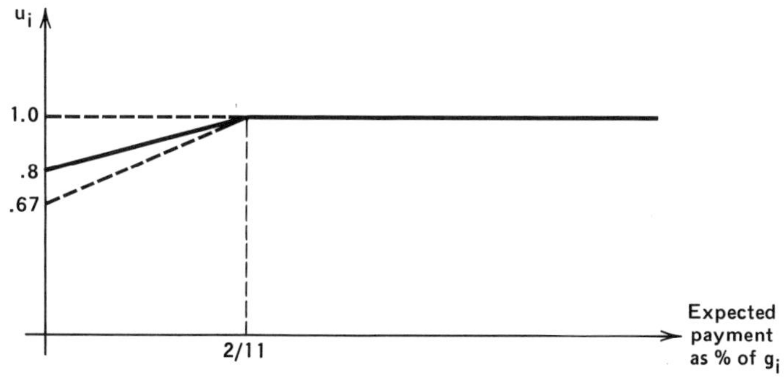

Figure 2.5
Graphic Representation of *u* Function:
Attrition as a Function of Payments

the most direct way in which the priorities of policymakers, as distinct from those of researchers, can be reflected in the experimental design. On the one hand, the policy space is defined broadly enough to encompass some "extreme" possibilities that no one currently thinks feasible so as to leave some scope for shifting political and social conditions affecting the acceptability of programs; on the other hand, the policymakers' assessment of current political/social priorities is reflected in a differential weighting of points *within* the space.

Watts[15] has said that the original policy weights were determined by James Lydey and Robert Levine at OEO early in the design process although these original policy weights were altered several times as plans were included and excluded from the final policy space, and there seems to have been very little subsequent discussion either internally or with OEO about the final weights used in the final allocation.[16]

We have been unable to discover in the internal memoranda written by Watts, Conlisk, and others any pure test of alternative policy weight assignments since each new run of the model reported involved several simultaneous changes in constraints and parametric specifications. It seems worth noting, however, that the variation in weights (from 3 to 10) is not obviously insignificant, and, when normalized so that the squares of the weights sum to 1, the range becomes substantially larger (11 to 1 rather than 3 to 1). The same is true of the two main center points on which most

[15] Notes on visit to Mathematica, February 4, 1974, interview with Harold Watts.

[16] The changes from original to final weights reflect the efforts of Mathematica to find ways to shift more observations into the interior of the policy space. Although it is quite likely that OEO would have largely agreed with the underlying reasons for the effort, it is not clear that anyone at OEO was ever formally asked to consider or approve the final policy weights as they emerged from the process of internal controversy among the researchers.

Table 2.3
Policy Weights: Original and Final Versions

Design Point	*Original Policy Weights*	*Modified (Final) Policy Weights*
A	0	0
B	3	3
C	5	4
D	6	6
E	10	10
F	4	3
G	7	10
H	3	3
I	5	5
(J)	(2)	—

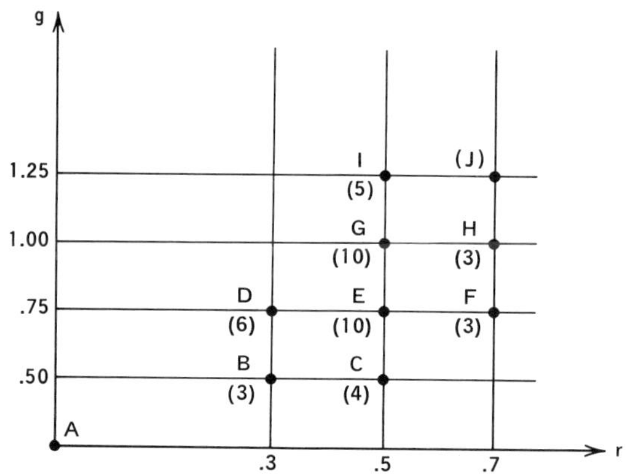

SOURCE: Heather Ross, "An Experimental Study of the Negative Income Tax" (Ph.D. diss., MIT, 1970) and John Conlisk, IM 10.

political interest centered; that is, the range of difference in policy interest between points E and G and their adjacent plans is two to four times greater when the normalized squares of the selected weights are used.

CHOICES AMONG ALTERNATIVE MODEL ALLOCATIONS

As the internal debate wore on, Conlisk used the Watts-Conlisk model with some incorporated modifications to generate a series of alternative sample allocations that were presented for discussion in early 1969. These runs differed in the form of Z, the positioning of M, maximum assumed attrition rates, administrative costs of control versus experimental observations, the weighting of work and income responses in the C_i function, the assumption of error variance across plans, and a variety of direct constraints placed on minimum cell size, maximum total and control sample size, distribution of N by income stratum, and the maximum budget share allocated to high-payment plans. Table 2.4 displays five of these allocations made with the same or similar model specifications and under varying sets of constraints including the final Tobin allocation. Their characteristics in terms of total N, the objective function (Q), an index of total response variance, and the average variance per observation are shown at the bottom of the table.

It is clear that, in terms of the objective function, a number of constraints can be placed on the basic Watts-Conlisk efficiency allocation without driving its cost in terms of increased variance as high as that of an equal allocation. The relative costliness of an equal distribution is also reflected in the total number of observations that can be afforded under a fixed budget constraint: With no constraints (other than B) on the pure efficiency allocation more than three times as many observations can be had than under the equal schema. Constraining the allocation to a minimum cell size of twenty for each plan reduces the total sample size slightly and increases total variance about 30 percent, primarily by shifting control, and some high-payment observations, into plans B and C, so that the budget share going to high-payment families (plan I) is somewhat reduced.

Placing additional constraints on total N, the high-payment budget share, the size of the control group, and the distribution by income stratum dramatically increases the average cost in terms of variance of an observation by shifting many more controls and a few high-payment observations into plans C and G, but even this allocation is twice as efficient in terms of the objective function as the equal distribution.

The O'Hare allocation (named for the meeting place where it was first suggested) incorporated most of the parameters of the basic Watts-Conlisk model but set $M = g/r$ thereby drastically limiting the number of observations at the upper end of the income scale and reducing the budget share of high-payment plans by ten percentage points (to 23 percent). The allocations to plans C, D, and E in the lower left corner of the policy space were also sharply increased with a much larger budget share going to plans D and C. This increased the total sample size to 1,561, correspondingly reduced the control share (from 70 percent with no constraints to 27 percent!), and increased total and average variance per observation substantially. While the relative efficiency of the O'Hare allocation is still 50 percent above that of the equal distribution, it is substantially lower than the Multiple Constraints allocation, all of whose constraints it incorporates.

Table 2.4
Consolidated[a] Sample Allocations Calculated For Different Sets of Parametric Assumptions and Constraints by Watts-Conlisk Model (All allocations within budget constraint: B ≦ $1,450,000)

	Tax Plan *g*	*r*	*Equal* ϕB	*No Constraints* ϕB	$n_i \geqslant 20$ ϕB	*Multiple Constraints*[b] ϕB	*O'Hare* ϕB	*Tobin*
A	0	0	97 (.01)	2031 (.10)	1610 (.08)	430 (.02)	416 (.02)	650
B	.5	.3	96 (.07)	6 (.01)	60 (.04)	60 (.03)	61 (.03)	48
C	.5	.5	96 (.03)	27 (.02)	60 (.02)	172 (.03)	222 (.07)	71
D	.75	.3	96 (.14)	99 (.12)	90 (.12)	100 (.13)	144 (.21)	94
E	.75	.5	96 (.09)	127 (.11)	158 (.09)	140 (.13)	193 (.07)	98
F	.75	.7	99 (.07)	172 (.04)	162 (.05)	90 (.04)	158 (.06)	64
G	1.0	.5	99 (.19)	60 (.09)	60 (.12)	110 (.18)	108 (.21)	76
H	1.0	.7	99 (.14)	179 (.06)	157 (.11)	70 (.09)	173 (.11)	70
I	1.25	.5	99 (.27)	186 (.47)	147 (.38)	128 (.33)	88 (.23)	138
Controls as % of N			11	70	64	33	27	50
Total N			876	2889	2502	1300	1561	1309
Q (000's)			5647	1773	2296	2798	3599	2500
Avg. Q/obs.			6446	614	918	2152	2306	1910
Efficiency Relative to ANOVA (Based on Q's)			1.00	3.18	2.46	2.02	1.57	2.25

[a] Allocations in table are consolidated over four sites and three income strata.
ϕB = budget share
ϕY = income-stratum share
N = total sample size
n_i = size of cell i
Q = objective function (index of total variance of response-cost ests.)
Assumptions of the alternative model runs are displayed in following table.

[b] Multiple Constraints:
$n_i \geqslant 20$
$N \leqslant 1300$
$\phi Y = .3, .3, .4$
control $N \geqslant 1/4, \leqslant 1/3$
high-g $\phi B \leqslant 1/3$

SOURCE: Memo, John Conlisk to NJ Experimenters, February 1, 1969 (IM 10): ANOVA allocation, p. 14; No constraints allocation, p. 15; $n_i \geqslant 20$ allocation, p. 17; Multiple constraints allocation, p. 22; O'Hare allocation, p. 23; Tobin allocation from memo, James Tobin to Harold Watts and William Baumol, "Sample Design for NIT Experiment," May 1969, pp. 4–11.

Table 2.5
Assumptions of Alternative Model Runs

Parameters	*"Basic" Watts-Conlisk*	*O'Hare*	*Tobin*
Z	$f(U^2, U^3)$		$f(U, U^2)$
C_i	½ [zero wk. response + zero income response] $C_i = \frac{u_i c_i + (1 - u_i) c_i}{3}$	½ [zero wk. + zero income resp.]	[(1 — .5r) zero wk. resp. + (.5r) zero income resp.]
M	$(1.3 + r)g/(.1 + r)$	$g/r = Y_b$	
u_i (or max. attrition rate)	.5 (controls), max. 33 (expers.)	.5 (controls), .33 max. (expers.)	.20 max. (expers.)
Admin. Cost per Observation	\$105 (controls) \$185 (expers.)	\$105 (controls) \$185 (expers.)	\$205 (controls) \$425 (expers.)
Number of Plans	8	8	8
W or ϕ Y's	.7, 1.15, 1.4	.7, 1.15, 1.4 .3, .3, .4	.7, 1.14, 1.4 .3, .3, .4
Error Variance	uniform σ^2 across all plans	uniform σ^2 across all plans	uniform σ^2 *except* when $\left\{\begin{matrix} Y_o > Y_b \\ Y_o < g \end{matrix}\right\}, 2\sigma^2$
Population Frequency	male-headed households in U.S. 1967 under age 65	male-headed households in U.S. 1967 under age 65	male-headed households in U.S. 1967 under age 65
ß	single ß all sites	single ß all sites	site specific $ß_1, ß_2, ß_3, ß_4$
Policy Weights	3, 4, 6, 10, 3, 10, 3, 5	3, 4, 6, 10, 3, 10, 3, 5, 2	3, 4, 6, 10, 3, 10, 3, 5
Constraints			
Budget	$\leqslant$ \$1,450,000	$\leqslant$ \$1,450,000	$\leqslant$ \$1,377,500
N	none		$\leqslant 1300$
n_i	none		$n_i = 0$ or $\geqslant 5$
High-g ϕ_B	none		33%
Maximum Control N	none	Distributed .3, .3, .4 over income strata	

DECISION-THEORETIC APPROACH

A rough decision-theoretic process was applied by Conlisk (IM 8 and IM 9) to estimate the "damage" (in terms of cost inefficiency) done by choosing a wrong design specification under six different assumptions about the "true" response surface. Eight different design specifications were tested against six "true" states of nature and the value of Q_i calculated for each potential mismatch.

As Ross reports when minimax and maximum-expected-loss criteria were applied: "It happened that each action had quite sizable losses for some states of nature, and that no action dominated the others in the sense that it showed the smallest loss for all the states of nature." As might have been expected, the equal allocation showed up in these tests as very robust to misspecifications of the true state of nature. The argument was simply pushed back to a subjective disagreement over the probabilities of finding the various states of nature to be true; *in fact,* the Wisconsin team assigned much higher probabilities to the U, U^2 family of specifications while Mathematica was inclined to hold a much wider range of functional forms equally probable.

Having pushed the basic argument to a stalemate, it was finally decided to get a binding opinion from an outside source and James Tobin was consulted.

THE TOBIN SOLUTION

The Tobin allocation was the one finally agreed upon and reflects a number of different assumptions about the model parameters themselves (see Table 2.5) including $Z = f(U, U^2)$, costs relating the probability of a zero work response to the tax rate of each plan, higher administrative costs for both experimentals and controls, a maximum 20 percent attrition rate, and different σ^2 across plans. The Tobin allocation, disaggregated by income stratum, is shown in Table 2.6. (Table 2.1 shows the Tobin final allocation disaggregated by site and income stratum.) This distribution reflects a number of "judgmental adjustments" to the allocation generated by the model that had the effect of shifting some observations into plan G (1.0/.5), on the reasoning that this was an important central plan for which one did not want to have to rely heavily on interpolated response, and boosting assignments to plan I (1.25/.5) in order to gain more information on the administrative costs of "borderline" families in a national program.

Nowhere in the internal documentation have we been able to find a state-

Table 2.6
Recommended Final Allocation of Sample Households
(The Tobin Solution)

	g/r Treatment	*Income Stratum* I.	II.	III.	*Total*
A	0/0 Control	238	165	247	650
B	.5/.3	5	31	12	48
C	.5/.5	29	37[a]	5[a]	71
D	.75/.3	30	14	50	94
E	.75/.5	5	57	36	97
F	.75/.7	13	51[a]	0[a]	64
G	1.0/.5	22[a]	34	20	77
H	1.0/.7	11[a]	26	33[a]	70
I	1.25/.5	50[a]	8[a]	80	138
	Total	403	423	483	1,309

[a] Indicates the cells Tobin identifies as high-variance (i.e., having a variance at least twice that of the other cells).

SOURCE: Adapted from Tobin memo addressed to Harold Watts and William Baumol, dated May 1969, p. 4. (See also Tables 2.1 and 2.2.)

ment of the Tobin allocation *before* his ad hoc adjustments although Tobin[17] himself reports that the efficiency "costs" of his adjustments "appear to be about a 1 percent increase in the variance of the desired estimate"; if the constraint limiting the maximum budget share going to plan I is raised from 33 percent to 36 percent, the variance is increased 3 percent or 4 percent. He presents this as the estimated price of insurance against model misspecification and accommodation of a number of secondary objectives. The problem with which he had been presented was particularly untidy because the original sample households had already been chosen and assigned across the eight treatments in Trenton. This sample proved to contain too few whites to give valid tests of racial differences and some difficulty was encountered in finding enough qualified families in the lowest income stratum to fill out the sample.[18] Hence a decision had been made to add a number of families in Scranton and Jersey City. The problem presented to

[17] Tobin, "Sample Design for NIT Experiment."

[18] That is, those with a working male head of household under 65 years of age, whose income did not exceed 150 percent of the official poverty level. Ross, in "An Experimental Study of the Negative Income Tax," reports that the ratio of eligible poor families to those contacted was less than 2 percent in all four cities. (The *Final Report* contains a higher figure; see Chapter 3.)

Tobin, after considerable in-house debate, was how to distribute these additional observations over new and old sites and across experimental and control groups to minimize the estimated variances for the sample as a whole. His recommended allocation is shown in Table 2.5.

Note that in making this allocation he was faced with *both* a sample size and a budget constraint: The size of the total sample had been previously determined and some portion already assigned, and it had been agreed with OEO that no more than 33 percent of the total budget should be used for the most expensive point, I (1.25/.5), in the policy space. This allocation results in 788 out of 1,309 or 60 percent of sample households at the extremes of nonpayment control group or high-payment, nonpoor households. At the same time, there is some coverage of interior points which, it was hoped, would yield sufficient information to determine the curvature of the response surface.

The dilemma of the optimization approach lies in the fact that its greater efficiency in using a limited budget and number of observations to produce estimates with smaller variance depends on selecting the proper functional form at the start. If we assume a linear surface and consequently test no interior points when the response surface is, in fact, convex, we run the risk of overlooking a highly effective policy package represented by some intermediate combination of *g* and *r*. As Tobin has expressed it, the parametric approach

> . . . will pick at a minimum enough [sample points] to match the number of parameters to be estimated, and at a maximum this number plus the number of effective constraints. Thus there will in general be several cells to which no observations are assigned. . . . The trouble is that the identity of the empty cells changes with the specification [of the response function], and we are not sure about which specification is correct.[19]

Branson (IM 23) has pointed out that this dilemma is logically equivalent to a choice between Type I and Type II errors in specifying a form for the response function since such a specification is equivalent to testing a hypothesis about the response of households to the parameter values. The Watts-Conlisk formulation is a design to minimize Type I error around the postulated function on the assumption that this has been correctly specified.

> But if the prior specification is incorrect, one of two things can happen: (a) the estimated parameters are significant when in fact the response surface is nonlinear but we can't see the nonlinearity; (b) the parameters are insignificant and we are led to the conclusion that there is no appreciable reaction to the tax variables. If the specification of the reaction function is

[19] Tobin, "Sample Design for NIT Experiment," p. 14.

changed, we would get a different pattern of assignment of tax variables peculiarly appropriate for testing that hypothesis, but the problem would still remain.

Procedures for hedging against misspecification risk have been suggested by Branson (IM 23), Orcutt and Orcutt,[20] Conlisk,[21] and Morris.[22] Branson suggests assigning observations under two sets of constraints, one on the acceptable probability of Type II error and the second to minimize Type I error. In practice this would mean assigning observations to each of the design points until the expected variance of the mean response at each point is reduced to some specified level and thereafter assigning the remaining observations to the most efficient points as picked out by the Watts-Conlisk model. The Orcutts suggest that a process of sequential sampling before the experimental design is set can help to reduce uncertainty about the assumed shape of the response surface. And Morris, in specifying a design for the Rand Health Insurance Experiment, proposes a sequential design in which half the sample is allocated randomly over all points, while the remaining families are assigned to specific plans by a "finite selection model," really an algorithm that scans the remaining families on the list, calculates for each one its cost-effectiveness at each design point, and selects that family that will contribute the greatest reduction in variance per dollar of program cost. Conlisk suggests three possibilities: constraining each cell size to a minimum n_i, minimizing the expected loss calculated for each functional form versus a "true" alternative state, and placing upper and lower bounds on the amount by which estimated responses at adjacent points may differ from one another. As noted, the Branson and Conlisk suggestions were used as the basis of several of the alternative allocations generated during the design process.

In a more recent look at the problem, Hall[23] has suggested that the efficiency of experimental design could be increased substantially over that of the regression allocations discussed by "letting subjects be their own controls." His argument is that family-specific differences among families of the same racial and income characteristics assigned to the same plan are so much greater than the group mean differences between plans that the best

---

[20] Guy Orcutt and Alice Orcutt, "Incentive and Disincentive Experimentation for Income Maintenance Policy Purposes," *American Economic Review* 58 (1968): 754–772.

[21] John Conlisk, "Choice of Response Functional Form in Designing Subsidy Experiments," *Econometrica* 41 (1973): 643–656.

[22] Carl Morris, "Statistical Design Aspects for the Health Insurance Study" (RAND working paper, August 1973).

[23] Robert Hall, "Labor Supply and the Negative Income Tax Experiment" (Xeroxed paper presented at the Brookings Institution Conference on the New Jersey Income Maintenance Experiment Results, April 29–30, 1974), p. 50.

guide to what the behavior of an experimental family would have been in the absence of participation is its own pre-enrollment behavior, *not* the behavior of another family over the same time period.

To test this, Hall formulates a theory of individual work choice behavior and applies it to the white male subsample of the NIT data using the pre-enrollment values as control observations contrasted with experimental observations. His results suggest that in most instances the variance of the estimators could have been reduced and the same information acquired with one-sixth the number of observations (slightly fewer than 200). To do this would have required simply delaying the start of payments for half the sample for six quarters, so that half the sample "would have six quarters of control observation followed by six quarters of the program (payments), and the other half the reverse."[24]

While a number of practical problems are presented by this approach, it is not inconceivable that it could offer substantial efficiencies in future experiments where time trends and attrition present fewer difficulties.

Enough has been said in this chapter to indicate the very high level of technical skill that went into the design of the NIT as well as the very considerable contributions it has made and induced others to make to the literature on experimental design. In the next chapter we turn to the design and organization of the fieldwork for the experiment.

Appendix to Chapter 2

References to the memoranda in the text will use the following numbering system.

Internal Memos—circulated between IRP and Mathematica, arranged by date.

IM 1. John Conlisk to William Branson and possibly others, "Reaction to Branson Proposal for Sample Design," April–May 1968.

IM 2. Harold Watts to GWIE staff, "Comments on the Optimal Allocation of Experimental Households by Income Strata," May 10, 1968.

---

[24] It should be noted that Hall's suggestion is a standard technique in experimental designs in biology and psychology. See Donald T. Campbell and Julian Stanley, *Experimental and Quasi Experimental Designs for Research* (Chicago: Rand McNally, 1963). David Kershaw et al. have stated that, in their opinion, Hall's approach would not have been feasible for the NIT because: 1) payments could not have been switched in this way; 2) it was not known *ex ante* that seasonal effects would be unimportant so that pre-enrollment values could be used; and 3) Hall's approach would have accentuated attrition bias in the sample.

IM 3. William Branson, "Sample Selection and Assignment of Tax Plans, Continued," May 15, 1968.

IM 4. Harold Watts to W. Branson, Letter (Watts' answer to Branson memo of May 15, 1968), May 28, 1968.

IM 5. William Branson and Stephen Goldfeld to Harold Watts (No title—comments and questions on Watts' memo), June 10, 1968.

IM 6. Heather Ross to GWIE staff, "Improving the Experimental Design," September 9, 1968.

IM 7. Harold Watts to GWIE staff, "Ross Memos of Sept. 4 and Sept. 9," no date.

IM 8. John Conlisk to NJE researchers, "Further Work on the Sample Design Study Described in 'Sample Design for the Negative Tax Experiment by John Conlisk' and Appendix, 'The ANOVA Model'," January 16, 1969.

IM 9. John Conlisk to NJ experimenters, "Amended Design Results to 16 January Memo," January 24, 1969.

IM 10. John Conlisk to NJ experimenters (No title—model allocations under various constraints on n_i, ϕ_β, N), February 1, 1969.

IM 11. Harold Watts to GWIE staff, "Strategy for Use of Optimization Models for Allocating Experimental Households, and Results of Most Recent Runs of Conlisk-Watts Model," February 1969.

IM 12. Harold Watts, "An Elementary Explanation of the Design Optimization Model," February 1969.

IM 13. Stephen Goldfeld to NJ experimenters, "Comments on the Design Model," March 14, 1969.

IM 14. Princeton NIT to John Conlisk and Harold Watts, "Further Runs," March 20, 1969.

IM 15. Heather Ross to members of NIT, "Notes on Memo of March 20," April 17, 1969.

IM 16. Harold Watts to Albert Rees, "Final Sample Allocation," April 24, 1969.

IM 17. Albert Rees to James Tobin, "A General View of the Design Model," May 1, 1969.

IM 18. Stephen Goldfeld to James Tobin, "Design Model for the Negative Tax Experiment," May 2, 1969.

IM 19. Harold Watts to GWIE staff (No title—alternative runs of the model for different positionings of M), May 14, 1969.

IM 20. Mathematica NIT (David Kershaw and Jerilyn Fair) to James Tobin, "Allocation Proposal," May 23, 1969.

IM 21. Harold Watts to James Tobin, "Mathematica's May 23, 1969 Memo," May 27, 1969.

IM 22. Harold Watts to Stephen Goldfeld and John Conlisk, "Explanation of Model's Assignment of Families to No Payment Cells When M is Set Equal to the Break-Even Point," May 1969.

IM 23. William Branson, "A Proposal for the Assignment of Tax Plans to Experimental Units," March 1968.

Chapter 3
Fielding and Administering the NIT Experiment

INTRODUCTION

Since the development of techniques for the sampling of human populations in the 1930s, sample surveys covering a wide variety of topics administered to very diverse sets of universes have become a standard tool for the gathering of social data for social science and policy purposes. A field experiment of the sort contemplated by IRP and Mathematica had many points of resemblance to panel sample surveys: A specified population was to be sampled, recruited to participate, and periodically contacted by interviewers for the purpose of obtaining information.

The NIT field operations differed from the more usual sample survey in several important respects: First, the population to be sampled—intact families whose income was below 150 percent of the poverty line—is hard to locate and difficult to interview. Second, participating families were to be contacted frequently for a relatively long period of time. Previous experiences with panel studies, involving repeated interviewing of the same respondents, had not been very successful: Attrition rates often depleted panels by close to half the original group within a short span of time. Finally, the families recruited were not only to be interviewed, but those in the experimental group were also to be given payments conditioned by their incomes and by the plan to which they had been allocated, a mixture of activities that might be a source of problems.

Neither IRP nor Mathematica had had much (if any) experience in fielding large-scale surveys. Although survey fieldwork is not either highly technical or esoteric, it is one of those arts in which experience is the best teacher. Neither organization (nor any other social research organization for that matter) had any experience in administering NIT plans.[1]

The first step that the researchers undertook was to separate out the payments from the research function. A Council for Grants to Families (CGF) was incorporated as a separate organization to administer payments. After a disappointing experience with subcontracting, Mathematica decided to set up its own survey organization as a subdivision with the harmless name of Urban Opinion Surveys. Payments and income reports were to be handled by the council while research interviews would be done in the name of Urban Opinion Surveys.

However, at the outset of the NIT Experiment, Mathematica was not going to handle the fieldwork directly. After some consultation with survey experts, initially it was decided to subcontract the research fieldwork to an experienced survey organization. Bids were solicited from several organizations[2] with the Opinion Research Corporation of Princeton, New Jersey, being selected as subcontractor. Within the space of a few weeks, it became obvious that the subcontractor was not able to conduct the initial tasks properly. As a consequence, Mathematica decided to undertake the fieldwork itself. From late 1968 to the end of the experiment in 1972, payments administration and research interviewing were handled by the staff at Mathematica.[3]

Expert advice on field operations was sought from National Opinion Research Center (NORC) and Survey Research Center (SRC) field personnel, among others. But the state of the art of fieldwork involving long-term surveys with a poor and near-poor population was not very well developed. It would be some years before the major survey organizations had developed sufficient experiences of the relevant sort. Hence, by and large, the staff at Mathematica were on their own.

---

[1] Bids were solicited from the two main academic survey organizations, The National Opinion Research Center at the University of Chicago and the Survey Research Center at the University of Michigan. According to David Kershaw, SRC responded by saying that they were too busy with their own research to submit a bid, while NORC responded with a bid that was so high, it was difficult to take the bid seriously. To anticipate the narrative somewhat, the costs of the research overran by 100 percent original estimates, so that it is difficult to judge at this point whether NORC's estimates were so far off the mark.

[2] Of course, existing welfare agencies, the Social Security Administration, and other agencies had experience in the administration of payments system. Since these organizations were negative models for the NIT plan, the experiences of these organizations were not sought.

[3] Mathematica's Urban Opinion Surveys has become the subcontractor on two of the subsequent NIT experiments in Denver and Seattle.

SCREENING FOR ELIGIBLE FAMILIES

The research plan called for obtaining approximately 1,300 intact (husband and wife) families whose head was not in school, under 21 or over 58, or permanently disabled, and whose income was below 150 percent of the then (1968) poverty line in four sites (initially three but later expanded to four by the addition of Scranton, Pennsylvania). The initial task before Mathematica was to locate families who were eligible and willing to participate. The obstacles to be overcome were as follows: First, eligible families constituted a small proportion of the populations of households in the four sites, and although such households can be expected to cluster in subareas characterized by low average incomes, even within those areas, the eligible proportions would be very small. The poverty line was set by the Bureau of Labor Statistics on the basis of national household income distributions and hence could be expected to be cutting somewhat lower in the relatively higher income areas of the urban Northeast. In addition, large proportions of poor households would not be eligible by reason either of age or the absence of an employable male.

Second, it is only under very unusual circumstances that close to perfect cooperation can be obtained from households. Sample surveys of the general adult population undertaken by nongovernmental research organizations tend to get cooperation rates from between 70 percent and 85 percent, with lower rates in urban areas and lower rates among the very poor.[4]

Since no adequate lists of eligible families existed, it was necessary to go door-to-door in the four sites to locate eligible families. The search was facilitated somewhat by concentrating in low income census tracks, but even so, close to 49,000 households were screened in order to locate a sufficient number of eligibles. Table 3.1 contains a summary of the field experiences through enrollment.

Of the 48,614 dwelling units approached, 43,722 were occupied. Among the latter, 63 percent ended in a successful screening interview. A little more than one out of three (37 percent) households could not be contacted or refused to be interviewed on initial contact. While this is a very high proportion of uncompleted contacts, it is not very different from the experiences reported by experienced survey organizations operating within large metropolitan areas. It should be noted, however, that it is large enough to be potentially quite biasing.

The screening interview administered to more than 27,000 households who were willing to be interviewed was designed to eliminate obviously

---

[4] There is some evidence that cooperation rates in sample surveys have declined in the past decade.

Table 3.1
NIT Screening and Enrollment Results

A. *Screening Experience*		
1. Total Housing Units Listed	48,865	
2. Total Screening Interviews Attempted	48,614	
3. Vacant Housing Units	4,892	
Total Occupied Housing Units		(43,722)
Results of Screening Attempt		
4. Family Repeatedly Not at Home	8,414	(19.2%)
5. Refused Screening Interview	7,958	(18.2%)
6. Terminated Screening Interview[a]	9,851	(22.5%)
7. Completed Screening Interview	17,499	(40.0%)
		100.0% = 43,722 occupied D.U.'s
Among Completed Interviews		
8. Ineligible	14,379	
9. Potentially Eligible	3,124	
10. Proportion Potentially Eligible of Total Screening Interviews Terminated or Completed (line 9/lines 6 & 7)		11.4%
	No.	%
B. *Pre-Enrollment Experience*		
11. Total Pre-Enrollment Interviews Attempted	2,953	
12. Moved, Could Not Find	401	13.6
13. Refused Interview	205	6.9
14. Other	6	.2
15. Completed Pre-Enrollment Interview	2,341	79.3
16. Ineligible for Enrollment	828	28.0
17. Eligible for Enrollment	1,513	51.2
C. *Enrollment Experience*		
18. Total Enrollment Attempts	1,316	
19. Moved, Could Not Find	30	2.3
20. Refused	62	4.7
21. No Longer Eligible	8	.6
22. Successful Enrollment	1,216	92.4

[a] Screening interview could be terminated by interviewer if household was clearly ineligible (e.g., over-age, no employable male present, etc.). Presumably these terminated interviews were of patently ineligibles.

Table 3.1 (Cont'd)
NIT Screening and Enrollment Results

	No.	*%*
D. *Some Summary Statistics*		
23. Proportion Eligible of All Completed Contacts (line 17/lines 6 & 8 & 15)		5.7
24. Proportion Refused or Unavailable of All Potentially Eligible[b]		44.0

[b] Computed by assuming that eligibility rate (line 23) applied to all refusals, not-at-homes, and moved at every level of contact (i.e., [lines 4 + 5 + 12 + 13 + 14 + 19 + 20] × .057 divided by line 22 + [4 + 5 + 12 + 13 +14 + 19 + 20] .057).

SOURCE: Adapted from *Final Report,* vol. IV, Table 2. The explanation given in text for differences between lines 7 and the sum of 8 and 9 and lines 17 and 18 is that only sufficient numbers were contacted at each succeeding step to fulfill the needs of the NIT design.

ineligible households. A series of questions were asked about the presence of an employable male between 18 and 58, about whether the household had an estimated annual income above or below 150 percent of the poverty line for a household of its size, and so on. When a household was shown to be obviously ineligible, the interview was terminated.[5] Only 11.4 percent of the screening interviews yielded potentially eligible households.

To make a more precise determination of eligibility, the potentially eligible households turned up in the screening interviews were visited again with a pre-enrollment interview, an instrument that asked for more detail on labor force activities, earnings, sources of non-earned income, and some base-line measures of other variables. Again, on this round, some households were not at home and others refused to be interviewed, amounting to 21 percent of those contacted. A final determination of eligibility left 1,513 families in the eligible pool.

Finally, families were approached to ascertain their willingness to participate in the experiment. At this stage, considerably fewer fell along the

[5] The screening interview, conducted with an adult member of the household, consisted of a series of questions on these critical points. Although a respondent could eliminate the household from eligibility by giving the appropriate answer to any one of the screening questions, it is doubtful that many deliberately did so since the interview did not reveal what was a disqualifying answer. However, since the interviewer did know what were the criteria for disqualification, it is possible that some interviewers disqualified some troublesome households by recording responses that indicated an interview was terminated by reason of ineligibility.

wayside: 7 percent either could not be contacted or refused, leaving a total of 1,216 who agreed to be enrolled.

It is clear from this account and a careful reading of Table 3.1 that the proportion of eligible households in the poorer census tracts of the four sites was quite small[6]: Of those who were successfully contacted, 5.6 percent proved to be eligible. It is also abundantly clear that a very large proportion of households either refused or eluded the interviewers' attempts to reach them. Applying the 5.6 eligibility rate to those who refused or were not reachable[7] to obtain an estimate of the eligibles among households not contacted, it appears that 44 percent of the potentially eligible households either refused or were not reachable.[8]

The fact that two out of five potentially eligible households fell out of the sample before being asked to cooperate is *potentially damaging* to claims of external validity for the experimental findings. One must emphasize the phrase "potentially damaging" in the previous sentence because there is no way of estimating whether in fact a bias existed.[9] If, for example, those who cooperated were no different in any way from those who refused or were repeatedly not at home, then the absence of such families is not serious. On the other hand, if non-cooperating families were different in some relevant way, e.g., more likely to regard leisure as a "normal good," then the experimental results may be badly flawed.

It should also be noted that the proportion of all households successfully contacted who were eligible, 5.6 percent, is very small. It is not at all clear

---

[6] Mathematica originally included some non-poor tracts in Trenton to pick up eligible families who were living in relatively affluent tracts. According to David Kershaw and Jerilyn Fair (*Final Report,* vol. IV), the yield in such tracts was so low that this strategy was abandoned as too expensive.

[7] It is not at all clear whether this estimate is a conservative or liberal one. On the one hand, one may argue that potentially eligible households were drawn disproportionately from life cycle stages in which cooperation rates are usually higher and hence that the estimate is probably high. On the other hand, one might argue that because better educated respondents are more likely to cooperate, poor households whose members have lower levels of educational attainment might be more likely to refuse cooperation, in which case the proportion eligible among the non-cooperators is underestimated. It is impossible to choose between these two arguments.

[8] The refusal rate is probably an underestimate since control families were not solicited to enroll after the pre-enrollment interview. They were contacted again for the first quarterly interview at which point some refused to participate further. Hence the controls refusing at first quarter should be added to the refusal rate at the final stage of enrollment to obtain a measure of initial refusal rate beyond determination of eligibility.

[9] It should be noted that the *Final Report* is far from candid in reporting the enrollment experiences of NIT. Accounts tend to gloss over all but the refusal rate at enrollment (line 20) emphasizing that of those asked to enroll only 4.7 percent refused to do so. The very large proportions who refused at earlier stages are rarely mentioned.

to what population this proportion should be referred: The tracts sampled within each of the sites were ones in which a relatively high potential yield was expected, tracts being selected in which the median incomes for 1960 were below the poverty level. This low yield suggests that in the four sites eligible families are unusual among poverty populations. Indeed, as we can see in Table 3.2, the sample families are unusual.

Table 3.2
Selected NIT Sample Characteristics at Time of Enrollment

Average Family Size—5.9 persons
Average Age of Head of Household—35.8 years
Average Educational Attainment of Head of Household—8.7 years
Average Duncan SES Score—19.1
Proportion on Welfare (1968)—10.6%
Proportion Who Own Their Homes—12.6%
Average Family Income (1968)—$4,024

SOURCE: Assembled from David Kershaw and Jerilyn Fair, *Final Report,* vol. IV, and Seymour Spilerman, *Final Report,* vol. II.

Perhaps the outstanding characteristic of the sample families is their low age and high family size. Given the definition of eligibility as conditioned by family income relative to family size, this end result is quite understandable. The extent to which family size differs from the general poverty population at the experimental sites was calculated by Taussig at 1.8 persons.[10] Taussig notes that family income was not as much at variance from the general poverty population suggesting that it was their large average size that led the sample families to be eligible for participation.

A similar calculation for educational attainment indicated that households in the sample had almost two years (1.8) less education than the general poverty population in the area. Finally, if we consider the earnings of the NIT sample household heads, a calculation by Spilerman[11] indicates that persons holding down similar occupations in the New York-Newark metropolitan area earned about $3,500 more per year than members of the NIT sample.

The occupational prestige scores of the occupations held by household heads (also shown in Table 3.2) indicate that the jobs held by household

[10] Michael Taussig, *Final Report,* vol. III. Comparison is with the non-aged poverty population in 1969.

[11] Seymour Spilerman, *Final Report,* vol. II, calculated from 1970 Census tapes containing detailed earnings by occupation.

heads were on the average very low in the occupational prestige hierarchy: Occupational titles with approximately the same Duncan SES scores were "Auto service and parking attendants" (19), "Painters" (18), "Operatives, beverages" (19), "Housekeepers" (19), and "Bartenders" (19).[12]

Finally, as shown by Wooldridge,[13] the proportion of homeowners in the NIT sample is considerably below the proportions found in census tracts from which the NIT sample was selected.

The eligibility requirements and the enrollment procedures produced an NIT sample whose household heads were working in very low occupations but earning considerably less than average for such occupations in the New York-Newark SMSA. Sample families tended to be considerably larger than the usual poverty families in the experimental sites. Household heads tended to be younger and less well educated than other poor families.

Assuming that these results are not a product of the completion rate described earlier, there is no reason to regard these sample characteristics as in any way peculiar. They represent the fact that in the urban areas in question, the eligibility criteria screened out smaller households, older household heads, etc. One may argue, however, that the eligibility criteria applied are not entirely appropriate to these urban areas since income levels in the urban Northeast tend to be higher than those for the nation as a whole, and hence the poor and near-poor as defined by NIT are relatively poorer in their communities than households eligible by the same criteria in the nation as a whole. In other words, the criteria cut somewhat lower in the four sites in the distribution of income weighted by household size in the nation as a whole. But this argument is not a very strong one: A national program that sets a single standard for the entire country for the definition of a target program would also tend to cut lower in that distribution in the four sites. Only location conditioned target population definitions in a national program would tend to make this sample unrepresentative of the poor and near-poor that would be eligible in the four sites.

One may also argue that it is not necessary for the NIT sample to be representative of the eligible population that might be defined under a specific national program. Since the goal of the experiment is to measure the work response surface defined over the policy surface represented by the experimental treatments, as long as the population sampled is one that is unbiased and covers the eligibility definitions of proposed NIT plans, the resulting computed response surface could be used to provide unbiased estimates of the work responses under such plans.

---

[12] Otis Dudley Duncan, "A Socio-Economic Index for all Occupations" in Albert J. Reiss, *Occupations and Social Status* (Chicago: The Free Press, 1961). The average Duncan score reported in Table 3.2 was calculated by Spilerman, *Final Report.*

[13] Judith Wooldridge, *Final Report,* vol. II.

THE CONSEQUENCES OF SITE SELECTION

The adoption of the "test bore" strategy of sampling was based on the assumption that a national sample would have been too difficult to administer. The obstacles that stood in the way were partially logistic—the difficulty of administering research interviews and income report forms at great distances—and partially political—the difficulty of negotiating with possibly half a hundred welfare departments. In contrast, the state of New Jersey seemed very attractive: A sympathetic administrator headed the state welfare department, New Jersey had a welfare plan that did not include aid to intact families of the working poor, and, of course, New Jersey was close at hand.

It is not at all clear that this decision was the wisest possible. A number of alternatives might have been better. To begin with, a national sample poses no more difficulty to administer as a research operation than several local samples.[14] Payments might have been more difficult to handle at a distance but not impossible. Besides, a national plan would most likely be centralized at least to a regional level. Negotiating with a number of welfare departments would be an obstacle, but it is not at all clear what has to be negotiated. Certainly, if one is going to offer payments to a large number of households within a department's jurisdiction it would be courteous, wise, and prudent to notify the department of this fact. A national sample, however, would deal with only a small number of households within any department jurisdiction, perhaps obviating the necessity for such notification.

Other types of more dispersed samples might have been considered. For example, a sample that covered the urbanized areas of the United States or just the urbanized areas of states that did not have AFDC-UP might be more appropriate. Other universes of interest could be carved out of regions, urbanized areas of various sizes, etc.

The consequences of using a sampling strategy that dispersed interviews among a number of sampling sites might have been very beneficial: First, vulnerability to local events would be reduced. Within a few months of the start of the experiment, the state of New Jersey changed its welfare laws to allow payments to families in which there was an employable male, a change that was to spoil experimental treatments for at least the two least generous plans and to muddy the waters considerably regarding other experimental treatments. Spreading families among a number of state jurisdictions would have preserved at least some of the experimental groups for analysis.

---

[14] Subcontracting to a national survey organization would have immediately made available to the researchers an experienced stable of interviewers and the capability to train the special interviewers this study may have required.

In addition, while negotiations with a small number of welfare officials are easier than relations with a much larger number, so is political vulnerability increased. The trials of Mathematica with the county prosecutor for Mercer County (Trenton) and his demands for access to names of participating families exemplifies this political vulnerability. (See Chapter 8.)

Perhaps the most important consequence of the selection of "test bores" as a sampling strategy was the resultant ethnic distribution of the sample. The 1960 Census led the experimenters to expect that the sample would have a large proportion of black families, but the difficulty of locating eligible white families in the original three sites was not discernible. Nor was it possible to appreciate the considerable increase in the Puerto Rican[15] populations of the three sites that occurred between 1960 and 1968–1969. As a consequence, the experimenters were forced to pick another site with a higher yield of poor white families and to cut back on the original sample allocations in Jersey City and Paterson-Passaic.

The resulting confounding of site and ethnicity is quite severe as Table 3.3 shows. Almost three-fourths of the whites in the NIT sample are from

Table 3.3
Ethnic Distribution Among Four Sites

Site	*Ethnicity*						*Totals*
	Black		*Puerto Rican*		*White*		
	No.	*%*	*No.*	*%*	*No.*	*%*	*No.*
Trenton	105	21	29	7	25	6	159
Paterson-Passaic	193	39	249	60	48	11	490
Jersey City	199	40	139	33	52	12	390
Scranton	3	0	0	0	315	72	318
Totals	500	(100)	417	(100)	440	(100)	1,357[a]

[a] Includes 141 additional control families added to original sample under the Tobin compromise (see Chapter 2).

Scranton, three-fifths of the Puerto Ricans are from Paterson-Passaic, while there are only three black and no Puerto Rican households from Scranton.

A more diversified sampling strategy would not have been as vulnerable

[15] We use the term "Puerto Rican" throughout to refer to those families identified in the *Final Report* of the experiment as Spanish-speaking. This usage emphasizes the fact that virtually all the Spanish-speaking families in the sample sites were ethnically distinct from other segments of the United States' Spanish-speaking population, such as Chicanos.

to inter-censal changes. Furthermore, a diversified sampling strategy that regarded whites and blacks as separate target populations would have produced sample subgroup sizes as desired. As things stand now, Puerto Rican households are apparently an unanticipated subgroup that is separately analyzed because the subgroup size is too large to ignore.

It should be noted that ethnicity was not taken explicitly into account in the sample design of the experiment. From all accounts it appears that the experimenters were concerned when the three New Jersey sites produced few eligible white families, but there was no goal set for a division of the sample among the three ethnic groups. Indeed, one searches in vain throughout the documentation for any statements on this issue until it becomes apparent that were the New Jersey sites alone to be used for filling out the NIT sample, few whites would be included. Nowhere is there a rationale for the heavy representation of Puerto Rican families, a group of some interest in its own right, but scarcely one that makes up a very large proportion nationally of the very poor or the working poor.

The particular form taken by the ethnicity effect (to be discussed in greater detail in Chapter 4 of this volume) is counterintuitive and hence was unlikely to have been anticipated by most social scientists. But, it is not counterintuitive to expect some effect of ethnicity. Further, the three ethnic groups identified in the analysis by no means exhaust the full range of ethnicity to be found in the ethnically heterogeneous urban Northeast. Indeed, one might speculate that the whites of Scranton may be predominantly drawn from among the descendants of eastern and southern European immigrants who came to Scranton in its heyday of anthracite mining and hence may not represent fairly poor and near-poor whites in general.

THE PROCESS OF RECRUITMENT AND ASSIGNMENT

Pre-enrollment interviews that probed in some detail into labor force participation, earnings, and other sources of income (as well as auxiliary topics) were the bases on which final determinations about eligibility were made. Once classified as eligible, families were assigned randomly to experimental groups and particular plans or to control groups.

Once assigned, experimental group families were again approached to be enrolled in a plan as predetermined earlier. Families to be enrolled in the experimental group were told about the plan they were under, presented with a check for their first payment (calculated on the basis of pre-enrollment interviews), asked to sign an agreement to participate, explained carefully their rights and obligations under participation, and were left brochures explaining the plan in detail. Families who had no payments coming were left a check covering a fee for participating.

Families assigned to the control group were told at the first quarterly interview that they were chosen to participate in a long-term study of how families managed their lives and told about the fees they would earn for answering quarterly interviews.

The efficacy of the enrollment procedures can be seen in the low refusal rate, as shown in Table 3.1. Refusals tended to be among the slightly older and less well educated. In addition, the average payment offered to refusals was lower than that offered to those who agreed to enroll, a finding that suggests that controls were less likely to agree to participate.

RESEARCH INTERVIEWING

The basic data collection operation called for a quarterly interview administered to both experimentals and controls. In addition, an annual interview, mainly focused on yearly income records, was administered to both control and experimental families.

Thirteen quarterly interviews were administered to the NIT sample. Each interview consisted of a core section whose content remained much the same from quarter to quarter and a supplement whose content varied from interview to interview. The core section contained questions on household composition, labor force participation of household members, earnings, hours worked, other sources of income, occupation(s), job changes, mode of transportation to work. The supplemental parts of the quarterly interview ranged widely from topics close to the purpose of the experiment, such as health status, inventories of durable goods possessed and purchased, housing, attitudes toward work, and those that were somewhat removed from the experiment, measures of political attitudes, anomie, self-esteem, and so on.

Initially the core interviews centered around the week's experience prior to the interview, being a replication of the Current Population Survey's labor force measurement instrument. Finding that NIT sample families experienced considerable short-term fluctuations in work experience and in income, the time span covered by the core interview was later extended to cover the four weeks prior to the time of the quarterly interview.

Evaluation of the quarterly interviews is crucial to an appreciation of the worth of the experiment since the basic dependent variables of the experiment were measured in the core portions of the quarterly interviews. Discussion of this issue will be postponed until Chapter 4 where the definitions of earnings, hours, and income are taken up.

It may be useful to note here that the core section of the survey questionnaires passed through four revisions each of which was introduced at different times in each of the four sites as shown.

	Quarters In Which Used			
	Old Core	*New Core*	*Revised New Core*	*Final Core*
Trenton	Pre–6	7	8–9	10–12
Paterson	Pre–5	6	7–8	9–12
Jersey City	Pre–3	4	5–8	9–12
Scranton	Pre–2	3	4–8	9–12

The old core instrument asked only for data concerning the previous week's activities and income; the new and revised new core and the final core questionnaires changed this format to ask about each of the four weeks of the previous month. Only the final core asked for overtime and hourly wage *rates,* as opposed to hours and earnings from which rates were calculated. The papers constituting the *Final Report* use series from all four survey forms but confine their analyses to data for the week immediately preceding the interview.

INCOME REPORTING AND PAYMENT ADMINISTRATION

Payments to eligible families in the experimental group were conditioned on filing an Income Report Form (IRF) every four weeks on which earnings of household members and other income received was to be reported. The Income Report Form was to be filled out by the head of the house and sent into the Council for Grants to Families along with pay stubs of employed household members.

Payments to families were calculated on the basis of averaging over the previous three four-week Income Report Forms and mailed to families every two weeks.[16] This method of averaging was employed to smooth out income flows and to avoid overpayment to families and subsequent heavy repayment schedules.

Field offices were maintained on each of the four experimental sites to which inquiries about Income Report Forms were referred by the Council for Grants to Families and to which families could refer for help in filling out the monthly income reports. Experimental families were paid a monthly fee of $20.00 for filing their IRFs. In addition, families were required to submit copies of their annual income tax returns to CGF. Income tax re-

[16] The actual computations also took into account the extent to which the family had been above their particular break-even point in the past forty-eight weeks and the amount of any overpayment in that period of time, payments being reduced proportionately if either condition obtained. See David Kershaw and Jerilyn Fair, *Final Report,* vol. IV, for a more detailed account of the procedures used.

turns were used to calculate reimbursements to families for income taxes paid by families below a certain level of income.

The payments transmitted to qualifying families were not inconsiderable, as Table 3.4 shows. Qualifying families received $1,183 on the average

Table 3.4
Payments Experience in Experimental Group
(Continuous husband-wife families: N = 693)

A. *Average Payments for Four-Week Period by Plan (Second Year)*[a]

	Tax Rate		
Guarantee Level	*30%*	*50%*	*70%*
125%	no plan	187.28	no plan
100%	no plan	183.72	66.07
75%	103.54	44.17	34.91
50%	46.23	21.66	no plan

B. *Average Payments For Each Year*[a]

	First Year	*Second Year*	*Third Year*
Four-Week Period Payments	$91.03	$93.25	$96.84
Annual Payments	$1,183	$1,212	$1,259

[a] Computed only over payments above zero.

during the first year of the experiment, rising somewhat in consonance with increased inflation to $1,259 in the third year of the experiment. (See section B of Table 3.4.)

Of course there was considerable variability in payments according to the plan in which a qualifying family was enrolled: On the most generous plan (125–50) non-zero payments to families averaged $187.28 for a four-week period (or $2,435 per year) and on the least generous plan (50–50) payments averaged $21.66 for a four-week period (or $282 per year).

For families on a given plan, payments, of course, varied according to their income, as computed over the three months previous to a payment period. Since families were allocated to plans differentially according to their income level, families with higher incomes tended to be located in the more generous plans, but at the same time, they were more likely to be over the break-even point and hence not eligible for payments.

The payments received, obviously, were not merely tokens. For many families, particularly those allocated to the more generous plans, the monies received could mean augmenting family income by as much as one-third or one-half again as much as their normal income. In short, the treatment is on the face of it a significant one.

THE PROBLEM OF ATTRITION

Any panel study in which persons are repeatedly contacted over a period of time can expect to run up against the problem of attrition. There are many reasons why respondents who are initially willing to cooperate change their minds. For some, the decision to cooperate is made without sufficient resolve behind it. For others, changed circumstances make cooperation seem less attractive than initially. Still others find answering the questions of the interviewer more irritating than initially anticipated. And so on. The end result is a sample depleted by those who drop out along the way.

The NIT Experiment was no exception to the attrition expectations. At the end of the experiment 81.8 percent of the originally enrolled households were still with the study (see Table 3.5). The proportion that left the study started with a low 4.7 percent at the first quarter and climbed to its maximum of 19.2 percent by the end of the twelfth quarter.

As one might have expected, attrition was greater in the control as compared to the experimental group, 24.4 percent as compared to 15.6 percent. For those who received actual payments or who potentially might have received payments if their incomes dropped below the break-even level, cooperation was apparently more attractive.

Some families left the NIT sample and returned at a later point in time. Section B of Table 3.5 shows the number of quarters missed by households (left-hand column) and the number of quarters in which one or more spouses were not present in the household. At least one-quarter was missed by 27.4 percent of the households, and in 39.3 percent of the households, one spouse was absent or the entire interview was missed.

Up to this point, most of the analyses of the experimental results were performed on a group of households for which there were at least six quarters of interviews and to which the husband and wife were present in the household during the entire span of the experiment. The total number of such households is approximately 690.[17]

The preceding data and that presented in Table 3.5 allow varying expressions of the amount of attrition experienced in the NIT Experiment. A low estimate is presented by the number of families still cooperating in the

---

[17] Different analysts employing slightly different criteria of inclusion have used numbers of households varying by a small number around 690.

Table 3.5
Attrition Experience of NIT Experiment

A. *Numbers and Percents Absent From Sample in Each Quarter*

	Experimental Group		*Control Group*		*Total Sample*	
Quarter	*No.*	*%*	*No.*	*%*	*No.*	*%*
1	18	2.5	39	7.9	57	4.7
2	33	4.6	53	10.8	86	7.1
3	52	7.2	58	11.8	110	9.0
4	57	7.9	60	12.2	117	9.6
5	76	10.5	71	14.5	147	12.1
6	83	11.4	75	15.3	158	13.0
7	87	12.0	88	17.9	175	14.4
8	94	13.0	97	19.8	191	15.7
9	95	13.1	100	20.4	195	16.0
10	96	13.2	112	22.8	208	17.1
11	108	14.9	116	23.6	224	18.4
12	113	15.6	120	24.4	233	19.2
Total NIT Sample	725	100.0	491	100.0	1,216	100.0

B. *Number of Quarters Missed*

Number of Quarters Missed	*Entire Family Interview Missed*	*Interview Missed or One Spouse Missing*
0	880 (72.5%)	695 (60.7%)
1	74	60
2	30	34
3	19	31
4	14	32
5	20	28
6	26	36
7	17	25
8	17	29
9	26	39
10	20	38
11	30	42
12	40	56
Number Missing at Least One Quarter	333 (27.4%)	450 (39.3%)
Base N =	1,213	1,145

experiment at the end of the twelfth quarter (983 or 81.8 percent of the sample initially enrolled). Since many of the analyses were based on the so-called continuous husband and wife subsample, another (and less charitable) estimate is 693 or 57.1 percent. Either the high or low estimates of retention are serious.

An analysis of attrition reported by Peck (*Final Report,* vol. III) indicated that the following household characteristics were predictive of attrition: site, family structure, being in the control group, being in a less generous plan, having a high income, having a low educational attainment, lesser hours of work per week, being on welfare, and being a resident of public housing.[18] In short, families that broke up, were high earners, were on less generous plans, were in the control group, had lower educational attainment, or were on welfare, were more likely to have missed quarters than those with the opposite characteristics.

Certainly the group of families on whom most of the analyses have been run are a self-selected subsample of the families initially enrolled. Peck concludes that analyses in which variables predictive of attrition are not included are likely to be biased against showing an experimental effect. Such variables, however, are routinely included in most analyses in the *Final Report.*[19]

Of course, more serious effects would occur if the variables predictive of attrition were also correlated with the error terms in regression analyses, but such seems unlikely.

Seen against the background of the experiences of other sample surveys in which households were repeatedly contacted over a long time period, it must be said that the NIT experiment did as well or better than most. This is an especially noteworthy accomplishment given the lack of experience of the staffs of Mathematica and IRP in the conduct of such studies. Whether average or slightly above average performance is enough is still another question. Even more perplexing, this last is a question to which there are no hard and fast answers.

A SUMMARY VIEW OF FIELDWORK AND NIT ADMINISTRATION

The fielding experiences of the NIT Experiment illustrate dramatically the very real difficulties that lie in the way of field experimentation that lasts

---

[18] These are *net* effects, computed by regressing number of quarters missed on a large number of household characteristics.

[19] Most of the analyses, in fact, routinely included such factors and hence corrected for this possible source of bias.

for any appreciable period of time. First, if the intended subjects of field experiment are a relatively rare subgroup, the task of locating eligible subjects can be a very time-consuming and costly task. Furthermore, one's vulnerability to the hazards of low completion rates is increased. Our best estimate is that in the end about 40 percent of the eligible families who were approached were either repeatedly not at home or refused to be interviewed.

Second, a field experiment that sets up a set of apparently reasonable eligibility requirements for participation should be wary that these requirements may mean that those who qualify may not be exactly those who are optimally desired. It does not appear that the experimenters anticipated that eligibility requirements would produce larger than average families with very low levels of adult female labor force participation and persons in very marginal jobs.

Third, the strategy of "test boring," while having an appealing name, is one that increases the vulnerability of an experiment to the idiosyncrasies of particular places where the test bores are sunk. In the case of the NIT Experiment, the site-ethnicity confounding was one unanticipated result. Another was political vulnerability as exemplified by the attempted actions of the Mercer County prosecutor's office.

Finally, attrition is an extremely serious hazard. Despite the fact that the experimental treatment is intrinsically attractive and hence should motivate those in the experimental group to remain in the experiment, there are many events exogenous to the experiment that can fundamentally alter a family's best intentions. One in five families had left the experiment by the end of the three-year period and even larger proportions missed one or another of the research interviews. In the end, more than two out of five families either radically changed their internal composition or had missed too many quarters so that the group of continuous husband and wife families upon which much of the analysis of the experimental results were performed constituted less than three out of five of the group of families initially enrolled.

The difficulties summarized are ones that might mean that the experiment is fatally flawed, but not necessarily so. A judgment in this respect has to be suspended until better replications either confirm or contradict its findings. The clearest implication of these operational failings is that experimental findings must be set about with a large number of caveats: The findings apply primarily to the four sites chosen to be test bores, to families that are poor because of their life cycle position and their large size, to families that self-select themselves into cooperation, and to families that remain stable and cooperative over a three-year period.

Chapter 4

Defining the Experimental Treatments

INTRODUCTION[1]

In the early, pre-experiment discussions of negative income tax proposals, only superficial attention was given to the administration of such plans. Milton Friedman envisaged at first an annual settling of accounts with families whose annual income tax returns showed them eligible for payments receiving a check covering payments for the annual accounting period involved. A later proposal by Friedman suggested that eligible families be sent payments on the basis of filing an estimated income for a tax year.

Other accounts of proposed negative income tax plans were agnostic about how the plans were to be administered although there was considerable agreement that the Internal Revenue Service was probably the most logical agency to administer the plan, as the term, negative income tax, suggests. After all, the Internal Revenue Service had considerable experience in mailing out checks, an activity in which the federal government was

---

[1] This Chapter relies very heavily on the following documents: David Kershaw and Jerilyn Fair, *Final Report*, vol. IV; Irv Garfinkel, *Final Report*, vol. III; and Henry Aaron, "Lessons from the New Jersey-Pennsylvania Income Maintenance Experiment," multilithed (Paper prepared for Brookings Institution Conference on the New Jersey-Pennsylvania Income Maintenance Experiment, April 1974).

thought to excel and which was seen as the major administrative task in NIT.[2]

The administration of a negative income tax plan in operation is by no means as simple as some early advocates thought. The operating rules of the New Jersey-Pennsylvania Experiment that deal with questions of eligibility, accounting of income, definitions of terms, procedures for income reporting and similar issues are contained in a manual that is several hundred pages in length. In practice the "treatments" that are outlined in the experimental design have to be spelled out in considerable detail, so that all contingencies are met that conceivably might develop in the real world of households with fluctuating incomes, that change in size, are more or less punctual in filing required reports, and move about from place to place with surprising ease.

It is the first main purpose of this chapter to provide sufficient descriptions of the field operations of the New Jersey-Pennsylvania Negative Income Tax Experiment, so that the readers may get a view of how the experimental treatments worked out in practice. The second main purpose is to provide a comparison between the experimental treatments and their main "competitor," the existing welfare plans in the states of New Jersey and Pennsylvania. The option of going on welfare was open to both experimental and control households with the experimental group households having to choose between payments from the experiment or welfare. The coexistence of welfare and the experimental plans conditions to some extent the external validity of the experiment since some versions of national plans would replace welfare and not coexist with it.

THE PAYMENT SYSTEM AND ITS OPERATION

If the incomes of poor households were relatively constant or predictable over time, the devising of a payment system that was equitable would be quite simple. All one would need to do is to ascertain a predicted income for a period, determine the appropriate payments, and set up a check writing routine that would make checks available at given intervals. But the incomes of poor families are neither constant nor predictable: The jobs[3]

---

[2] According to Harold Watts and David Kershaw (Personal interview, February 1974), the Internal Revenue Service has shown virtually no interest in negative income tax plans and in the New Jersey-Pennsylvania Experiment. Furthermore, when Nixon's proposed Family Assistance Plan was designed, administration of the plan was left to the Social Security Administration. Indeed, HR-1, the administration's bill, was phrased as amendments to the basic Social Security legislation.

[3] The average occupational prestige score of participating household breadwinners was approximately 20, indicating that the typical breadwinner was a semi-skilled operative. One-third of the breadwinners were laborers or service workers. (See Chapter 3.)

held by wage earners are ones in which hours can vary widely over time, in which layoffs are frequent, and in which voluntary job shifts occur.

The payment system administered by Mathematica was separated administratively from the research activities of the experiment by setting up a separate corporation, the Council for Grants to Families. Payment checks were issued by CGF. All household income reports that related to payments were made to CGF. Income reports that were made in response to quarterly research interviews were ignored in computing payments.[4]

An equitable payment system can be defined as one that would be sensitive to income shifts and at the same time prevent overpayment at the end of any accounting: The system devised tended to be somewhat sluggish in its response to monthly shifts in income but did not lead to long-term under- or overpayment. Experimental households were paid bimonthly on the basis of the averages of their income over the previous three months less carry-over amounts by which their previous forty-eight weeks income exceeded the break-even points for their plans. Accumulated carry-over amounts during the previous forty-eight week period were deducted from payments due according to the three-month moving average, so that accounts were always tending toward balance rather quickly.

Incomes for a given month were determined on the basis of a report form filed monthly by each household.[5] Monthly Income Report Forms[6] (IRF) were to be accompanied by pay stubs for wages paid to household members in the report pay period. The forms also called for recording income from other sources as well as certain types of expenditures (e.g., child care) that were deducted from income.

For families whose income over the previous forty-eight weeks did not involve carry-over amounts, payments during the two pay periods following the receipt of a monthly report form were calculated by averaging that report month with the previous two months. Thus such a family reporting no income for a given month would receive two checks during the next month, each equivalent to 1/26 of its guarantee if its income for the previous two months had also been zero. If the family had some income for the

---

[4] They were not ignored, however, in auditing payment-related income reports. Large discrepancies between the two income series were considered grounds for conducting a field audit.

[5] The period actually used was four weeks. To avoid clumsy phraseology we will use the term "month" in appropriate contexts to refer to the four-week reporting period and the term "bimonthly" to refer to the two-week payment schedule.

[6] Monthly Income Report Forms underwent a major revision early in the experiment. The initial version did not stress strongly enough the distinction between gross and net income (it was gross income that was desired) and also underplayed earnings from secondary wage earners and income from sources other than earnings. The final version of the Income Report Form was intended to correct these deficiencies.

previous two months, its bimonthly payments would be less than 1/26 of the guarantee level, the exact amount depending on the amount of income received during those two months. Thus a month of unemployment and zero income would not be responded to for a minimum of forty-five days after the zero income was first experienced, and the immediate payment response did not bring the family up to the guarantee level, only reaching that level after three and one-half months of unemployment.[7]

Unlike most existing welfare programs, no provisions were made for emergency payments to tide a household over until eligibility could be established administratively. Thus a household that experienced a sudden plunge in income and that did not have any reserves to draw upon would be immediately worse off than under welfare although long-run prospects might be better on experimental plans. Of course, we do not know whether such situations of zero income and zero resources actually occur or how frequently.

Households were given a period of two weeks in which to file a monthly report form: Kershaw reports that 89 percent of the households filed in compliance with this requirement. Households that did not file within that time had their bimonthly payment held up. If reports were not filed within an additional two weeks, both payments for that month were forfeited. Only a small portion of families exceeded this additional grace period. A family that had forfeited its rights to payments could be restored to the rolls if it filed the missing report forms. Two forfeiture incidents, however, were sufficient to remove the family from the rolls of the experiment.[8]

It is instructive to compare this report procedure with that required by welfare departments. Typically, eligibility for welfare once having been established, no regular income reports are filed, the household being required only to report changes in income, household composition, etc., as they occur. Eligibility is reestablished by episodic checks on income and assets, the frequency of which usually being a matter of administrative practices within local welfare agencies. A family may go as long as six months to a year without having to reestablish its eligibility.

The points of contrast between welfare and NIT are important. First, welfare typically relies on the client to produce information about changes

[7] Actually the response time is even slower if the household received unemployment compensation since such payments were counted as income and hence figured into the three-month moving averages. The averaging used to compute payments, while assuring that families would not be grossly over- or underpaid, also assured that the connection between earnings and payments would not be patently clear to the families. A period of zero income would not immediately mean payments of $g/26$, nor did payments immediately stop after a family exceeded its break-even point in income.

[8] The final report does not tell how often this occurred nor if families who were removed from the rolls of the experimental group as far as payments were concerned remained on the rolls as far as research quarterly or annual interviews were concerned.

in eligibility, a system that might be appropriate if one would assume few or minor changes over time in a household's income and composition but sure to work inequities if there are many fluctuations. Second, welfare is a system that provides many opportunities for discretionary actions on the part of welfare department personnel. Some departments or subunits or caseworkers may pursue redeterminations of eligibility more diligently than others with a resulting inequity in benefits across clients and possibly across communities. In contrast, NIT operates with a minimum of discretionary possibilities: Benefits are calculated according to a firmly fixed formula, and adjustments in payments are sensitive to short-run changes. If the discretionary aspects of welfare operations are a source of dissatisfaction with the welfare system, then NIT appears to be a definite improvement. This would be especially important if coverage under income maintenance plans is extended more widely to the working poor as well as the unemployed, the former being families more likely to show many short-run changes in income.

All experimental group households, whether receiving payments or not, were required to file monthly Income Report Forms and accompanying validating pay stubs. For filing report forms, experimental families received $20, delivered in two installments either as a bimonthly $10 check in the case of families that did not get payments or added onto payments for other families.[9]

In addition, experimental families that received payments were reimbursed for the positive income taxes (federal) they paid up to the break-even point of their plan. The reimbursement was made on the basis of W-2 and 1040 forms filed by the household and took place annually. Kershaw writes that such reimbursements were not very "effective" since the time lag between the experience of the positive income tax and reimbursement was so great.

Families that were enrolled in the control groups were not required to fill out monthly Income Report Forms. Their incomes were ascertained in the quarterly research interviews. Hence the only income and labor force response measurements that are common to both the experimental and the control groups are derived from the quarterly and annual research interviews. The main analyses of labor force responses are therefore based on the quarterly research interview income series.[10]

---

[9] The monthly filing fee was raised from $5 to $20 early in the experiment in an effort to reduce attrition among families that did not receive payments. Such payments did not count as income for the purposes of the experiment and were subject to income tax.

[10] A comparison among the three income series is made in Chapter 5 of this report. Monthly income reports tend to understate income relative to income reported quarterly or annually.

The payments given to eligible households are not inconsiderable especially when considered against the average incomes of these families.[11] The reader is referred to Table 3.4 which shows the average payments made to "continuous husband-wife families" who were eligible for payments under the various plans. The average annual payment was around $1,200, or about $47 per bimonthly period with considerable variation by experimental plan.

It should be recalled that in addition to these payments, each family in the experimental group received filing fees of $20 per month ($260 per year) for turning in monthly Income Report Forms and $5 for each quarterly interview for a total of $280. Such fees were not exempt from positive income taxes but could be received in addition to welfare payments without affecting welfare eligibility. Thus payments averaged closer to $1,500, and every experimental group family received at least $280 per year (less taxes). Given the low average family incomes of the families in NIT, the filing fees represented a not insignificant increase in income of up to about 5 percent to 6 percent. Filing fees were given only to families in the experimental group, but controls also received some payments for quarterly interviews and address notifications amounting to $116 per year. In short, the experimental treatment at minimum consists of a $12 per month (difference between experimental and control group interview and filing fees) increase in income for each family over and above payments, if any. It is difficult to judge whether this experimental-control differential is important. We bring our readers' attention to this additional feature of the experiment, because it does not receive much attention in the *Final Report* as part of the experimental treatment.

POLICING INCOME REPORTS

One of the features of proposed negative income tax plans that was attractive to liberal critics of the existing welfare system was its promise to avoid some of the more distasteful aspects of welfare's means tests. Eligibility for welfare is based typically upon eligibility criteria that involve marital status, assets, and sometimes proof of unemployability. In contrast, the negative income tax proposals discussed in the early 1960s were to be strictly income based, as modified to take into account the size of a household unit. The allegedly intrusive caseworker who drops by to check on "the man in the house" was to be eliminated completely along with other criteria that tend to stigmatize and degrade.

---

[11] Average annual income for all households was $4,250 for 1968.

Of course, no one ever suggested that there be no checks on household income, but only that the content of the checks be restricted primarily to income. A negative income tax plan had to have some requirement for disclosure of income and some proofs of income had to be obtained. The NIT Experiment opted to express these requirements in the form of the monthly IRF form and accompanying pay stubs as discussed previously. Additional features of the NIT Experiment supplemented the IRF forms.

The pre-enrollment interview may be regarded as the NIT analoguc to the application for welfare payments.[12] Indeed, much of the same information was required: Families had to estimate their income over the year, indicate their monthly rentals, ownership of homes, mortgages, possession of cars and household appliances, show sources of income other than wages and salaries, etc. Quarterly interviews at various times repeated these questions and asked others that dealt with matters that would be of concern to the intrusive caseworker—family composition changes, job and employer shifts, bank balances, as well as purchases over the previous period.

While the quarterly interviews were explained to the NIT families as research and not as payment qualifying instruments, an interpretation reinforced by the division of the two operations between different organizational entities, it is unclear to which extent this separation was believable and understood. While all reasonable attempts were made to nullify misperception of the quarterly interviews, it is possible that some of the families were unable to perceive the differences between the research and the payments operation.

Once enrolled and filing monthly income reports, a household became subject to an auditing system designed both to increase the accuracy of income reporting and to detect possible fraud. The purposes of the income audits were mixed: They were designed to assess the accuracy of measurement of income as reported in the IRF forms and also to deter and detect fraud.[13] Kershaw reports that the audits seldom were pursued to the point where repayments were sought from participating families, and only one household was dropped from the NIT Experiment in Jersey City toward the

---

[12] A major and crucial difference between the pre-enrollment interview and application to AFDC-UP was that a family did not know at the time what would be the consequences of their answers to the questions asked. As a corollary, of course, they did not know how to guard their interests, i.e., whether it would be better to exaggerate or underestimate income and assets.

[13] In a comment on the penultimate draft of this chapter, David Kershaw objected strongly to the interpretation we have given to the auditing procedures of the experiment, claiming that the auditing procedures had mainly a research purpose. The relevant portions of Volume IV of the *Final Report,* we believe, are not clear on this point: For example, the opening paragraph of Chapter XI describes the auditing procedures as follows, "The first three audits were applied to the experimental group only and were designed to deter as well as to detect and measure misreporting."

end of the third year because of repeatedly detected strong possibilities of fraud. Yet the audits did lead to contacts with participating households and hence such contacts, however slight they may be, may also be regarded as part of the experimental treatments that were especially important for families receiving payments.[14] Income Report Forms were checked for internal inconsistencies, compared with previous months for continuity of income sources (e.g., sudden drops in income or earnings from sources that had been reported regularly). If inconsistencies were found or if families did not enclose paycheck stubs with their monthly reports, a series of contacts were initiated with the household starting with a form letter and ending with a visit from a local office if the inconsistency could not be cleared up easily.

Kershaw reports that sometimes information was obtained about possible misreporting through someone observing that the household wage earner was in a work uniform when he reported that he was unemployed or from information received from a neighbor or in newspaper reports. Unfortunately we do not know how frequent such reports were.

Cases of suspected fraud were referred to an Audit Review Panel consisting of five staff members of CGF who reviewed the entire file on the household in question and came to a conclusion about whether fraud was involved.[15]

One hundred and sixty-five cases of suspected fraud were reviewed by the Audit Review Panel of which 72 percent were judged to be "possible, probable, or confirmed fraud." Families so judged were contacted and

[14] In a table presenting results as averages for a month in the middle of the experiment, Kershaw and Fair show that contacts with the families were not inconsiderable, at least in volume. For 668 families, contacts and time per contact were as follows:

	Average Number of Contacts	*Average Time per Month per Family*
Note or Letter	67.3	(Not applicable)
Telephone Contacts	132.9	2.01 minutes
Office Visits	21.9	.99 minutes
Home Visits	32.6	2.55 minutes

It should be noted that these contacts include all contacts, and most involved IRF omissions and errors. Some portion of the contacts were initiated out of the auditing procedure, although it is not possible to tell from the text of Volume IV how large these proportions were.

[15] Although the description given by David Kershaw of the auditing process does not indicate whether or not the auditing for fraud was limited to households receiving payments, it seems clear that if a household misreported income above the break-even point, no fraud is involved and no sanctions can be applied. Hence, whatever auditing was done of Income Report Forms from households above their break-even points must have been concerned primarily with the adequacy of reporting and with inconsistencies that appeared to cast doubt on the accuracy of reporting.

warned that additional offenses would result in forfeiture of payments. Kershaw reports that only one family was removed from the NIT Experiment on these grounds.

A Review Board was also provided for in case households wanted to appeal the decisions of the Audit Review Panel. The Review Board was never used.

There are several important characteristics of this aspect of the auditing procedures. First, the review was conducted entirely within CGF with the household not present or apparently unable to introduce evidence on its behalf. Second, reviews were conducted in a rather large proportion of the cases: The 165 cases represent 22 percent of the families in the experimental group and close to 50 percent of the families receiving payments. Kershaw's account does not indicate how many cases are repeat "offenders" nor what sanctions were imposed.

A second form of audit was instituted after it was discovered that some families in Trenton in the earlier months of the experiment had accepted payments from both welfare and the experiment and underreported such payments to both sources. (See Chapter 8 for a fuller account of these incidents.) Every quarter at each site, the field office manager met with a representative of the community's welfare office to compare rosters of persons receiving payments. Families that were discovered to be accepting welfare payments then entered the regular auditing process (through the Audit Review Panel,[16] amounting to about 18 percent of families on experimental plans and about 40 percent of families receiving payments). In 68 percent of the welfare audit cases, a finding of "possible, probable, or confirmed fraud" was made. Kershaw's account does not indicate whether there were any special dispositions made in these cases that distinguished them from other cases sent before the Audit Review Panel: We may assume that the same actions, as described, were taken.

Without knowledge of the overlap among cases, it is difficult to estimate how many families were caught up in the welfare audit review procedure. Assuming no overlap, the proportion covered is about 40 percent of the experimental families and 90 percent of the families receiving payments. Assuming that families whose cases appeared before the board had an average of two encounters each, these proportions would be lowered by one-half. These two sets of proportions are plausible limits on the amount of detailed scrutiny into the financial affairs of households receiving payments.

Assuming that the lower limits actually prevailed means that one in five of the experimental group households and close to one-half of the households receiving payments were subject to some question concerning the

[16] Note that these 138 cases are *not* included among the 165 reported earlier.

truth or falsity of their Income Report Forms. Furthermore, about one in ten of the families receiving payments were exposed to possible legal prosecution for welfare fraud.

It is difficult to judge from this position and at this time how these investigations were perceived by participants. It is clear that the differences between the NIT Experiment and welfare turned out in practice not to be as great with respect to means tests, although somewhat different in focus as some of the earlier proponents had hoped.

Income and earnings qualifications were tested much more frequently than would be the case under welfare. Inaccuracies and intentional or inadvertent "fraud" were detected through the auditing system that operated with a frequency that far exceeded what would ordinarily be the case for any welfare payment system.

The problems of income reporting can be seen in other perspectives from two additional comparisons between income series made by the Mathematica staff. For 1970 a comparison was made between IRS Form 1040 income (based on copies of returns furnished by participants) and income as reported on the Income Report Forms. Approximately 12 percent reported 15 percent or more income on their IRS 1040s than on the CGF Income Report Forms. A comparison for the same year (1970) with Social Security earnings indicated that about 20 percent of the households misreported (actually underreported) their earnings by 15 percent or more, and about 65 percent of both the experimental and control groups were credited with more earnings by Social Security than they reported on their Income Report Forms. A startlingly large proportion (20 percent) underreported their wages and salaries earnings by 50 percent or more. Overall, however, only 4.2 percent of Social Security earnings in the aggregate was underreported.[17]

In short, income misreporting was widespread among the families participating in the experiment. Of course, any measurement is subject to some error, a condition that is not necessarily fatal to usefulness of the measure. We may regard the errors in this case as generated by a variety of factors, including misunderstanding of the Income Report Form requirements,[18] by the fact that sources of other income may not provide reminders, such as pay stubs, that would increase accuracy on IRF forms, by the fact that Social Security income may be in error, or that Form 1040 incomes may also be in error, and so on. Errors that are important from a research view-

[17] It should be noted that Social Security taxes cover only income from wages and salaries, sources of income that are probably better reported than such non-wage income as interest, transfer payments (e.g., unemployment compensation and public assistance of all kinds), and payments in cash for work on uncovered jobs.

[18] Particularly crucial in this respect is the difference between gross and net income, especially for earnings backed up with paycheck stubs.

point or from a payments viewpoint are those that lead to biased estimates of response or payments over a period of time that are too high or too low. Reviewing the evidence from the various checks made, it does appear that biases are in the direction of understatement of earnings. If we take Form 1040 income and Social Security income as more accurate measures, then IRF income is a slight (under 5 percent) underestimate of "real" income with some families making quite serious underreporting errors.

We can expect that any NIT program that goes into operation will be scrutinized carefully for any resulting evidences of fraud in income reporting. The main lesson that can be drawn from these comparisons is that such concern for fraud will undoubtedly encounter some validating instances when income reports are audited. Such instances will reinforce the strains for developing some sort of strong auditing procedure in an operational negative income tax plan; hence such plans can be expected to develop auditing procedures that blur the differences between negative income tax plans and welfare plans in these respects.

Of course, one may question whether the means tests and income surveillance are as much of a negative feature of our current welfare system as had been supposed. There is much qualitative evidence in the form of reporters' accounts and some from qualitative observers of the welfare system to justify that position.[19] On the other hand, a major study of the welfare system of Wisconsin brings that position into question: Handler[20] finds that welfare clients (at least in Wisconsin) do not find that their contacts with caseworkers are unpleasant or demeaning. The NIT Experiment leaves this question still in an unsettled condition.[21]

Some of the critics of the present welfare system object not so much to the means test as they do to the discretionary powers of caseworkers. NIT did reduce discretionary powers of payments administrators considerably.

---

[19] See, for example, the participant-observer study by Joseph Howell, *Hard Living on Clay Street* (New York: Doubleday–Anchor Books, 1973), for a view of welfare as a constant reminder to clients of their marginal and unspeakable position in our society.

[20] Joel F. Handler and Ellen J. Hollingsworth, *The "Deserving Poor"; A Study in Welfare Administration* (Chicago: The Markham Publishing Co., 1971).

[21] Qualitative remarks from NIT participants, as reported in Kershaw and Fair, *Final Report,* vol. IV, do not refer to the administrative aspects of the experiment as sources of irritation or annoyance, even from participants who dropped out of the experimental group. Negative remarks were recorded about the quarterly interviews but not concerning the auditing system.

This body of evidence tends to support Handler's findings (*The "Deserving Poor"*) although such qualitative remarks are difficult to interpret since their contents are highly dependent on interviewer probes. Furthermore, Kershaw and Fair show only some subportion of the remarks primarily as illustrative, a selectivity that may underplay comments critical of the audits review system.

The rules of eligibility were clear, presumably uniformly applied, and left little or no room for negotiation between an individual family and any representative from CGF. If the objection to discretionary powers is that such powers may be used unfairly to influence the behavior of participating families, then NIT is clearly an advantage over existing systems. If, however, the main objection is to the use of means tests and continual income monitoring, then NIT tends to be possibly marginally different from the existing welfare system and may, in fact, require more rather than less surveillance.

NOMINAL AND ACTUAL TAX RATES

Although marginal tax rates (r) were set in the experimental plan designs, the implementation of the plan to some extent vitiated the tax rates set. Actual tax rates experienced by families participating in the plan differ from nominal tax rates because the three-month moving average payment smoothing device tends to lower the marginal tax rates (at least in the short run) and because some types of income are "forgiven" (e.g., child care payments). In addition, payments are based on income as reported on the monthly Income Report Forms that underreport income as given in the quarterly interviews. Obviously, unreported income could not be subject to the experimental plan tax rates.

A computation of the estimated actual tax rates by Garfinkel[22] yielded the following estimates:

Nominal Tax Rate	*Estimated Actual Tax Rate*
30%	32%
50%	54%
70%	67%

The estimated and actual tax rates are quite close for all of the three tax rate plans indicating that the administration of the experiment was successful in implementing in practice what was intended in the way of actual tax rates.

Garfinkel's estimates of actual tax rates were computed by regressing payments on actual incomes (as reported in quarterly research interviews). Regression coefficients for unearned income (i.e., non-wage and salary in-

[22] Garfinkel, *Final Report,* vol. III. The computations of the actual tax rates shown in earlier versions of Garfinkel's paper showed very striking discrepancies between actual and nominal tax rates. It is upon the earlier versions of this paper that the discussion in Henry Aaron's paper is based. Henry J. Aaron "Cautionary Notes on the Experiment," in *Work Incentives and Income Guarantees,* eds. Joseph A. Pechman and P. Michael Timpane (Washington, D.C.: The Brookings Institution, 1975).

come) were taken as estimates of the marginal tax rates for families receiving payments. Garfinkel claims that these coefficients are biased toward zero, and hence tend to underestimate the actual tax rates. If his claims in this last regard are correct, then the administration of the NIT plans actually imposed slightly more stringent tax rates for the two low tax rate plans than had been intended.

WELFARE AND THE NEGATIVE INCOME TAX TREATMENTS

As envisaged by its advocates, a national negative income tax plan would replace the existing welfare system at least as far as general assistance and AFDC goes. The more "radical" proposals call for replacement of Old Age and Survivors' Insurance (i.e., Social Security) and such categorical assistance plans as Aid to the Blind and possibly some of the veterans' pension plans as well.

The New Jersey-Pennsylvania Experiment, however, could not replace existing welfare plans in those states. Hence, the experiment is to some degree compromised by taking place in a context in which the experimental plans had to "compete" with existing programs, some of which were designed to be available to at least some portion of the same population to which the experiment was directed.

One of the reasons New Jersey was chosen as a site for the experiment was because at the time (1968) that state did not have an AFDC-UP plan. Hence, initially, intact households (husband and wife both present) were not eligible for AFDC support, although such households were, if eligible, covered for some support under the state's general assistance plan.[23] Indeed, one of the motives for restricting the experiment's coverage to intact households was to remove the experiment from competition with the New Jersey welfare system. However, shortly after the experiment was launched in Trenton, the New Jersey legislature elected to change its welfare system to include intact households under an AFDC-UP plan. The new plan also

---

[23] The main differences between general assistance and AFDC lie in the source of funds—a large part of the AFDC costs are borne by the federal government while general assistance costs are borne totally by the states—the terms of eligibility, and the levels of support. Generally, the levels of support provided under general assistance are not as generous, and eligibility is usually somewhat more difficult to establish. Understandably, states have tended to shift households from general assistance to AFDC when possible.

Another reason for picking New Jersey was because the head of the state welfare system was regarded by the experimenters as sympathetic to the aims of the experiment. Ironically, this sympathy arose out of the same liberal intentions that led him to push for the liberalizing change in the state welfare system in the direction of extending benefits to families with unemployed male parents.

established quite generous levels of support for families in which the main breadwinner was either unemployed or worked less than 100 hours per month.

The changes in the New Jersey welfare system went into effect before recruitment of families in the other two New Jersey sites, so that for most of the experimental period the treatments existed side by side with a competitive New Jersey welfare system.

Pennsylvania's welfare system had an AFDC-UP plan in effect throughout the entire experimental period with the effect that participating households in Scranton had options, if otherwise eligible, to either take the experimental payments or apply for welfare.

The competing welfare plans in New Jersey and Pennsylvania were quite generous at the outset, although New Jersey was to cut back on its guarantee level and tighten up its administrative rules toward the end of the experimental period. Differences between welfare and the experimental treatments existed in a number of respects, as follows.

1. An eligible household on the experimental plan receives payments as long as Income Report Forms are filed. To obtain welfare payments, a household has to apply, report changes as they occur, and submit to episodic reassessments of eligibility.
2. Eligibility for welfare depends not only on income but also on other criteria, e.g., unemployment or underemployment of major breadwinner. Furthermore, eligibility is established administratively by welfare officials who have some degree of discretion in their judgments.
3. Although the nominal tax rate under AFDC-UP is 67 percent, discretion, a number of income forgiveness features reduce the actual tax rate to 47 percent in New Jersey and 34 percent in Pennsylvania.[24] A main source of the difference between nominal and actual tax rates on welfare plans lies in the generous forgiveness features of the plans. For example, the first $30 of monthly earned income is "forgiven." In addition, certain expenses that are work-related (e.g., transportation, work clothes, meals eaten away from home, etc.) are exempt from computation in figuring benefits.
4. In addition to payments, welfare recipients are entitled to certain non-cash benefits, among which the more important are coverage under Medicare and participation in the food stamp plan.[25] Benefits under Medicare can be quite considerable in the case of catastrophic and/or prolonged illness.
5. Income eligibility levels for welfare are usually lower than the break-even points for welfare. Thus a family would have to be poorer to get on

[24] As computed in Garfinkel, *Final Report,* vol. III.

[25] Participation in food stamp plans, initially restricted to welfare and other assistance plan participants, was extended to low income families in general during the experiment in 1971. Hence food stamp plan participation distinguished between the experiment and welfare only for a portion of the experimental period.

welfare initially than it would have to be for welfare payments to cease entirely.

6. Families participating in the experimental group of NIT received payments automatically when their monthly Income Report Forms showed eligibility. In contrast, to go on welfare a family had to apply and establish eligibility. In the existing welfare system considerably more families are eligible for payments than are receiving payments, a condition that is especially prevalent for the "working poor," the group from which the NIT sample was drawn most heavily.[26]

Many of these differences between welfare and the negative income tax plans used in the experiment are hard to incorporate into a systematic comparison between the two plans. Some of the differences are optional choices, e.g., filing for welfare benefits or participation in food stamp plan; others are obtained only under certain circumstances, e.g., forgiveness for work-related expenses; and others are difficult to convert into cash equivalents, e.g., Medicare coverage.

For these reasons, any comparisons between welfare plans and the NIT plans are fraught with possible error. The comparisons that follow are based upon certain assumptions that vary in fragility. First, we assume that the computations of the actual tax rates presented by Garfinkel in the *Final Report* are good estimates. Second, we assume that it is as easy to get on welfare as it is to receive payments under NIT, an assumption that ignores the element of administrative and caseworker discretion that we know exists in the real world. Finally, we ignore the important fact that there are other benefits whose impact is not shown. Hence, when we refer to *systematic differences* between welfare and NIT payment plans, we only refer to the impacts of guarantee levels and estimated actual tax rates.

The systematic differences among experimental plans and competing welfare plans[27] that can be calculated are shown in Table 4.1. Note that the computations are shown for a household of four persons. Larger or smaller household sizes are subject to guarantee levels that vary from those shown.[28]

Given the numbers shown in Table 4.1, it is clear that the New Jersey

---

[26] The "involuntary" nature of payments among NIT experimental families raises the question of whether the experiment is a fair test of NIT plans that might be enacted. It is difficult to envisage an enacted NIT plan that would require that all families (or even those below a certain income cutoff point) be required to file monthly Income Report Forms. Hence enacted NIT plans would most likely be "voluntary" in the same sense that current welfare plans are. Some commentators, noting this administrative problem, propose tying NIT plan administration to place of employment using the existing withholding mechanism in reverse to supplement earnings, a device that ties payments to wages and not to family incomes.

[27] Aaron, *Income Maintenance Experiment.*

[28] The NIT plans do not provide any additional payment for households that are larger than six persons while welfare plans continued to increase payments beyond that household size.

Table 4.1
Real, Nominal Welfare, and Negative Income Tax Guarantees, Tax Rates and Break-Even Levels[a]

Program	*Guarantee*	*Nominal Tax Rate*	*Nominal Break-Even*	*Eligibility Level*	*Actual Tax Rate*	*Actual Break-Even*[b]
Welfare						
New Jersey Pre-cut	$4,164	.67	$6,192[c]	$4,248	.47	$ 9,219
New Jersey Post-cut	2,592	.67	4,608[c]	3,310	.47	6,235
Pennsylvania	3,756	.67	5,994[c]	3,756	.34	11,407
Negative Income Tax Experiment Plans						
50–50	$1,984	.50	$3,968	$3,968	.54	$3,674
50–30	1,984	.30	6,613	6,613	.32	6,200
75–70	2,976	.70	4,251	4,251	.67	4,428
75–50	2,976	.50	5,952	5,952	.54	5,511
75–30	2,976	.30	9,920	9,920	.32	9,300
100–70	3,968	.70	5,668	5,668	.67	5,923
125–50	4,960	.50	9,920	9,920	.54	9,185

[a] Computed assuming a family of four persons.
[b] Computed taking into account exemptions noted in footnote c and actual tax rates.
[c] Assuming $360 exempt from tax rate in New Jersey pre-cut and Pennsylvania and $720 exemption in New Jersey post-cut.

pre-cut welfare plan dominated all of the experimental plans, except the 75–30 plan, with respect to break-even points. The Pennsylvania welfare plan dominated all of the experimental plans in that respect having a higher break-even point than any of the experimental plans. Even the post-cut New Jersey plan dominated most of the experimental plans, four out of seven.

Of course, the break-even points are not the only comparative features to dwell upon. In order to receive payments a family must fall below the eligibility levels shown in Table 4.1. In this respect, the experimental plans were usually more accessible, the eligibility levels of the experimental plans dominating both New Jersey and Pennsylvania welfare plans with the sole exception that it was easier to get on the New Jersey pre-cut plan than to get on the least generous experimental plan (50–50).

Tables similar to Table 4.1 can be constructed for other household sizes. Indeed, the point can be made that there are considerably more than eight treatments since each household size has a different guarantee level and correspondingly different break-even and eligibility points on each of the eight experimental plans. Without computing out the relative advantages of NIT payments and welfare for different family sizes, it is not at all clear whether the pattern of inferiority-superiority shown for four-person households would obtain for other household sizes.

What is clear, however, is that the NIT plans are *not* uniformly superior to the existing welfare plans. Furthermore, if we assume the computed tax rates, as shown in Table 4.1, the plans for at least some of the household sizes are largely inferior in some important respects to the existing welfare plans that obtained for most of the experimental period.

As one might expect from the nature of the criteria for eligibility imposed by the experiment, a rather large proportion of the families enrolled were eligible for welfare payments. According to computations made by Avery[29] (shown in Table 4.2) 44 percent of the families in the experimental group and 45 percent of those in the control group were eligible for welfare on the basis of income alone for at least four quarters of the experiment. Section A of Table 4.2 also shows eligibility levels among ethnic subgroups within the experimental and control groups. It is apparent that control group blacks had the highest eligibility level (59 percent) while control group whites had the lowest (33 percent), a fact that may reflect differential attrition among whites (see Chapter 3) and the fact that black controls showed an unexplained steady decline in fortunes during the experimental period (see Chapter 5).

Section B of Table 4.2 shows the proportions who have ever been on welfare during the experiment among those who were eligible and among those who were not eligible (by virtue of income levels). Perhaps the most

[29] Robert Avery, *Final Report,* vol. II.

Table 4.2
Welfare Eligibility[a] and Welfare Participation[b]
(Continuous husband and wife sample: N = 693)

A. *Welfare Eligibility*

	Experimental Group		*Control Group*	
	Percent Eligible	*100% =*	*Percent Eligible*	*100% =*
Whites	42%	[181]	33%	[129]
Blacks	42%	[151]	59%	[83]
Puerto Ricans	52%	[93]	52%	[56]
Total	44%	[425]	45%	[268]

B. *Welfare Participation*

	Experimental Group Percent Participating Among				*Control Group Percent Participating Among*			
	Eligible	*100% =*	*Not Eligible*	*100% =*	*Eligible*	*100% =*	*Not Eligible*	*100% =*
Whites	36%	[76]	14%	[105]	81%	[43]	23%	[86]
Blacks	47%	[64]	17%	[87]	53%	[49]	18%	[34]
Puerto Ricans	42%	[48]	18%	[45]	41%	[29]	22%	[27]
Total	42%	[188]	16%	[237]	60%	[121]	22%	[147]
Average Number of Quarters on Welfare	6.4		4.5		8.4		5.7	

[a] Welfare eligible: Families whose total income (excluding transfer payments) fell below the relevant eligibility levels for one-fourth of the experiment and whose income fell below relevant break-even levels for at least one-half of the experimental period.

[b] Welfare participation: Family was on welfare at least once during the period of the experiment.

surprising aspect of this portion of Table 4.2 is the fact that income ineligibility is apparently not a barrier to welfare participation.[30] Among the ineligible experimental families 16 percent were on welfare at least once, and among ineligible control group families 22 percent had been on welfare during the experimental period. A sizable difference in welfare participation between experimentals and controls among eligible families (42 percent

[30] It should be noted that classification into the eligible group was based on having family incomes below eligibility for at least four quarters. Some of the ineligible families may have been below the eligibility level for shorter periods of time and applied for and received welfare during those shorter periods of ineligibility. In addition the measurement of family income used by Avery is an estimated value (see Chapter 5) and these families may simply have lower *actual* incomes than estimates would predict.

and 60 percent) shows the extent to which payments under NIT were preferred to welfare by the experimental families.

Whites were apparently more likely to go on welfare if eligible and in the control group than either blacks or Puerto Ricans. This finding highlights the confounding between site and ethnicity since the concentration of whites in Scranton makes it nearly impossible to decide whether this response is a difference due to ethnicity or due to the perhaps greater ease of entry into the welfare system of Pennsylvania as opposed to that of New Jersey. Experimental-control group differences in welfare participation for blacks and Puerto Ricans were small indicating that most of the experimental-control group overall differences in participation were accounted for by a very great differential among whites.

The findings shown in Table 4.2 clearly indicate that the potential competition between welfare participation and accepting payments from CGF was significant. These findings also indicate that the aggregate response to that competition is made up of quite different response tendencies in the three major ethnic subgroups of the NIT sample, confounded with possible site differences.

At this point it may be useful to digress from the presentation of this chapter to consider some of the implications of Table 4.1 for the ethics of future experiments. While the experimenters were aware early in the experiment that there would be some competition between welfare and NIT, the full extent of this competition came to light when analyses had been undertaken that revealed the relative attractiveness of the experimental plans and local welfare payments. As a corollary, we can assume that the experimenters were also unaware of the extent to which participation in the experiment for some families was not to their advantage and that some would have been better off applying for welfare and foregoing CGF payments.

However, let us consider the following issue: Suppose that the experimenters had known at the start that the plans were inferior in benefits for some families, what obligations would they have had to inform the families that they would be better off foregoing payments? Furthermore, would they have had an obligation to compute for each family the relative advantages to be gained from participation in the NIT experimental group and to inform the families of the results of such computations? The general rule that researchers should not expose unnecessarily a subject to harmful conditions can be applied in this case only by making some assumptions about how much and how necessary is such harm done to a family by withholding information of this sort. Certainly, withholding information about welfare eligibility when a family is eligible and is not aware of the eligibility is not doing positive harm: It is simply not providing a benefit, an act for which there exists no positive rule. Hence one might properly take the position that informing a family about relative advantages is also not an act of positive harm. Yet, one may also take the position that the offering of participation in an experimental plan alters the situation somewhat and hence that there is a positive obligation to point out that they could be better off applying for welfare payments.

We do not pretend to be skilled ethicists. All we can point out is that the NIT Experiment presents some ethical dilemmas that are worthwhile considering since identical or similar situations may occur under future experimentation with social programs that are designed to coexist with prior plans.[31]

It is difficult to assess precisely what are the effects of this pattern of unclear differences between experimental treatments and existing welfare plans. Table 4.3 shows the proportion of households on each of the plans that were on welfare, on NIT payments, or above the break-even level for NIT. Table 4.3 also shows dramatically where NIT payments were clearly inferior, as in the case of the least generous plans (see rows 2 and 5), households opted for welfare. It is also clear that even on the most generous plans (see rows 3 and 7) some households opted for welfare, possibly because of non-cash benefits, e.g., Medicare or food stamps.

Since welfare was available to both experimental and control groups, the experimental treatment represented by the least generous plans can hardly be said to obtain. Indeed, it may be only for the most generous plan, 125–50, that NIT payments were a clear experimental treatment for households in the experimental group.

Aaron[32] suggests in his paper that the "true" experimental treatment by each family is the difference between NIT plan payments and welfare payments for that family. Although this suggestion has a certain appeal to it, there are some cogent objections to it as well. First, welfare does require some effort on the part of the household in applying. Second, welfare does have a means test that takes into account assets that are completely ignored under NIT plans. Third, the income eligibility levels for welfare are often lower than the corresponding eligibility levels for the NIT plans. Fourth, welfare eligibility is tied to unemployment and underemployment, conditions that are ignored in NIT computations. In short, while welfare may be more generous in its payments, it may be considerably less attractive

---

[31] This problem has been encountered in a more compelling form in the design of the RAND health insurance experiment where some participants are asked to accept inferior medical coverage for the experimental period. A system of side payments may meet the ethical objections by muddying the treatment.

[32] Aaron, *Income Maintenance Experiment.*

Table 4.3
Distribution of Families by Welfare, NIT, and Break-Even Status Among NIT Plans and Control Group
(Unweighted average percents over twelve quarters)

Plan	*Percent on Welfare*	*Percent Above Break-Even*	*Percent on Welfare or Above Break-Even*	*Percent on NIT*	*Percent of Those Below Break-Even on Welfare*
50–30	21	28	49	51	29
50–50	18	76	94	6	75
75–30	8	9	17	83	10
75–50	12	47	59	41	23
75–70	18	72	90	10	64
100–50	12	15	27	73	14
100–70	13	41	54	46	22
125–50	7	6	13	87	7
All Experimental Households	12.1				
Control Households	23.2				

in other respects and, for many households that are not already on welfare, unavailable because of eligibility rules.

A clue to the overall relative attractiveness of welfare and the NIT plans is afforded by the overall average proportions of the control and experimental families who were on welfare, as shown at the bottom of Table 4.3. Of the experimental families, 12.1 percent on the average were receiving welfare payments in any given quarter; the comparable proportion for the control group households was 23.2 percent, almost twice as high.[33] Since there is no reason to believe that control group families were any more likely to be eligible to participate in welfare plans than experimental households, the difference between the two proportions indicates that NIT participation was largely preferable to and/or easier to get than welfare. The last column of Table 4.3 modifies this generalization somewhat by showing that when welfare payments were clearly superior to those obtainable from NIT plans, as in the cases of the least generous plans, experimental households elected to be covered by the welfare system.

[33] Note that these average participation rates are not the same by definition as the proportions ever on welfare shown in Table 4.2.

WHAT WAS THE EXPERIMENT?

The essence of an experiment is control exercised by the experimenter over the content of the treatments and the ways in which those treatments are administered to appropriate groups. In the best of experiments, the treatments are clearly defined and as far as possible uncontaminated with non-treatment elements. A nominal treatment may be severely compromised by the way in which it is administered to experimental groups and by the presence or absence of elements in the real world that may interact with treatments to vitiate the nominal content of treatments. The discussion of this chapter illustrates that the New Jersey-Pennsylvania Experiment has not been exempt from problems in these respects.

Obviously, no single experiment can fulfill the requirements of an ideal experiment in these terms. A treatment has to be translated into operations that only more or less faithfully represent the treatment as envisaged by the experimenters. Any instance in which an experiment is tried or any context in which it is administered is to some degree unique and hence capable of interacting with the treatment in ways that are hard to anticipate in advance and harder to disentangle after the experiment is over. Hence one of the major products of an experiment are additional experiments, each motivated by the desire to clarify the nature of the treatment by varying some aspect of it or to test the generality of experimental results by extending the experimental target to other populations. The NIT Experiment is no exception to this tendency for a single experiment to broaden into an experimental program: The recently completed rural NIT experiment conducted by Lee Bawden and the Seattle, Denver, and Gary experiments extend NIT to different populations and define the treatment parameters differently.

The work response to negative income tax plans will be better assessed when the results of all experiments are in and as carefully analyzed as the present NIT Experiment. In the meantime, it is important, we believe, to examine the form of the NIT experimental treatments as we have in this chapter in order to provide an assessment of the limitations that might be properly placed around the interpretations of the NIT experimental results. There are several features of the experimental treatments to which we want to draw attention.

First, it should be clear that the experimental treatment as administered is not merely payments but rather a system of income reporting, auditing of reports, *and* payments. This is unavoidable; any national negative income tax plan would contain administrative elements as well as payments. The question remains, however, whether a different administrative system would produce a noticeably different response. For example, a negative income tax plan with compulsory work or manpower training provisions may have a different impact on households. Or, an income accounting procedure that was based on a quarterly income report from families might be met with a different response. The experimenters implicitly assumed that the important aspects of a negative income tax plan were guarantee levels and tax rates; hence these were systematically varied in the experimental design. From the New Jersey-Pennsylvania Experiment it is impossible to disentangle administrative components from guarantees, tax rates, and payments.

Finally, the experiment was transformed fundamentally by the fact that its treatments were undermined by the existence of competing welfare plans. As the discussion in the chapter tried to show, it is not at all easy to discern the impact of this competition on the experimental treatments. It is clear, however, that the experimental results ought to be interpreted as the labor force response to a negative income tax plan in competition with relatively generous welfare programs. The findings then may be interpreted as the labor force response that can be expected from NIT over and above the labor force response already engendered by generous welfare plans of the sort administered by New Jersey and Pennsylvania during the experimental period.

It should be noted that this qualification on the interpretation of findings may vitiate the experiment's relevance to economic theory. Whatever work response that has been generated by existing welfare plans is not measured by the experiment: Hence if the total work response of a population subject to a variety of g's and r's is the point at issue in economic theory, the experiment only provides part of the answer. On the other hand, the competition between welfare and experimental payments does not undermine the experiment's relevance to social policy. An enacted negative income tax plan would most likely supersede existing welfare plans. Hence if the relevant policy question is how much *more* of a labor force response can be expected under such an enacted plan, then the NIT Experiment does have something to say on the issue. Properly qualified, the findings of the experiment provide important information on labor force response to NIT as a *replacement* for generous welfare plans.

Chapter 5

Measurement of the Dependent Variables in Analyses of the Labor Supply Response

INTRODUCTION

Measures of the labor supply response of NIT families form the basic data from which estimates of experimental effects were constructed. The quality of the data obtained in raw form from the families and the ways in which such data were transformed into indices and constructed variables are obviously crucial to an evaluation of the NIT Experiment. It is to these issues that this chapter is devoted.

The labor force responses of the NIT families were derived from three raw data series.

> *Family income:* Earnings of individual wage earners plus other sources of income, collected quarterly in family interviews.
>
> *Labor force participation:* Employment, unemployment, withdrawal from labor market for individual members of family, collected quarterly.
>
> *Hours worked:* For employed persons, hours worked on each of the jobs reported, collected quarterly.

For the most part, discussions of the quality of these data series are dispersed throughout the *Final Report*.[1] A degree of professional anarchy prevails in the chapters of the *Report* manifested in a tendency for authors to pick and

[1] Volume III of the *Final Report* is devoted primarily to technical evaluations of the data series, but discussion of the issues involved is contained in many of the more substantively oriented chapters in the other volumes.

choose among data series and to construct new variables in ways that may vary from author to author. We will not look at all the ways in which the basic raw data series were used, preferring to dwell upon the most commonly employed series.

Particularly crucial to the understanding of the main analyses of labor force response are two constructed independent variables $\hat{Y}$ and $\hat{w}$, measures, respectively, of the "normal" income and wage rates of individual wage earners *in the absence of experimental participation.* Since these constructed variables are used throughout the *Report* on the right-hand side of labor force response estimating equations, they are especially important to an understanding of the mode of analysis used throughout the *Report.*

Measures of non-labor force responses of families to the experiment are discussed in detail in Chapter 7.

DEPENDENT VARIABLES—MEASURES OF RESPONSE

Four direct measures of labor supply response were collected in quarterly interviews.

1. *Labor force participation:* defined consistent with BLS practice as those who are employed or actively seeking employment during the week(s) prior to the interview.[2]
2. *Employment status:* not in labor force, unemployed without a job, unemployed with a job (i.e., temporarily laid off), employed but not at work in previous week(s), employed and working, unknown.
3. *Hours worked:* total hours worked in the previous week(s) at all jobs, hours worked at main job only, and regular hours worked at main job only (i.e., excluding overtime).
4. *Earnings:* total gross cash income for labor services of the previous week(s) including overtime, sick pay, and vacation pay *before* taxes and other deductions.

Each of these measures was obtained in the quarterly research interviews administered to families in both the experimental and control groups. The questions used underwent several transformations during the experiment, a final version of the core questionnaire being adopted after experience with three earlier versions. The initial version of the core questionnaire, replicated from schedules used in the Current Population Survey labor force participation monthly survey, concentrated on the measurements of behavior during the week previous to the interview time. The final version of the

---

[2] David Horner and Harold Watts, *Final Report,* vol. I, esp. pp. 20ff., and Robinson Hollister, *Final Report,* vol. I. Only data for the previous week were analyzed in the *Final Report* papers.

core interview, adopted in 1970, extended the time coverage to include each of the weeks during the month previous to the interview. Although the extension of coverage to the month previous was designed to iron out the fluctuations in earnings that result from concentrating on only the previous week, to restrict the analysis only to data in the final version of the core meant giving up data collected during the first year and one-half of the experiment: As a consequence most of the analyses have been restricted to data obtained concerning the week previous to the quarterly interview.

As discussed in Chapter 2, experimental group families also reported earnings and other income on the monthly Income Report Form. The resultant data were used primarily for payment purposes: They cannot be used for analysis of labor responses since control families were not required to submit monthly reports. Such data have been used, however, to estimate the reliability of earnings and income reports of experimental families, as noted subsequently.

In addition to these four dependent variables, two independent variables for normal income ($\hat{Y}$) and normal wage rate ($\hat{w}$), were constructed econometrically, the first to give a smoothed income series net of experimental effects to be used in both labor supply and non-labor supply equations, the second to provide an independent measure of wage-rate effects free of any bias inherent in calculating wage rates from the reported data for earnings and hours worked, which may themselves contain substantial measurement error. In the *Final Report* analyses of labor supply response, normal income ($\hat{Y}$) and the normal wage rate ($\hat{w}$) are used as independent variables determining labor supply as measured by labor force participation, employment status, and hours worked—earnings were dropped from some analyses when it was discovered that this variable included a large reporting error.

The next section examines the quality of the reported data series for the four dependent variables, followed by descriptions of how $\hat{Y}$ and $\hat{w}$, the independent variables, were constructed; the last section draws together some critical observations on these measures and attempts to indicate some improvements in the formulations of both the dependent and independent variables that could have had substantial impact on analysis of the final results.

QUALITY OF THE DATA SERIES

Although information on the quality of the basic data series is rather spotty throughout the final papers,[3] it appears that quality varies consider-

[3] An exception is Walter Nicholson's paper on the income data series, *Final Report,* vol. II.

ably. Data on labor force participation and employment status come from relatively straightforward and well-tested questions used by the Bureau of the Census so that errors in these series are likely to be minimal arising out of respondent dissimulation or defects in data handling. While the *Final Report* papers say very little about possible incentives for misreporting labor force participation and employment status, we may surmise from the data themselves and their close parallel to national participation figures that neither conceptual nor reporting errors were very significant in these two dependent variables. Greater scope for error is presented in the hours worked and earnings measures, and these are the subject of some specific discussion where they appear in the labor supply analyses of the *Final Report.*

Reported Hours Worked

The final versions of the core questionnaire distinguished total hours worked from overtime and double jobs, but the final labor supply analysis was based only on the most comprehensive measure, "hours worked at all jobs, including overtime." There are at least two sources of possible bias in this measure, neither of which is discussed in the final analyses. First, straight-time and overtime are commonly (though not always) paid at differing rates, so that when the aggregate "total hours worked" is used to calculate an observed wage rate (w) the result will be some average hourly wage that is a combination of the straight-time and overtime rates.[4]

Whether the worker makes his labor supply decisions on the basis of some average wage or consciously calculates the effect of a higher marginal wage from overtime is ignored in this treatment.[5] In the final analysis of the labor supply responses of married men, Watts finds evidence that the 5 percent reduction in hours worked by white males on the "middle plan" was accomplished by a contraction of hours worked within the same employment level, an adjustment made presumably by reducing overtime work, but he is unable to analyze the adjustment in terms of a difference in marginal wage rates or to say anything more specific about the way overtime is used by the working poor. This omission is particularly regrettable when one attempts to draw some conclusions about the ability of the national working population as a whole to make small adjustments in what is commonly a fixed work week.

---

[4] Regular and overtime pay *rates* were collected for the final year of the experiment but to our knowledge these data have not yet been exploited, at least in part because they are not available for the full three-year period of the experiment.

[5] It might be noted that this decision process is of particular interest to those who argue that an increase in the minimum wage or a direct wage subsidy to employers are superior anti-poverty policies.

A second possible source of error in hours worked arises out of the way in which the question concerning hours was asked. The revised version of the new core interview on which the *Final Report* analyses are based ascertained hours worked through the following question.

> I would like to find out about the work you have done on your *main* job in the past month. Could you tell me about how many hours you spent working for each week in the *past month?* I want the total number of hours, including overtime, if you had any. Does that include any overtime? If so, how many hours of overtime did you work that week?
>
> Did you ever have more than one job at the *same time* during the *past month?* If so, about how many hours per *week* over the *past month* did you work on the extra job(s). . . ?[6]

It is possible that some respondents who were paid at time-and-a-half overtime rates reported an hour and one-half for each hour of overtime. Without knowing the conventional rhetoric in which hours worked is discussed by typical blue collar workers, it is difficult to evaluate whether this question is a sufficiently well-phrased one.[7]

A related problem has been noted with respect to the accuracy of reported hours of those working at irregular and part-time jobs.[8] Such hours may well be understated since there was clear incentive to underreport earnings (which became subject to the marginal tax), and this would have been much easier to do for jobs involving no formal time-card punching or pay stubs. Families in the experimental group were supposed to support their

---

[6] Harold Watts, Dale Poirier, and Charles Mallar, "Concepts Used in the Central Analyses and Their Measurement," *Final Report,* vol. I, p. 89, fn. 2. They are quoting items 3, 4, 18, and 21 from the revised new core Questionnaire. A later revision of the questionnaire asked for more detail on overtime rates, but these were not used in the final analyses.

[7] Since hours and earnings were known from the very start to be critical dependent variables it is surprising that some pretesting was not undertaken on alternative ways of asking these questions. In effect, the original core questionnaire, administered over the first year, became the pretest for three subsequent changes in the survey instrument.

[8] Albert Rees has commented that a significant number of the male heads in the sample "held part-time jobs full time," that is, combined several part-time jobs into the equivalent of a thirty-five to forty hour work week and, indeed, this may have been what permitted the adjustment of hours within constant employment levels. Unfortunately it is not possible to obtain from the *Final Report* any estimates of how frequent such double job holding might be among the NIT families. Indeed, the *Final Report* is distressingly vague on what it was that NIT wage earners were doing on their jobs, the variability of hours worked, or earnings and other descriptive data that might help to place NIT families into our understanding of the overall patterns of the occupational structure or of the world of work.

Information on this and a number of other work aspects, such as the frequency of job interruption by slack demand, equipment downtime, labor disputes, and the cost and mode of transportation to work, were collected but not exploited in the *Final Report* analyses.

monthly income reports with pay stubs and W-2 forms and to request written records from casual employers, but the quarterly research interviews required no such documentation. Simple recall error (especially for earlier weeks in the month) plus a possible perceived financial disincentive to accurate reporting[9] suggest strongly that the reported hours may be understated in a pattern such as that found in the income series (discussed in the next section). In contrast to the extensive discussion of the income data, the *Final Report* papers do not discuss the quality of the hours data in any detail so it is difficult to form a judgment from this source as to how much more (or less) reliable this series may be as a measure of labor response.[10]

Reported Income and Reporting Error

The quality of the reported income data is extremely important to interpretation of the experiment, not only because income is an argument in the theoretical model of labor supply response, but also because it enters almost all analyses as an independent variable.[11]

There were three sources of income data reported to the experiment: *monthly* Income Report Forms, filled out by experimental families only (not by controls) that formed the basis for payments calculations to eligible families; *quarterly* questionnaires filled out by both experimentals and controls every three months; and an *annual* Income Supplement.[12] From each of these, six income measures were compiled: 1) total income (including non-earned income), 2) total earnings, 3) total other income (transfers, interest, rental income, etc.), 4) earnings of male heads, 5) earnings of female heads, and 6) earnings of others (children and other adult family members).

Comparison of the average reported income figures for 1970 collected for

---

[9] Payments were explicitly not tied to quarterly interviews in explanations given to NIT families. However, discrepancies between monthly income reports and quarterly interviews could be the basis of a family audit (see Chapter 3).

[10] Of course, it was the existence of three separate income series plus the possibility of comparison with Social Security earnings that made it possible to conduct a relatively extensive evaluation of the earnings statements. To make comparable analyses of the hours series would have required collecting alternative measures of hours worked. For example, it might have been sensible to conduct sample checks with employers to ascertain whether the hours reported for the week previous to quarterly interviews were accurate. It should also be noted that some pay check stubs indicate hours worked and hourly rates. This again underscores a criticism made earlier that technical research on the reliability and validity of hours worked was not undertaken to the extent possible.

Watts has written: "The notion of cross-validating hours measures with employer reports was carefully considered and rejected because we did not want to disturb an often tenuous employment relationship by asking employers about particular workers." (Private communication, July 9, 1975.)

[11] These analyses include experimental effects on education, health, consumption of housing, food, consumer durables, and family fertility (*Final Report,* vol. II).

[12] Annual income supplements were also accompanied by inspection of IRS Form 1040.

each of the three survey instruments[13] indicates that the greatest variance across sources occurs in the total other income (3) and earnings of others categories (6), and somewhat surprisingly, that the monthly and quarterly series produce figures in much closer agreement than either compared to annual income figures. Table 5.1 displays the average income figures re-

Table 5.1
Average Income in 1970 as Reported in Alternative Sources
(Continuous husband-wife families: N = 693)

Item	*Annual Supplement*	*Quarterly Questionnaire*	*Monthly Report Form*
Total Income	6,449	6,407	6,198
Total Earnings	5,616	5,659	5,520
Total Other Income	833	747	678
Male Earnings	4,874	4,913	4,988
Female Earnings	491	441	392
Earnings of Others	259	303	140

SOURCE: Walter Nicholson, "The Income Data Series in the Graduated Work Incentive Experiment: An Analysis of Their Differences," *Final Report,* vol. III.

ported in the three sources for 1970 roughly midway through the experiment.

CHOICE OF INCOME SERIES FOR LABOR SUPPLY ANALYSES

A first thought might be to adopt the annual figure on the argument that some families have an incentive to underreport in any case and the highest total income figure is probably less biased than the other, lower figures. But on inspection it is evident that the difference between the annual figure and the others lies largely in the total other income and earnings of others categories, the exact compositions of which are not reported in the analyses. In early quarters the value of non-earned transfers was imputed from a variety of sources, so that it is not clear to what extent non-cash but work-conditioned payments, such as the value of food stamps or the imputed value of subsidized housing, may have been reported in total other income.[14] Indeed,

[13] Nicholson, *Final Report,* vol. III.

[14] Mallar discusses the various items of non-earned income collected on the new core questionnaire for later quarters. The largest differences between experimentals and controls occurs in business income which experimentals reported at twice the level of controls (Harold Watts, Dale Poirier, and Charles Mallar, *Final Report,* vol. II, p. 79, et passim, especially Table 22).

on the same argument about underreporting bias, a better choice might be the monthly series since the major policy interest in the experiment focused on the behavior of male heads and only secondary interest attached to responses of wives and subsidiary earners in the family.[15] The difficulty with this is that controls did not file monthly reports so that analyses based on differential responses of experimentals and controls cannot make use of these data.[16] The decision made in most of the *Final Report* analyses is to use data from the quarterly reports: For each family there are thirteen data points available covering the three-year experimental period.

RELIABILITY OF THE SERIES

Since there is no "true" income figure against which to compare the reported series, the validity of the data was assessed by two indirect tests, a calculation of the internal variance among the three series and an external comparison of the earnings for male heads with federal income tax and Social Security reports. Averaging the inter-series variances for each pair of income series suggests that reporting errors in the data range from 10 percent–40 percent of the variance in the income series and are larger for other earnings and income of others than for earnings for male and female heads. The variance in reported earnings across the three series appears to bear no consistent relation to income types, that is, the tendency to underreport females' earnings on the monthly reports relative to the quarterly and annual series has no correlation with under- or overreporting of monthly figures relative to quarterly and annual data for earnings of males or other earners. Efforts to find correlates of inter-series reporting error among the experimental parameters were also unsuccessful.

External comparisons of the reported income series against IRS and Social Security reports reveal that, relative to the IRS reports, earnings are quite accurately reported in the monthly and quarterly series but that income from interest, rentals, and businesses (largely unearned income) was heavily underreported to the experiment. A comparison of the annual series with the Social Security reports revealed that approximately 65 percent of the male heads underreported their earnings to the experiment (about 20 percent of male heads underreported by more than 10 percent) and that a disproportionate number of small (less than 10 percent) underreports came

[15] Walter Nicholson suggests three possible explanations for the fact that earnings of other family members relative to male heads are underreported on the monthly survey: deliberate underreporting to avoid *r*, believing it unnecessary to report the income of other members, and a tendency to bunch irregularly earned income into the more comprehensive period reports.

[16] Monthly income reports were used to calculate payments to experimental families.

from the Paterson-Passaic sample. No evidence was found that these deviations were correlated with a desire to escape the implicit tax; indeed, the controls were slightly *more* likely than experimental families to underreport males' earnings relative to the Social Security files.

REPORTING ERROR IN THE INCOME SERIES

As preliminary analysis of the income data was begun, evidence of another and more systematic source of reporting error emerged. Observed wage rate differentials for experimentals versus controls (calculated from reported income divided by reported hours worked) show a substantial jump in the early quarters of the experiment tapering off in the later quarters, suggesting a "learning effect" in the reporting process. This was traced to a confusion in the minds of respondents between gross and net income—the interviews asked for gross income before taxes and deductions but many respondents apparently reported their net (take-home) pay until checked by the field staff—compounded by the differential reporting frequency of experimentals and controls. The result was that experimentals who reported monthly had more opportunities to learn the gross-net distinction and to revise their reported income upward than controls, who reported only quarterly and annually, so that spurious positive wage rate effects were generated in the labor supply analyses. These spurious differentials were initially larger for blacks and Puerto Ricans than for whites, mainly located in Scranton, who entered the experiment later and benefited from more experienced interviewing. The evidence of such reporting error was so strong that it was finally decided to drop earnings response from many of the final analyses.[17]

CALCULATION OF NORMAL INCOME ($\hat{Y}$) AND NORMAL WAGE RATES ($\hat{w}$)

Economic theory requires that labor response be measured relative to the individual's or household's permanent income or wage rate free of transitory windfalls or shortfalls, so that some means had to be employed to separate from reported figures the income or wage rate the household

[17] In addition to this reporting error hypothesis, Harold Watts and John Mamer (*Final Report,* vol. II, pp. 20ff.) discuss, but reject, two other possible explanations for the large observed wage differential: that the differential results from a greater drop-out response to payments at lower wage levels among experimentals; that it reflects a higher rate of job change among experimentals in search of better paying jobs. The empirical evidence supports neither of these alternatives.

would have received on average over the long run in the absence of the experiment.

In some cases, this was done by utilizing pre-enrollment income and wage rates in the response function as a proxy for normal levels and in others by employing an estimate of normal $\hat{Y}$ and $\hat{w}$ derived from the controls or from the total sample of experimentals *and* controls and attributing deviations from these levels among the experimentals to the NIT treatment. The constructed values $\hat{Y}$ and $\hat{w}$ were considered preferable for use in response functions containing interaction terms of income and wages with the treatment parameters and for controlling for normal earning power within income strata. However, should the normal income and wage rate estimates be contaminated by the presence of some experimental effects, the labor response functions in which they appear as control variables would misstate experimental response by an indeterminate amount. As will be seen in Chapter 6, the final estimated responses were in general so small that such an estimation bias in the constructed independent variables is a significant issue. For this reason, the precise procedures for estimating $\hat{Y}$ and $\hat{w}$ are discussed in some detail.

Estimation of $\hat{w}$

The procedure for estimating a predicted wage for an *individual* ($\hat{w}_{it}$) consists of decomposing a sample of observed wage rates into average normal wage (w^*) and experimental wage effect ($\tilde{w}$) components and then adjusting the normal wage estimated for an individual with specified socioeconomic characteristics derived from the sample by the addition of an individual deviation term to get an individual respondent's predicted wage ($\hat{w}_{it}$). In short,

$$\text{(V.1) } w = w^* + \tilde{w} + E \text{ (for the sample)}$$
$$\text{(V.2) } \hat{w}_{it} = w^*_{it} + d_i \text{ (for an individual)}$$

The normal wage rate variable used in the labor response functions was estimated from the observed wage rates of a sample of male-headed, full-time working families, both experimentals and controls, using a generalized least squares procedure to generate a predicated (equilibrium) wage from which experimental effects are netted out. The formulation for decomposing the observed wage is given in equation V.1, where the observed wage (w) is a function of the normal wage (w^*) and an experimental wage effect ($\tilde{w}$) plus a two-part error term (E) composed of time-persistent individual effects and "true" cross-sectional variance. A third source of error, secular time effects, is included explicitly in the estimates of w^* and $\tilde{w}$ (rather than in E) on the argument that both the sequential enrollment of sites and the experimental treatments themselves might be expected to have explicit time effects that would be of interest in assessing national program effects.

It can be seen from this process that the accuracy of the labor response analyses is made to depend crucially on capturing all experimental treatment effects completely in $\tilde{w}$; if w^* is contaminated with experimental effects, it cannot be reliably used as a control variable in the response function. For this reason, the next sections report in some detail the results of analyses of the determinants of w^* and $\tilde{w}$; special interest attaches to the evidence of experimental impact on wage rates in $\tilde{w}$.

Analysis of the Determinants of w*

The normal wage (w^*) for a household head was estimated as a function of seven variables representing personal and job characteristics of the reporting household head: age, education completed, industry code, occupation code, site, employment status of spouse, and calendar time. The age and education variables were entered in the form of a bilinear spline variable with knots at 25 and 45 years of age and at eight years of completed schooling.[18] Site effects are measured as deviations from the observed wage in Trenton. Spouse's employment status was entered as a dummy variable reflecting her labor force status of the prior week. A time variable, included to measure general economic and labor market conditions common to all sites, was entered as a cubic spline[19] with knots at zero, sixteen, thirty-two, and forty-eight months from August 1968, the first Trenton enrollments.

The results of estimating w^* for 618 male heads indicate that as determinants of their normal (equilibrium) wage, age and education separately are very important for all subgroups; however, the *structure* of the age-education effects varies across the surface such that education beyond the eighth grade has an important effect for blacks under 25 but little effect for other ethnic groups or for the combined sample of workers under 45. Occupation and industry are significant for all ethnic groups, but site is significant only for whites in Scranton where the labor market is apparently different from the New Jersey sites. Employment status of spouse is insignificant across the board. A significant rising time trend in normal wage rates was found for all ethnic groups, the only distinction being that the rate of increase for blacks is slower than for whites and Puerto Ricans.

---

[18] For a description of the spline technique see Harold Watts, *Final Report,* vol. I. It is useful to think of the "knots" as joints or break-points at which the estimated function changes slope. A brief summary of the spline technique as applied in the NIT is provided in an appendix to this chapter.

[19] For a technical description of cubic splines see Dale Poirier, "Technical Note on Cubic Splines," *Final Report,* vol. I, Part E.

What all this amounts to is that an individual male head's expected or normal wage rate during the experimental period was determined most importantly by his age, education, industry/occupation assignment, and the general rate of growth in wages in his regional labor market between 1968 and 1972. Except for blacks, the difference made by completion of high school was negligible and in no case did the employment of his spouse have any effect on the male's wage rate. None of this is unexpected.

Analysis of Determinants of $\tilde{w}$

While there are no surprises in the factors determining the normal wage rate (w^*), there are some puzzles presented by the analysis of determinants of the experimental wage rate effect ($\tilde{w}$).

The influence exerted on the wage rate by experimental treatment is estimated as a function of g and r, entered as a bilinear spline measuring deviations in response from the "central" ($g = .75$, $r = .50$) treatment plan, and experimental time, entered as a cubic spline with knots at zero, two, six, and twelve quarters.

The results of estimating $\tilde{w}$ for male heads indicated that the g-r interactions had no significant effect on the wage rates of any ethnic group but that time-on-the-experiment had a significant influence that varied drastically by race. Experimental-control wage rate differentials for the Puerto Rican group rose over the first year, then fell dramatically over the following five quarters, and finally rose again in the last half year to wind up not significantly different from zero. Whites followed a pattern of much sharper increase in the wage differential over the first year of the experiment followed by a steady decline toward zero over the remainder of the period—a pattern consistent with the "reporting error" suspicion described earlier for income. Blacks followed the wage rise of whites almost exactly for the first year but continued to increase the wage differential between experimentals and controls to the end of the experiment.

It is difficult to think of any plausible explanation for these time trends in $\tilde{w}$ and none is offered in the final analyses.[20] These results are rather disconcerting; the experimental wage effect turns out to have no significant and systematic relation to the experimental parameters, which are supposed to have produced it, and its one significant correlate, experimental time, shows a pattern apparently without explanation and differing widely among ethnic subgroups.

---

[20] Henry Aaron, "Lessons from the New Jersey-Pennsylvania Income Maintenance Experiment," multilithed (paper prepared for Brookings Institution Conference on the New Jersey-Pennsylvania Income Maintenance Experiment, April 1974), has suggested that this confusing pattern may result from a misspecification of the treatment plans such that the average responses for each cell may be masking greater differences in effective tax rates within than among treatment groups.

Analysis of the error components indicates that differences in the predictability of wage rates for the three ethnic groups stem primarily from differences in the cross-section variance within groups rather than from individual error effects. Not surprisingly, the white subsample shows the greatest cross-section variance since this group includes a few whites from the predominantly black inner-city poverty tracts in New Jersey combined with a much larger group of whites from a different labor market in Scranton.

Estimation of Females' Wage Rates

A similar procedure was followed for decomposing observed wage rates for females (wives only, since no initially female-headed families were included in the sample); except that because the total number of working wives in the sample was so small,[21] data for ethnic groups were pooled. This produced a sample of 129 females as compared to the 618 males used to estimate determinants of wage rates described previously.

Results of the estimates for females' normal wage rates (w^*) differ from the results for males in that, in addition to significant age and education effects taken singly, there are also significant age-education interactions. The influence of age tapers off sharply after 25 for whites and Puerto Ricans but increases sharply for black females over 25. The industry/occupational assignment of women is also significant with jobs in the manufacturing and services sectors serving to *lower* their wage rate relative to the "miscellaneous" category. Similarly, women whose husbands worked showed a reduction of expected wage rate below that for wives without working spouses. Females' wage rates were also highly responsive to the experimental-time variable, showing a decline relative to pre-enrollment wages in Trenton during the first few months but rising sharply over time thereafter until at the end of the experiment they were 20 percent above the Trenton base value. In short, this evidence suggests that females' wage rates are more sensitive than males' to age-education interactions, occupational assignment, and spouse's employment status and further, that these determinants affect wage rates for black females differently than those for whites and Puerto Ricans.

Estimating a Predicted Wage ($\hat{w}_{it}$) for Individuals

The analysis of wage rate determinants described was based on average characteristics for male and female samples estimated separately. But the

[21] The small sample of wives is the result of the income measure used to define initial eligibility (total family income) which resulted in the truncation of the sample since the wives' earnings were, in most cases, sufficient to bring total family income above 150 percent of the poverty level. Moreover, the working wives who did appear in the sample are those who work very few hours per quarter and are probably not typical of steadily working wives.

purpose of the attempt to construct an estimating equation for normal income and wage rates is to fill in missing data and to control for the basic earnings capacity of *individuals* (and family units). To do this a predicted wage ($\hat{w}_{it}$) is calculated for each individual, which excludes the experimental effects estimated earlier and substitutes for E an average individual deviation ($\bar{d}_i$) by which the earnings and hours reported by him over the course of the experiment differ from the average wage for individuals with similar characteristics as estimated by the wage regression in the previous section. The predicted wage for each individual is calculated from

$$\log_{10} \hat{w}_{it} = w^*_{it} + \bar{d}_i$$

where $\bar{d}_i = 0$ for individuals who are unemployed or otherwise report no earnings. $\hat{w}_{it}$, as constructed here, is the wage rate variable used in all the final labor supply analyses.

Estimation of Normal Income ($\hat{Y}$)

The previous section described the construction of a normal wage rate variable that was then used to estimate a predicted wage for *individuals* (or families), interpreted as that wage they could have expected to receive in the absence of experimental payments. This section describes the calculation of a parallel variable for normal income of experimental households.

The general method of constructing $\hat{Y}$ was analogous to that used to estimate $\hat{w}$ except that in decomposing the observed/reported incomes for families, normal income (Y^*) appears twice, once as a function of a string of socio-demographic characteristics and again in interaction with the experimental parameters. The following relation was estimated from the complete sample of 693 continuous husband-wife families, imputing for any missing variable its value in the immediately preceding period:

$$Y = Y^*(Z) + \tilde{Y}(Y^*, X) + E$$

where the observed value (Y) was taken as total gross income including all earnings as well as non-work-conditioned property and transfer receipts; Z is a vector of family characteristics; X is a vector of experimental parameters; and E is the two-part error term. The computation was carried out by substituting Y_o for Y^* and then iterating Y^* and $\tilde{Y}$ to a solution.

As Aaron[22] has commented, the analytical reports do not indicate that the Y^* resulting from this iteration process is invariant with respect to the start-

[22] Aaron, "Lessons from the New Jersey-Pennsylvania Income Maintenance Experiment."

ing point (i.e., would substituting some value other than Y_o in the beginning lead to a different estimate of Y^*?).

Determinants of Y*

As in the normal wage rate estimate, Y^* is estimated as a function of nine demographic variables: male head's age, male head's education, female head's age, female head's education, site, calendar time, month of the year (to distinguish seasonal variations), family composition (by age structure), and health of male head. The male head's age and education and the female's age and education variables are entered as bilinear splines as in the wage equation; calendar time is entered as a cubic spline; and the month of the year as a periodic spline. The results are too detailed and complex to summarize here, except to note that substantial seasonal and time trends are found which, for blacks, show a fall in Y^* over time.[23]

Determinants of $\tilde{\hat{Y}}$

Similarly, $\tilde{\hat{Y}}$ is estimated as a function of an experimental dummy, g, r, time, and family's normal welfare ratio $= Y^*/PL$. The results show systematic variations of $\tilde{\hat{Y}}$ by time, ethnic group, and g-level (at $r = .50$). The time pattern appears to be seasonal, peaking at the fourth month and bottoming around the eighth month for blacks. The same pattern holds only for Puerto Rican families on the $g = .75$ plan; on more generous plans the Puerto Rican group shows virtually no time response. Whites on the least generous plan exhibit an earnings pattern like that of blacks but shift sharply downward; on more generous plans whites exhibit a steadily declining income pattern over the full year.

Normal family income ($\hat{Y}$) was estimated as $log_{10}\ Y_{it} = Y^*_{it} + d_i$ where each of the terms is obtained analogously to their counterparts in the $\hat{w}_{it}$ equation. $\hat{Y}$ as derived here has been used in the final analyses of the labor supply responses for males and females, in the family consumption analyses, and as a continuous stratification variable to replace Y_o.

COMMENTARY: IMPLICATIONS FOR THE FINAL ANALYSES

Previous sections have described the measurement and quality of the four basic labor supply variables and the construction of two normal variables used as independent variables in the estimated labor supply response

[23] The interested reader is referred to Watts, Poirier, and Mallar, "Concepts Used in the Central Analyses," *Final Report,* vol. I, pp. 67–77, for the full results.

functions. Comments are here organized into those dealing with 1) the loss of the earnings measure and 2) specification of the constructed variables.

Loss of the Earnings Variable

In the *Final Report,* analyses of the response of male heads is measured by only three of these variables—employment, labor force participation, and hours. The earnings response, though one of the most interesting from the standpoint both of testing economic theory and a policy impact, had to be eliminated from serious consideration when the likelihood of substantial reporting error was discovered.[24] Failure to distinguish clearly between gross and net income in the early phases of the experiment resulted in dramatic increases in reported earnings as respondents learned to supply the amount of their earnings *before* taxes and other deductions in later interviews. By the nature of the reporting system, experimentals, who reported incomes monthly as well as quarterly and annually, learned this distinction faster than controls who reported only quarterly and annually, so that earnings response, measured as the control-experimental differential, is contaminated by some indeterminate amount of error. To the extent that earnings reports were in error, the wage rates calculated from them would also be contaminated—indeed, it was evidence of dramatically rising wage rate effects that first cued the experimenters that reporting error might be involved—so that the calculation of normal wage rate became imperative.

The weakening of the earnings variable as a reliable response measure is serious, because it undermines the one direct test that could be made of the power of an NIT to "induce people to work themselves out of the poverty category" and so weakens the evidence for those who would like to argue that the appropriate test of a guaranteed income policy is the extent to which it can increase the effective resources of recipients, rather than the extent to which it induces work per se.[25]

Elimination of the earnings variable threw the full weight of detecting a labor supply response on the hours-worked formulation since, especially for male heads, both employment and labor force participation are virtually

---

[24] Earnings results were reported for wives and families but carry the same doubt about their reliability.

[25] See the debate raised by Bette and Michael Mahoney at the Brookings Institution Conference on the New Jersey-Pennsylvania Experiment, April 29–30, 1974, and the response by Alair Townsend and James Storey. During discussion that followed, David Kershaw noted that during his testimony before the Senate during the Family Assistance Plan (FAP) hearings "all the committee members wanted to know was how many people we had raised above the poverty level."

It has been suggested that an approximation of the earnings effect can be calculated by multiplying hours worked by the normal wage rate (comments on draft manuscript), but this involves a circularity since normal wage rates are themselves calculated from the suspect earnings series.

constant over the experimental period.[26] That is, the only scope for adjustment in male heads' labor supply lay in the adjustment of hours worked within the same employment levels, so that careful definition and measurement of the hours variable became extremely important in the final analysis. On the quality of the hours data, the *Final Report* has very little to say.[27]

Specification of $\hat{Y}$ and $\hat{w}$

Finally, some comments on the constructed variables, $\hat{Y}$ and $\hat{w}$. Recall that these variables were constructed by decomposing their observed equivalents into a normal value, estimated as a function of a string of personal and job characteristics, and an experimental segment, estimated as a function of g, r, and time. Predicted wage rates and incomes for individuals were then calculated from the normal segment plus an average deviation of the individual from the group mean. $\hat{Y}$ and $\hat{w}$ are then used as independent variables in the labor supply equations.

Clearly, the accuracy of the final labor supply estimates depends heavily on both the quality of the reported data and on the specification of the initial regression.

In the specification of w^*, there are no measures of training other than years of formal schooling, no indication of union affiliation or the importance of union wage scales in the industry/occupation spline, and no attempt to isolate industry-site effects, as they might show up through the calendar time variable reflecting general regional economic conditions.[28]

Further, the procedure of estimating $\hat{w}$ from a combined sample of controls and experimentals and then extending the estimated $\hat{w}_{it}$ to all individuals whether they worked or not embodies an assumption that is pointed out but not defended by any particular logic in the analyses; namely that the wage determinants for workers in the sample are the same as those for non-workers.[29]

---

[26] Labor force participation rates for male heads in all ethnic groups ranged above 90 percent and employment rates close to 85 percent for male heads over the experimental period. See Watts, Poirier, and Mallar, "Concepts Used in the Central Analyses," *Final Report,* vol. I, Table 1, p. 5.

[27] The researchers have noted that it is possible to check for internal consistency between earnings and wage rate, but this would have to be limited to data for the last year since independent reports of the wage rate were not collected until the final core questionnaire was used. Prior to that, wage rates are *calculated from* earnings and hours so that such a "check" would be circular. In any case, no such internal check is reported in the *Final Report* documents.

[28] One might suspect, for example, that the Scranton whites are more heavily unionized in the coal and steel industries than the blacks and Puerto Ricans in the New Jersey sites, or at least that the union pay scale may set the general structure of wages in Scranton in a way that is not evident in the other sites.

[29] In addition, it is assumed that there is no interaction of experimental parameters with the local wage rate, that is, that labor supply adjustments made to experimental

The validity of these assumptions is called into question by at least two features of the experimental design: the truncation of the original sample at 150 percent of poverty level income, which raises the distinct possibility that the structural relation of the non-experimental variables to $\hat{w}$ and $\hat{Y}$ may be different for this sample than for the population as a whole; the non-random assignment of families to plans such that high income families were assigned to high guarantee treatments with the result that the coefficients of the Y^* and w^* determinants may well reflect experimental interactions with g. In a footnote to their analysis of male wage rates, Watts and Poirier[30] acknowledge that estimating $\hat{w}$ on the whole sample yields inconsistent parameters for the hours-worked equation since it is estimated on those who did not work and had zero wage rates, but they offer no defense of this and no clear reasons for working with the pooled sample rather than with the control group alone.

Similar questions might be asked about the $\hat{Y}$ estimate that is derived from a decomposition of reported income that is itself suspect. The appearance of experimental and/or calendar time and significant determinants of both Y^* and w^* lead one to suspect that this variable is picking up some treatment effects as well as catching some inter-site differences in regional labor market conditions and perhaps some differences in the way the experiment was administered as the interviewers learned in the field. Since it appears to be primarily with respect to this time trend that the counter-theoretical behavior of the black sample emerges, it is possible that more complete specifications of Y^* and w^* would suggest some explanations. In any case, the suspicion is strong that the estimated $\hat{Y}$ and $\hat{w}$ used as independent variables in the labor supply analyses may well be contaminated by experimental effects introduced by previous features of the experimental design and incompletely removed in the specifications of $\tilde{w}$ and $\tilde{Y}$.

Appendix to Chapter 5

Digression on Spline Technique[31]

A spline is a piecewise linear estimate of (in this case) a three-dimensional surface for which the function is permitted to change slope between specified nodes. It is a useful way to formulate tests of behavioral responses, which one

---

payments are not large enough to influence the local labor market—true in this case but probably not for a national program.

[30] Harold Watts and Dale Poirier, *Final Report,* vol. I.

[31] For a more complete description, see Harold Watts, *Final Report,* vol. II.

has some external reason to believe may be discontinuous with respect to one or more of the independent variables. For example, in estimating normal wage rates, it is reasonable to anticipate that the relationship between wage rates and education that holds for recipients with educations up to high school (eight years) may be structurally different for those with education beyond high school; or that in direct tests of the labor supply response to NIT payments the relation between, say, hours worked and g will differ depending on whether g is above or below the poverty level.

A spline variable is then constructed as

$$Z = a_0 + a_1Z_1 + a_2Z_2 + a_3Z_3$$

where between 0 and x_1, $Z = a_0 + a_1Z_1$; between x_1 and x_2, $Z = a_0 + a_1Z_1 + a_2Z_2$, etc. giving a kinked function the slopes of whose segments are as shown.

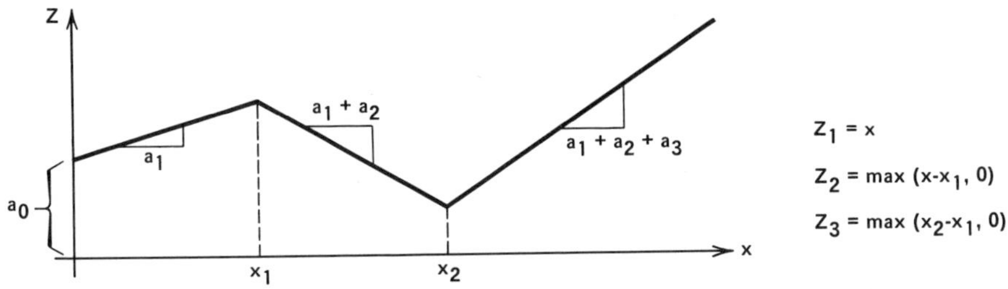

It is evident that the second derivative of this function is a discontinuous step function; cubic splines have continuous function segments wth constant third derivatives; and so on.

Notice further that it is simple and often very useful in facilitating interpretation of the results to shift the origin of the spline function in order to measure all effects from some point other than 0,0. In the NIT case, for example, the origin has been shifted to measure all labor supply effects from $r = .5$, $g = .75$ (a "central" plan) rather than from the relatively uninteresting case of zero guarantee and tax rate. The function plotted above is shown below with its origin shifted to x_2.

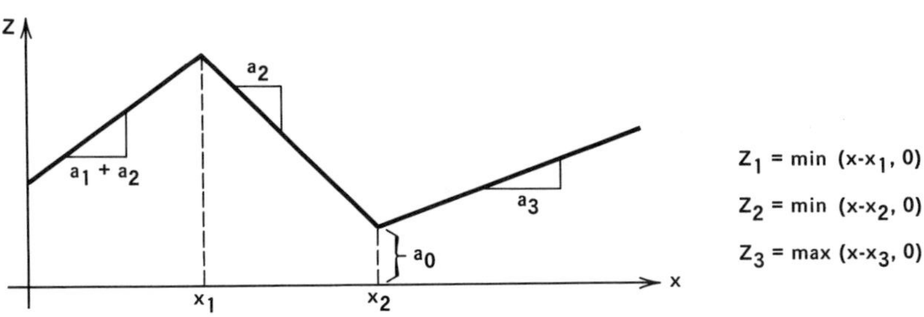

Clearly, as the number of elements in the spline formulation is increased, the estimated segments become smaller until, when the number of elements equals the number of design points, the formulation is equivalent to using a dummy variable for each treatment. The arguments advanced in support of the spline formulation over the use of dummy variables for each treatment are 1) the spline formulation allows easy interpolation for intermediate points on the surface, and 2) a spline formulation incorporates directly tests of interaction and nonlinear effects as indicated.

The standard splines incorporated in the final analyses of the labor supply responses to the NIT experiment are:

$S_1 = (1,0)$—a dummy variable to distinguish experimentals from controls

$$\left.\begin{array}{l} S_2 = (g - .75) \\ S_3 = (r - .50) \end{array}\right\} \text{ shift the origin to } g = .75,\ r = .50$$

$S_4 = \max(S_2,0)$—equal to zero when S_2 negative and to S_2 when $S_2 \geqslant 0$.

$S_5 = \max(S_3,0)$—equal to zero when S_3 negative and to S_3 when $S_3 \geqslant 0$.

$S_6 = \max(g - 1.0,0)$—equal to zero when $g < 1.0$ and to $g - 1.0$ when $g \geqslant 1.0$

(S_4–S_6 are used to catch any additive, nonlinear effects of g,r)

$$\left.\begin{array}{l} S_7 = S_2 \times S_3 - S_4 \times S_5 \\ S_8 = S_4 \times S_5 \end{array}\right\} \text{—multiplied combinations of other splines to catch any non-additive interaction effects.}$$

Chapter 6

Findings: Labor Supply Response

INTRODUCTION

There are at least three reasons why major interest in the experiment was focused on the labor supply response of NIT recipients: 1) the need to address a series of political-moral objections to guaranteed income plans that reflected the fear that the work ethic would be undermined; 2) the desire to make a realistic estimate of program costs of a national NIT; and 3) a desire for technical information on differential response to various parameters, information deemed useful for rationalizing the designs of future welfare programs. Emphasis on one or another theme varied with the particular population subgroup under scrutiny—less approbation is attached to wives dropping out of the labor market than to husbands, for example—so that the labor supply responses were examined separately for males and females and for families collectively. The moral-political objections centered not only on the feared loss of the traditional work ethic (generally assumed to be undesirable) but also on the specific fear in some quarters that the pool of low wage labor would be significantly reduced with consequent increases in wages for the remaining labor force. The ability to forecast the total transfer costs of a national NIT was also seen as an important element of the political battle, and this, of course, depended on knowing rather precisely the magnitude of any labor supply reductions and their effects on payments entitlements. To pin down these relations of payments to guarantee level, tax rate, eligibility criteria, and administrative arrangements, it was necessary to focus on the manner in which labor response varied among plans with different design features.

This chapter discusses how the researchers went about analyzing the labor supply responses for their sample, the results they found (or failed to find), and the extent to which these results are generalizable to the national scale. No attempt is made here to report exhaustively on the full range of tests and results for labor response found in the *Final Report* documents; rather, the focus is on linking the major analytical results to characteristics of the experimental design discussed in Chapter 2 and in setting the stage for thinking about the broad policy implications of the experiment for national reform discussed in the final chapter.

THE METHOD OF ANALYSIS

In sorting out the multitude of tests and results reported in the *Final Report* papers, it is useful to retain the notion, introduced in Chapter 2, of the labor supply issue as one of estimating a *response surface* for each of the various subgroups of interest (males, females, households, and so on) where response is measured by the dependent variables, hours worked, labor force participation rate, employment rate, and earnings as discussed in Chapter 5. As we discussed in Chapter 5, there are serious reasons to believe that some of these measures are less reliable than others, so that all estimates of response will not be of the same quality—a fact to be kept in mind when assessing the overall persuasiveness of the labor supply results.

Two methods of reporting results are adopted: simple tabulations of mean control-experimental differentials by demographic and ethnic subgroup (these are conveniently summarized in the HEW *Summary Report*[1]) and net regression coefficients along with relevant statistical significance tests. In general, the regression results confirm in detail what the gross comparisons of statistical means reveal more broadly. Because the regression analyses provide more explicit control for many external influences and a means of testing for sensitivity to each of the experimental parameters separately as well as in interaction, we focus for the rest of this chapter on the regression results.

The general formulation adopted for the labor response regression consists of a *control function* (containing a variety of demographic, ethnic, and normal income variables) and a *response function* (containing the experimental parameters); the former function picks up variations in labor supply resulting from influences common to both experimentals and con-

[1] U.S. Department of Health, Education and Welfare *Summary Report: New Jersey Graduated Work Incentive Experiment* (Washington, D.C.: December 1973).

trols, the latter function is intended to pick up variations traceable only to experimental treatment differences between the two groups. The model is

$$Y = f(C) + LR(X, XC) + u$$

where Y is the labor supply response in question, C is the control function, LR is the experimental response (a function of the experimental parameters, X, and any interaction, XC), and u is a random error.

The Control Function applied to the analysis of labor response of males, females, and families consists of seventeen variables measuring pre-enrollment hours and weeks worked, age, education, family size, health status, and the effects of normal income and wages in a complex subfunction

$$S = a_1\hat{W} + a_2\hat{Y}/PL + a_3/\hat{W} + a_4\hat{Y}/\hat{W}$$

where $\hat{Y}$ and $\hat{W}$ are derived by the estimation process previously described in Chapter 5, and PL is the poverty level for the family in question. The idea behind this subfunction is that, in addition to controlling an individual's response for his normal earning power in the absence of the experimental treatment (the first term shown), his response may also be conditioned by how close his normal income is to the poverty level (the second term); the third term allows for the possibility of a nonlinear wage effect (i.e., that one's normal earning capacity may have more influence at low wage rates than at high ones); and the fourth term picks up any interactions between normal income and wage rate.

A typical full control function, then, is

$$C = B_o + B_1(H_o) + B_2(W_o) + B_3(S_a) + B_4(S_e) + B_5(S_n) + B_6(H_1) + B_7(H_2) + B_8(S)$$

where H_o and W_o are pre-enrollment hours and weeks worked, S_a is a spline for age (with knots at 25 and 45 years), S_e is a spline for education (with a knot at eight years), S_n is a spline for family size, H_1 and H_2 are dummies for health status, and S is the complex subfunction of $\hat{Y}$ and $\hat{W}$ described earlier.

Site and ethnicity effects are analyzed in several ways, sometimes by the use of dummy variables, at other times by entering race and site as interaction variables in the response function or by running regressions on each of the ethnic samples separately.

The Response Function consists of six parameters including the experimental parameters, g and r, and a constructed variable, θ, designed to incorporate the assumption that responsiveness to experimental treatment tapers off as one's income rises above the break-even level.[2] This variable was scaled arbitrarily so that individuals whose incomes are more than twenty hours worth of work above Y_b have no response to the experiment and are treated as another control observation. The experimental parameters are entered as linear splines[3] so that their coefficients measure response differences from the central plan ($g = .75$, $r = .5$). The full response function is a quadratic in θ

$$LR = (a_{11} + a_{12}S_2 + a_{13}S_3)\theta + (a_{21} + a_{22}S_2 + a_{23}S_3)\theta^2$$

where a_{11} and a_{21} measure the height of the response surface at the central plan, and S_2, S_3 are splines for g and r respectively. Labor response (LR) is measured as the control-experimental differences in each of the four dependent variables described earlier.

When added together, these functions provide a flexible and efficient way to estimate the response surface subject to a large number of control factors. In interpreting the empirical results we are interested in both the *height* of the surface (the absolute control-experimental differential) and the slopes (derivatives) between plans; the first gives an idea of the gross magnitude of the experimental impact on work, the second gives an estimate of the direction and sensitivity of work adjustments to specific features of the program—the theoretical income- and substitution-effects. The elasticities of labor supply with respect to g, r, and actual payments are also of policy interest in determining optimal NIT design. (See appendix for summary of analytical techniques.)

THE DATA BASE

The labor supply analyses reported in the *Final Report* papers were based on a sample of 693 continuous husband-wife families (from the original 1,300) who filed at least eight quarters of reports during the three-year experimental period. Distribution of this sample by site, race, and plan is shown in Table 6.1. Two aspects of the continuous sample, its distribution by site and the composition of the controls, are worth mentioning.

The distribution of the sample by site exhibits a clear ethnic dimension:

---

[2] θ is defined as: $(M_{it} + 20\hat{W} - \hat{Y}_{it})/10\hat{W}_{it}$, where $M_{it} = (g_i PL_i)/r_i = Y_b$ and θ is distributed with a mean of 5 and a standard deviation of 3. The reason given for adopting this assumption is the belief that greater interpersonal comparability is achieved in labor responses when they are scaled to the respondent's position in the relative income distribution.

[3] For a brief description of the spline technique see Chapter 5, Appendix. Fuller discussions are available in Harold Watts, Dale Poirier, and Charles Mallar, *Final Report*, vol. I, pp. 14–18, and Poirier, *Final Report*, vol. III.

Table 6.1
Distribution of Sample Used in Final Report Analyses: Continuous Husband-Wife Families by Plan and Site

	Total	*White*	*Black*	*Puerto Rican*
	(Percent of relevant total in parentheses)			
Total	693(100%)	310(100%)	234(100%)	149(100%)
NIT Plan				
50–30	27(3.9)	13(4.2)	8(3.4)	6(4.0)
50–50	32(4.6)	11(3.5)	12(5.1)	9(6.0)
75–30	60(8.7)	22(7.1)	23(9.8)	15(10.1)
75–50	65(9.4)	24(7.7)	25(10.7)	16(10.7)
75–70	48(6.9)	24(7.7)	21(9.0)	3(2.0)
100–50	44(6.3)	20(6.5)	14(6.0)	10(6.7)
100–70	53(7.6)	21(6.8)	17(7.3)	15(10.1)
125–50	96(13.9)	46(14.8)	31(13.2)	19(12.8)
Controls	268(38.7)	129(41.6)	83(35.5)	56(37.6)
(New)	141	12	69	60
Site				
Trenton	60(8.7)	12(3.9)	38(16.2)	10(6.7)
Paterson-Passaic	158(22.8)	30(9.7)	59(25.2)	69(46.3)
Jersey City	236(34.0)	32(10.3)	134(57.3)	70(47.0)
Scranton	239(34.5)	236(76.1)	3(1.3)	0(0.0)

NOTE: New controls are those which were added to the sample as a consequence of the Tobin solution of the design controversy (see Chapter 2). They were enrolled after the start of the experiment in the New Jersey sites and so do not have a full thirteen quarters of reports; for this reason they were excluded from the sample used in the *Final Report* analyses.

SOURCE: Adapted from Harold Watts, Dale Poirier, and Charles Mallar, *Final Report,* vol. II, Tables 2 and 3, pp. 3–4.

Scranton is virtually all white; Jersey City and Trenton are over 50 percent black; and Paterson-Passaic is about evenly split between blacks and Puerto Rican households. A comparison with Census data for these central cities reveals that the black and Puerto Rican representation is disproportionately high even for the subareas sampled[4] and that the New Jersey sites in which they are concentrated are clearly part of a different labor market from the Scranton (white) sample. These differences are marked further by time (and administrative) differences in enrollments, since the Scranton sample was enrolled nearly a year later than the first New Jersey sites and presumably benefited from initial experience of the field administrators with

[4] Michael Taussig, *Final Report,* vol. III.

attrition, eligibility criteria, and the like. These site-ethnicity interactions reflect slightly more clearly similar relations in the original sample.

Concerning the composition of the control group in the continuous sample, it should be noted that the controls comprise a smaller percentage of the continuous sample (39 percent) than of the original sample (47 percent), reflecting partly a higher attrition rate among controls generally and partly the elimination from the continuous sample of the so-called "new controls" (those that were added as a consequence of the Tobin solution to the design controversy).[5]

Since both theory and experience suggest that work decisions are made differently by various members of the family, analyses were run for the labor response of male head, wives, and families in the continuous sample separately. The use of the continuous sample simplifies interpretation of the results by removing major changes in family composition (primarily splits which have the effect of creating a female-headed household unit) and missing data problems as additional sources of labor supply variation.[6] In a number of the analyses, observations drawn from the two least generous NIT plans (50–50, 10–50) were omitted, since other evidence suggested that these treatments were substantially dominated by competing welfare programs in New Jersey and Pennsylvania.[7]

LABOR SUPPLY RESPONSES TO EXPERIMENTAL TREATMENT

Experimental Effects on Labor Supply of Married Men[8]

Primary interest focused on the labor supply responses of married men because their traditional role as economic supporters of the family could

---

[5] Users of the full sample data should be aware that the inclusion of "new controls" in the data base may impart a site and ethnic bias to the sample since the new controls comprise a much larger fraction of black and Puerto Rican controls and were enrolled at a time point in the experimental cycle more nearly comparable to the original white controls in Scranton. This means, in effect, that any differences in attrition rates, the reporting of welfare payments, and receipt of larger reporting fees, improved field procedures and monitoring techniques, and the like related to the different enrollment dates for the sites will work to produce uncomparable control groups.

[6] No analysis of female-headed units emerging during the course of the experiment has been attempted so far. As noted earlier, there are substantial reasons to expect that the labor responses of wives analyzed here are *not* good descriptions of the responses that would be observed to the same experimental stimuli on the part of female heads. This suggests that the results for wives must be treated carefully and *not* relied upon to indicate the results of a national program among the large proportion of female-headed families in the current poverty population.

[7] See Chapter 4.

[8] This section summarizes the analyses reported in Harold Watts and David Horner, *Final Report,* vol. II.

not easily be abandoned without creating major social and economic readjustments feared by many. The vision of an NIT "goldbricker" was almost universally one of an able-bodied male with family responsibilities who dropped out of the labor force to live on his guarantee. But in a programmatic sense it is clear that, since males make up such a large part of the steadily employed labor force, even moderate reductions in their labor supply, if widely induced, could amount to a sizable reduction in national labor supply and a correspondingly large cost for a national guaranteed income program.

In fact, the measurable effect of experimental treatments on male heads was generally very small and almost never statistically significant. Tables 6.2 to 6.4 display summary data by plan, ethnic group, and income level.

1. *Labor force participation* rates for both experimentals and controls were above 90 percent throughout the experiment with experimentals aver-

Table 6.2
Experimental Response in Labor Force Participation Rates
Male Heads, Quarters 3–10, by Ethnic Group and Income Level

Plan		*Response at Mean Income*[a]	*Response at Lowest Income*[a]
		(Expressed in percentage points)[b]	
.75/.5	Whites	.3	—3.0
	Blacks	2.9	—1.6
	Puerto Ricans	—4.4[c]	—41.9
.75/.3	Whites	.5	.4
	Blacks	2.2	3.7
	Puerto Ricans	6.7[c]	7.0
1.0/.5	Whites	1.8	1.0
	Blacks	2.4	.2
	Puerto Ricans	—1.8[c]	—21.6
1.0/.7	Whites	1.6	—2.4
	Blacks	3.0	—5.1
	Puerto Ricans	—12.8[c]	—70.5

[a] Mean income refers to the mean of the relevant ethnic sample relative to the appropriate break-even level. Lowest income is one standard deviation below the mean.

[b] Entries in the cells of this table are net percentage points by which experimentals exceed controls in labor force participation.

[c] Response to experimental treatment parameters significant at the .01 level.

SOURCE: Harold Watts, *Final Report,* vol. II, Table 8, p. 26.

Table 6.3
Experimental Response in Employment Rates
Male Heads, Quarters 3–10, by Ethnic Group and Income Level

Plan		*Response at Mean Income*[a]	*Response at Lowest Income*
		(Expressed in percentage points)	
.75/.5	Whites	—1.5	—12.2
	Blacks	7.4	9.4
	Puerto Ricans	—18.7[b]	—81.5
.75/.3	Whites	.9	—1.5
	Blacks	5.4	11.0
	Puerto Ricans	4.1[b]	1.8
1.0/.5	Whites	.4	—4.4
	Blacks	6.7	8.1
	Puerto Ricans	—9.4[b]	—43.2
1.0/.7	Whites	—2.0	—15.1
	Blacks	8.5	6.3
	Puerto Ricans	—32.2[b]	—126.5

[a] Mean income refers to the mean of the relevant ethnic sample relative to the appropriate break-even level.
[b] Response to experimental treatment parameters significant at the .01 level.
SOURCE: Harold Watts, *Final Report,* vol. II, "Labor Supply Response of Married Men," Table 11, p. 32.

aging a percentage point or two *higher* than the controls.[9] The controlled regression function described previously, applied to the participation data by ethnic group, supports the finding of *no* significant experimental effects on the participation rate for blacks and whites but reveals strongly significant effects for the Puerto Rican subsample that are positive for individuals with incomes near break-even but increasingly negative below break-even. Virtually all the significant effects on the labor participation of the Puerto Rican sample occur in the first two years (see Table 6.2).

With the exception of the lower participation rates for the Puerto Rican sample, none of this is very surprising since it will be recalled that the eligibility terms for enrollment in the experiment required the male head to be in the prime age range (18–58) and free of mental or physical disabilities. Coupled with the strong social definition of male heads of households as primary earners and the corresponding tendency for the social status of males to be identified with their contributions to the production process, it is

[9] Harold Watts, "Labor Supply Response of Married Men," *Final Report,* vol. II, Table 1, p. 5.

Table 6.4
Estimated Response of Hours Worked to Alternative Plans
Male Heads, Quarters 3–10, by Ethnic Group and Income Level

Plan		*Response at Mean Income*[a]		*Response at Lowest Income*	
		Hours	*%*	*Hours*	*%*
1.0/.7	Whites	—1.6[c]	—4.6	—7.6	—21.7
	Blacks	5.0	16.5	1.9	6.3
	Puerto Ricans	—2.4	—6.8	—21.4	—60.5
.75/.5	Whites	—1.9[c]	—5.4	—7.2	—20.5
	Blacks	3.7	12.2	2.6	8.6
	Puerto Ricans	—1.1[d]	—3.1	—13.8	—39.0
.50/.3	Whites	—2.3[c]	—6.6	—6.9	—19.7
	Blacks	2.5	8.3	3.3	10.9
	Puerto Ricans	.3[d]	.8	—6.2	—17.5
1.0/.5[b]	Whites	—1.9[c]	—5.4	—6.4	—18.2
	Blacks	3.2	10.6	2.0	6.6
	Puerto Ricans	—2.1[d]	—5.9	—13.9	—39.3
1.25/.5	Whites	—.6[c]	—1.7	—1.6	—4.6
	Blacks	3.7	12.2	4.7	15.5
	Puerto Ricans	—.4[d]	—1.1	—3.8	—10.7
.75/.3	Whites	—3.8[c]	—10.8	—9.4	—26.8
	Blacks	4.0	13.2	8.9	29.4
	Puerto Ricans	.4[d]	1.1	—3.6	—10.2

[a] Mean income refers to the mean of the relevant ethnic subsample relative to the appropriate break-even level.
[b] This plan is approximately the mid-point on the hours worked response surface.
[c] Response to *g* significant at .10 level; response to *g-r* significant at .05 level.
[d] Response to *g* and *r* significant at .01 level.
SOURCE: Harold Watts, *Final Report,* vol. II, Table 18, p. 45. All percentages calculated on basis of mean work week values for controls in quarters 3–10 as reported in Table 1, p. 5: whites, 35.1; blacks, 30.3; Puerto Rican, 35.4.

to be expected that the availability of NIT payments on a temporary basis would not change significantly the labor force participation commitments of male heads.

Labor force participation rates reflect the percentage of those who are work-eligible and are employed or looking for work, but it is evident that this self-declared status is subject to a good deal of qualitative variation since one may look more or less vigorously for work and may be more or less choosy in accepting an offer. For this reason a more direct measure of labor actually supplied on the market is the employment rate.

2. *Employment rates* for male heads regressed on the same set of control and treatment variables reveal essentially the same overall results as participation rates but with a different pattern across subgroups: Whites and Puerto Ricans show slight *decreases* in employment relative to their controls while blacks show an *increase* in employment relative to the black controls (see Table 6.4). Further examination indicates that this pattern results from the fact that the Puerto Rican group both reduced their participation rate (see Table 6.3) and experienced a higher unemployment rate among those who remained in the labor force whereas the reduction in employment for the whites occurred despite roughly constant participation rates for this group. Blacks on the other hand mirrored the Puerto Rican group in increasing their employment rates both through higher labor force participation and a reduction in unemployment among this larger pool of black workers relative to their controls. These effects become stronger for poorer respondents. These employment responses to the experimental treatment can be converted into measurements of the traditional income- and substitution-effects by taking the derivatives of the response function (LR) with respect to g and r and evaluating them at specified points on the response surface. The results of such calculations[10] are statistically small and theoretically ambiguous figures, the tax (substitution) effect being negative for whites and Puerto Ricans but positive for blacks while the guarantee (income) effect is positive for whites and Puerto Ricans but negative for blacks. In short, the general impression of small and unstable results is strengthened.

A still more direct index of labor response might have been the earnings differential between experimentals and controls, of particular interest to those who would argue that the more appropriate test of the impact of an NIT is whether it succeeds in raising the disposable income of recipients rather than whether it causes them to work more per se. Unfortunately, this measure was lost to the analysis by the reporting error found in the basic data series described earlier so that the most direct measure of labor supplied is the data on hours worked.[11]

3. The differential response of experimental male heads in *hours worked* indicates a statistically significant overall average reduction in work time of 5 to 10 percent attributable to the experiment, but this average is generated by a more complex pattern of adjustments across ethnic groups than either participation or employment rates (see Table 6.4). In particular, at the central plan (75–50), whites show a statistically significant reduction in hours worked of about 6 percent (two hours on a thirty-five-hour

---

[10] Reported in ibid., Table 14, p. 39.

[11] Indeed, Watts refrains from reporting data on the earnings regressions for males although Robinson Hollister, *Final Report,* vol. I, reports the results of earnings analyses for families with a warning that they may be reflecting reporting error.

work week) ranging up to as much as six hours for those at the lowest end of the income scale. The Puerto Rican sample shows a similar reduction of about two hours at the middle of the income scale but ranges up to as much as fourteen hours (40 percent) reduction in work time for those at the poorest end of the distribution. Blacks, on the other hand, show an *increase* in hours ranging from three hours (10 percent) at the median sample income to two hours for the poorest in the black sample. When the results are examined across plans, it appears that the tax rate has the greatest disincentive effect for the Puerto Rican sample and none for whites and blacks (in the period examined); likewise, the guarantee level is significant primarily for the Puerto Rican sample and to a lesser extent for whites, where its disincentive effect tapers off as income rises relative to the break-even level.[12]

Translated into conventional income- and substitution-effects, these hours-worked adjustments imply that among those most sensitive to the experimental treatments (i.e., those at the lowest relative income levels) about 10 percent of the NIT check is spent to purchase additional leisure for the male head with the remaining 90 percent being available for other consumption. For the poorest whites in the sample, this would represent a 60 percent increase in attainable consumption. Additional analysis of the variance components in the white responses suggests that most of the reduction in hours worked by whites was achieved by reducing overtime *without* changing labor force participation or employment rates; reductions in the Puerto Rican sample were largely achieved by reductions in both participation and employment rates while the *increase*s in hours worked by blacks were achieved through increases in participation and employment rates relative to their controls.

Summary and Comments: Male Labor Responses

As might be expected, experimental treatments had little detectable effect on male heads' labor force participation or employment rates and only a small overall effect on hours actually worked by recipients. For the experimentals *as a group* there is virtually no statistically significant effect attributable to systematic variations in either the tax rate or the guarantee level. However, when the results are analyzed by ethnic group, it becomes apparent that the overall effect is the net result of significantly different responses by race, some positive and some negative. As Watts has stated:

---

[12] Details of the effects of *g* and *r* over the full range of the response surface can be found in Watts, Tables 15–17, pp. 41–43. The lack of any apparent and significant tax disincentive effect has been a puzzle and frustration to the experimenters who, as Watts has put it, "feel certain there *is* a tax effect which the data are not showing." Some possible reasons are discussed in a later section of this book.

> The outcome briefly restated . . . a general pattern of convexity in the response (surface) producing increasing and accelerating disincentive as the distance from the vanishing point, θ, increased. The convexity generally became more pronounced with higher guarantees. . . . ([F]or whites) the most prevalent response involved an adjustment in hours rather than in rates of job holding or job seeking. . . . [I]n the black sample the response was positive over most of the relevant range of θ. Pronounced and significant (negative) responses for the Spanish-speaking husbands were observed at all stages . . . (—the only response fully in line with theoretical expectations).[13]

The dilemma raised by these results, then, is that blacks showed a counter-theoretical response that cannot be easily interpreted.[14] Puerto Rican males show a theoretically "correct" response but are too small and unrepresentative a subsample to generalize to the nation;[15] and whites, who are the largest subsample, show mixed and inconsistent responses over time.

The ultimate effect of the existing design has been to permit relatively more exact tests of responses for small portions of the population than for the sample representing the majority of potential national recipients. Put another way, when analyzed by ethnic group, a labor supply response of a given magnitude can be detected as significant at a higher level of confidence for blacks and Puerto Ricans than for whites. As Watts expresses it, the result of having to analyze the sample by ethnic stratum has been to create

> . . . three separate but highly comparable sets of experimental evidence, each of which is smaller than the originally designed experiment. The precision available in each is sufficient to establish their dissimiliar findings but not enough to produce a satisfying degree of confidence in the results of any of them.[16]

Lack of response to the experimental parameters, particularly the tax rate, was somewhat surprising and equally frustrating since it was these individual design effects that the experiment with its range of plans was particularly designed to reveal. With regard to the apparent lack of a tax rate disincentive at least four explanations have been offered: 1) The experiment did not test widely differing tax rates; there should have been a 90 percent

---

[13] Ibid., p. 59.

[14] One reason is that the differential for blacks is largely the result of the experimentals resisting a general downward trend in employment and hours experienced by the black controls during this period, rather than in any dramatic increase in hours by black experimentals. Because of site-ethnicity confounding (discussed in Chapters 2 and 3), it is impossible to establish exactly what happened to blacks in these markets over the three-year period.

[15] Furthermore, Puerto Ricans do not constitute a significant portion of the national poverty population nor can they be considered representative of other Spanish-speaking groups, especially the large Chicano population of the Southwest.

[16] Watts, p. 57.

or even a 100 percent tax plan; 2) the non-random assignment of families to plans by income level had the effect of virtually excluding from the 70 percent tax plans all but a very few families who were actually receiving payments and so actually subject to the highest tax rate (most families assigned to the 70 percent plans either elected a better welfare allowance or were consistently above their break-even income); 3) the process by which observations were assigned to plans had the effect of creating cells with greater intra- than inter-group variations in effective tax differentials faced by participants so that *average* responses to *r* show no significant differences across plans (see Chapter 4);[17] and 4) the awareness by individual participants of their assigned tax rate and/or their ability to calculate what it implied about the advantage of additional work effort was very low; not understanding their tax status, participants could not react in any systematic way.[18] As indicated, some response was detectable to the level of the guarantee across plans, and experimental families seem to have been more aware of their guarantee than their tax rate.

Experimental Effects on Labor Supply of Wives[19]

The labor response of wives in the continuous sample is of interest for both theoretical and practical reasons. Since wives have a good (and socially acceptable) alternative to market work, namely work in the home, they are faced with a more flexible market choice and might be expected to be more responsive to the change in the marginal wage embodied in the NIT tax rate. Their response should show up more quickly and be more fully adaptive in the space of a short-term experiment than that of the male heads. In a practical sense, the growing labor force participation of wives in the national population makes their response important in estimating national program costs of an NIT.

The Wives' Sample

The sample of wives in continuous husband-wife families differs from the male sample in several important respects. First, the female sample is truncated by the eligibility criterion of total family income used for enroll-

[17] See Henry Aaron, "Lessons from the New Jersey-Pennsylvania Income Maintenance Experiment," multilithed (Paper prepared for Brookings Institution Conference on the New Jersey-Pennsylvania Income Maintenance Experiment, April 1974).

[18] Jon Helge Knudsen, John Mamer, Robert Scott, and Arnold Shore, *Final Report,* vol. III, examine the question of information levels of participants; in general, they conclude that awareness of plan parameters was very low or nonexistent, greatest information being reported for the level of payments received.

[19] This section summarizes Glen Cain, Walter Nicholson, Charles Mallar, and Judith Wooldridge, *Final Report,* vol. I. The likelihood that the wife's work pattern is decided jointly with the husband and other secondary earners in the family is explored in the family response analyses of Robinson Hollister, *Final Report,* vol. I.

ment, so that working wives whose earnings did not bring the family income above 150 percent of the poverty level are to be found only in certain kinds of family units, primarily those with large numbers of children. As would be expected under such circumstances, the average amount of work time spent outside the home by such women was relatively small even before the experiment. Second, female heads of families that split up during the experiment have not been included in the analyzed sample, so that all the women included in the final analyses were acting in the role of secondary earners. It is important therefore to remember that their responses cannot be extrapolated to predict the behavior of the growing number of female-headed poverty units in the nation. Third, while the sample of all wives shows a low participation rate, the experimental wives worked more than their controls at pre-enrollment. Fourth, the work patterns of the wives in the sample are very erratic—while 40 percent of the wives reported themselves in the labor force for one or more quarters, only half this number were working in any given quarter, so that the sample of working wives with continuous or stable work experience is quite small.

Since the sample used in the final analyses is of intact husband-wife families, the distribution of the wives over sites, races, and plans will, of course, be exactly the same as that for males and the total family sample displayed in Table 6.1.

We would expect the labor supply of wives to vary with number of children, husband's income, pre-enrollment income of the family, their own health, tax rate, family guarantee, and payments. Further, we would expect experimental wives to make larger adjustments in labor supply than their husbands because their usual jobs are more short-term, seasonal, and unseniority oriented. For wives, NIT payments act as a cushion, the tax rate reduces the opportunity cost of home work, so that greater sensitivity might be expected to the particular plan parameters.

The Model of Wives' Labor Response

The regression model employed was of the same general form as that for male heads but differs slightly in the specification of the control and treatment variables. Labor response is a function of independent control variables (X), normal income and wage variables (Z), labor supply in the previous period (L), treatment variables (T)—expressed as both dummies and individual experimental parameters, an interaction term (TZ), and an error term (u):

$$\mathrm{LR} = \mathrm{f}(\mathrm{X}, \mathrm{Z}, \mathrm{L}, \mathrm{T}, \mathrm{TZ}) + \mathrm{u}$$

The main differences from the male heads' regression are the inclusion of previous-period labor supply as a significant control variable and the specification of the experimental parameters both as plan dummies and as individual parameters for *g, r,* payments (P), and a tax rate restricted in effect to below break-even incomes (r').

The independent variables measuring labor supply are hours worked, the labor force participation rate (measured as the percentage of quarters in the labor force), and earnings; no employment rate is used because the nature of the wives' work patterns make this a highly erratic index. In addition to running the response regression on averaged data for the wives' sample, a pooled sample of time series cross-section data is constructed for components of variance analysis the results of which substantiate those from the averaged sample.[20] See appendix to this chapter for summary of analytical procedures.

Findings

The regression results (see Table 6.5) reveal some interesting differences between the wives' and the male response patterns. As anticipated, wives generally made much larger *percentage* adjustments in their labor supply calculated on a rather small initial base (pre-enrollment participation of about 16 percent and annual hours of about 250 for experimentals), and controls made larger adjustments than experimental wives. The statistically significant adjustments were made primarily by entering and leaving the labor force frequently (changes in participation) rather than by changing hours or earnings as did the males. With respect to treatment effects, some response is detectable to guarantee level and the size of payments, but there is none found with respect to the tax rate or among the plan dummies. Again, this is somewhat surprising since the expectation had been that the marginal tax rate would implicitly reduce the opportunity cost of home work, but further examination suggests that this function may be being served in a looser way by the guarantee and/or payments that may have been seen as a partial "substitute" for the wife's foregone earnings without any more precise calculation of the marginal effects.[21]

When broken down by ethnic groups, it is evident that the average ad-

---

[20] The pooled sample is essentially a panel of data moving through time in which each report (rather than each earner or family) is treated as a separate observation. This greatly expands the number of observations compared to the averaged sample in which all twelve or thirteen reports for an individual are averaged into a single data point and sidesteps missing data problems for individual units.

[21] Restricting the tax effect to those below break-even reveals a negative compensated tax effect as expected.

Table 6.5
Estimated Experimental Labor Supply Response of Wives in Continuous Husband-Wife Families, Quarters 3–10

	Response Calculated at the "Central Plan"			
	All Wives	*Whites*	*Blacks*	*Puerto Ricans*
Labor Force Participation (Percentage points) (Mean = .163)	—4.3[a]	—9.4[b]	.2[b]	.5
Hours Worked/Week (Hours) (Mean = 3.83)	—.940	—1.940[c]	.510[d]	—.800
Annual Earnings (Dollars)	$100.00	$206.50	$54.50	$85.00
	Response as Percent of Mean Value			
Labor Force Participation	—26	—58	1	3
Hours Worked/Week	—25	—51	13	—21
Annual Earnings	—25	—51	13	—21

[a] Response significant in *g* at the .05 level and to *g-r-T* jointly at .10 level.
[b] Response significant in *g* and *g-r-T* at the .01 level.
[c] Response significant in *g* at .05 level and in *g-r-T* at .10 level.
[d] Response significant in *g*-ethnic interaction at .05 level.
SOURCE: Glen Cain, Walter Nicholson, Charles Mallar, and Judith Wooldridge, *Final Report,* vol. I, Table 8, pp. 39–42. For details of variations in response over plans other than the "central plan" shown here, see the source tabulations.

justments shown in Table 6.5 are due to a relatively large reduction in labor supply by white wives (nearly 50 percent) with zero or positive responses by black and Puerto Rican sample wives. White wives show a reduction of nine percentage points in participation rates, 100 hours, and about $200 in annual earnings at the central plan; black wives show no change in participation, an *increase* of about twenty-five hours, and $50 in annual earnings; and Puerto Rican sample wives show about one-half of 1 percent *increase* in participation rates, a reduction of forty hours, and about $80 in annual earnings. These results prove to be robust with respect to welfare status of the household, its distance from break-even income, and experimental time.

While the researchers themselves attempt no explanation of these differences, several hypotheses come to mind. It may be that white wives are functioning in a different sociocultural milieu in which the basic attitude towards a working wife is quite different among the Scranton whites who are largely of immigrant east European stock than among the blacks and Puerto Ricans in the sample, or it may be that black and Puerto Rican wives are more likely to live in "extended family" situations where other members are at home to care for children.

Whatever the explanation, it is clear that labor response among wives is almost exclusively a white phenomenon, at least as far as the truncated sample can tell us. Had only the male head's income been used to determine eligibility, the total sample would surely have contained more working wives (in the continuous sample only 40 percent of the wives worked at some time and none of these steadily) whose work experience and patterns more nearly approximate those of women with fewer children (the average family in the continuous sample contained six persons)[22] in families with incomes above the effective break-even levels of the experiment.

The New Jersey Experiment was deliberately designed to focus only on male-headed families but, as we have seen, there is apparently little response to be expected from male heads; the response of females promises to be a larger and more sensitive determinant of national program costs, but broadly generalizable evidence on female labor responses cannot be derived from this NIT Experiment.[23] Other income maintenance experiments now under way in Gary and Denver include treatments that consist, in part, of day care for the children of working wives in recipient families and should provide additional information on the sensitivity of wives' labor response to child care duties in the home.

EXPERIMENTAL RESPONSE OF FAMILIES[24]

Previous sections have analyzed the labor supply decisions of husbands and wives as though they were made independently of one another although it is clear in practice that for most families these are joint decisions reflecting preferences and returns to the use of the total household labor resources. In addition, as noted earlier, the experimental families were chosen in such a way that they contain relatively large numbers of children and other adult

---

[22] Glen Cain, "The Effect of Income Maintenance Laws on Fertility," NJE *Final Report,* section D, ch. VII, finds no perceptible effect of NIT payments on either the number or timing of children in recipient families.

[23] In addition, it should be borne in mind that the quality of data on the earnings and hours of secondary workers in the NIT families is somewhat suspect. Income Report Forms and quarterly interviews both tend to understate the activities of wives and other secondary workers. (See earlier sections of this chapter.)

[24] This section discusses the analyses presented in Robinson Hollister and Charles Mallar, *Final Report,* vol. I.

dependents, some of whom represent potential additions to the family labor supply either for market work or for home work.

The analysis of family labor supply responses implicitly treats the labor supply decisions of its members as interdependent and examines the relation of *total* family hours and earnings to a series of control and treatment parameters. The result is *not* a simple weighted combination of the responses of husbands and wives as analyzed separately because: 1) The total family results contain some hours and earnings contributed by other members of the household; and 2) some shifting of the division of market work time among members can be expected in response to changes in the marginal earning power of individuals. Ordinarily, it would be most convenient to combine the hours worked by each member of the family by weighting their respective wage rates to get a total family labor supply measure functionally related to the individual contributions of the members. In this case, however, this procedure is suspect both because the wage rate may itself be a response to treatment and because the wage and earnings data show evidence of substantial reporting error.

THE DATA BASE

The family sample is drawn from the 693 continuous husband-wife families from which are dropped ninety-seven households assigned to the two least generous NIT plans dominated by state welfare programs. The 596 remaining families are further reduced by adjustments in the sample necessary to compute *Y*, so that the final sample (for the averaged data) is 530, composed of 228 white, 175 black, and 127 Puerto Rican families. There is no way to determine from the *Final Report* documents precisely how these families are divided by site or plan since it cannot be assumed that the sixty-six exclusions were distributed in proportion to the original sample.

Analyses are reported both for the averaged sample and for a pooled sample. Regressions run on the averaged sample reveal the major responses at the "central plan"; components-of-variance analyses run on the pooled sample confirm the regression results and detect some weak tax and payments responses around the central point of the response surface as described.

The regressions run on the averaged sample were of the following form:

$$\mathrm{LR} = f(\mathrm{T}, \mathrm{S_g}, \mathrm{S_r}, \mathrm{Sites}, \hat{\mathrm{Y}}/\mathrm{PL}, \mathrm{S_g}\cdot\hat{\mathrm{Y}}/\mathrm{PL}, \mathrm{S_r}\cdot\hat{\mathrm{Y}}/\mathrm{PL}, \\ \mathrm{T}\cdot\hat{\mathrm{Y}}/\mathrm{PL}, \mathrm{Health}, \mathrm{Health}\cdot\hat{\mathrm{Y}})$$

where T is a treatment dummy, S_g and S_r are the experimental splines, and

$\hat{Y}/PL$ is normal family income relative to the poverty level.[25] The pooled sample analysis includes, in addition, seasonal and experimental time splines. (See appendix to this chapter for summary of analytical procedures.)

Findings

The range of results for the averaged and pooled samples calculated at the central plan is displayed in Table 6.6. While the range is rather wide,

Table 6.6
Range of Estimated Experimental Response of Families at Mean Income and Central Plan (g = 1.0, r = s5)

	A. Control-Experimental Differential in			
	Hours		*Earnings*	
	Avgd.	*Pooled*	*Avgd.*	*Pooled*
	(In hours)		(In dollars)	
Whites	−2.19[a]	−3.40	− 1.66	−11.00
Blacks	+ .98	−1.26	+15.58	+ 9.40
Puerto Ricans	−6.12	−2.60[a]	− 9.26[c]	− 2.08[b]
	B. Percentage Differential in			
	Hours		*Earnings*	
	Avgd.	*Pooled*	*Avgd.*	*Pooled*
Whites	− 6%	−11%	− 1.4%	−15%
Blacks	+ 2	− 4	+13	+ 7
Puerto Ricans	−14	− 8	− 8	− 4

[a] Significant at the .05 level.
[b] Significant at the .01 level.
[c] Significant at the .10 level.
SOURCE: Section A adapted from Robinson Hollister, *Final Report,* vol. I, Tables 5–10, pp. 19–24. Section B adapted from Final Report, Vol. I, Table 4, p. 16.

Hollister suggests an average *reduction* of about 10 percent in both earnings and hours (significant at the .01 level) for white families; a reduction of about 9 percent in hours (significant at .05 level) and 8 percent in earnings for Puerto Rican sample families; and a zero change in hours and a 10 percent *increase* in earnings (significant at .01 level) for black families. No

[25] Normal family income ($\hat{Y}$) is calculated by Robinson Hollister on the control group alone rather than on the total sample of controls plus experimentals used by Watts. See Chapter 5 for a critique of the Watts procedure.

significant guarantee or tax rate effects were detected. The components-of-variance analysis on the pooled sample adds only three bits of further evidence: 1) The hours and earnings effects cited for the averaged sample show an increasing differential over the experimental time period; that is, the reductions (or increases) in experimentals' hours and earnings result from both controls and experimentals moving in the same direction but at different rates over time; 2) there is some weak evidence that white families' responses were more closely linked to their normal payment level (the NIT payment they could expect at their normal income, $\hat{Y}$) than to g or r; and 3) an interaction term for r and the normal variance of Y shows up as significant suggesting that family labor supply is more responsive to the tax rate for households whose expected incomes fluctuate a great deal and that this sensitivity increases with $\hat{Y}$. This last effect probably stems from the greater response of wives and may indicate a learning effect in which higher variance in income (and payments) produces greater awareness of plan parameters.

While husbands and wives account for the majority of family labor resources, additional earnings can also be contributed by other members of the household including children old enough to hold work permits (in most states, 16 years and older). The labor decisions made by young adults in experimental families are of particular interest, because they involve a choice between further schooling (investment in future earning power) and immediate earnings. Mallar[26] has tested the hypothesis that NIT payments will be used by families to keep children in school longer and found two weak effects: a slight increase among experimentals in the school enrollment of older youths and a slight increase in labor force participation of black and Puerto Rican youths.

CONCLUSION: GENERALIZABILITY TO A NATIONAL NIT

The preceding sections have outlined briefly the results of the labor response analyses for male heads, wives, and families as composite units.

While the degree of confidence one can have in particular results reported in the *Final Report* varies considerably, it is fair to say that the experiment gives us some information on the short-term responses of a particular sam-

---

[26] Charles Mallar, *Final Report,* vol. III; a critique of these results is found in Chapter 7 on non-labor force responses which suggests that the cut-off age of 18 used in the Mallar analysis is too low.

Mallar has subsequently reanalyzed the data for youths 19–21 at the end of the experiment and found much larger experimental responses on the order of thirty percentage points in the increased probability of youths in experimental families completing high school. (See Mallar, "The Educational and Labor Supply Responses of Young Adults on the Urban Graduated Work Incentive Experiment," mimeo, 1975.)

ple of large, stable, intact families most of whom were not poor in the sense of being below the official poverty level. The information is that the male heads of such families have rather firm commitments to work and show very little inclination to adjust their work pattern in response to an NIT that gave them payments averaging about 25 percent of their normal family earnings. Such adjustments as were made differed in both direction and magnitude by ethnic group; blacks showing an *increase* in work, Puerto Ricans showing a *decrease,* and whites exhibiting small and fluctuating responses, positive and negative, over time. The labor supply adjustments of males appear to be made through marginal changes in overtime and, to a much lesser extent, through more intensive job searches and improvement in wage rates.

The 40 percent of wives in these families who worked at all, worked very few hours in the year and cut this effort substantially in response to NIT participation apparently in order to substitute home work for additional cash income to the family. The fact that they had relatively large numbers of children at home and that their earning power was already very low (partly as a consequence of their limited and discontinuous work experience) doubtless made their original attachment to the labor force marginal and their departure from it easy when a partial substitute for their income was provided. In contrast to the male heads, the wives' response was almost exclusively a white phenomenon and was achieved by a relative withdrawal from the labor force compared to their controls. The non-response of black and Puerto Rican wives suggests that these women are, or see themselves as being, in a very different socioeconomic position within the family than do white wives. From the standpoint of those who concern themselves with the violence they fear an NIT would do to the traditional work ethic, these results should be reassuring. Male heads, particularly black, tend, if anything, to work *more* and to make only small adjustments in their overtime commitments while the relatively large *reductions* in work come from (white) wives who leave the labor force to shoulder heavy home and child-rearing responsibilities.

Neither wives' nor husbands' labor responses show any consistently significant relation to the experimental parameters separately; in particular, the finding of no-response to the tax rate is disturbing to those who have argued that the high implicit tax rates of existing welfare programs are a major evil to be addressed by an NIT. As we have seen, the evidence suggests that this may be largely an artifact of the experimental design—there is reason to believe that a sufficiently wide range of tax plans was not tested and awareness among recipients of which tax plan they were on seems to have been virtually nil. The greater awareness among participants of the guarantee and their greater responsiveness to the level of payments actually received suggests that what may count in constructing an NIT program is some index of joint effects rather than a fine tuning of its separate components.

Similarly, the distribution of a limited sample over a large number of plans designed to test response to plan parameters also had the effect of limiting severely the ability to establish with certainty an effect that did turn out to be significant—the ethnic response differences. It is possible to argue with hindsight that common sense or corollary information should have suggested that the rather gross differences of race would matter more than the rather subtle differences of plan parameters, but this is fruitless now; rather, the observation to be made is that the responses to be expected from an experimental treatment are smaller than was previously supposed and run along some rather obvious dimensions so that future experimenters must 1) give a good deal of attention to getting the most likely response parameters into their design initially and 2) adopt much larger and more divergent treatments than heretofore in order to elicit responses of a magnitude discernible with relatively small samples. This suggests some tension between the desire to use experimentation to test economic or sociological theory (a scientific objective) and the desire to acquire efficient information for the evaluation of national policy—two objectives that the NIT Experiment approached as complementary. A summary of overall findings is in the appendix to this chapter.

Four general qualifications apply in considering the experimental results as indicators of aggregate response to a potential nationwide income maintenance program.

1. *Time bias*—resulting from the expectation that respondents will react to experimental treatments with less than full adjustment of their work patterns as long as they are aware of the temporary nature of the experiment and do not expect it to be continued immediately in the form of a national program. Metcalf[27] has explored the theoretical implications of short-term time bias on the NIT results and concluded that the net result will be a tendency for the experimental responses to underestimate probable long-term national responses to an NIT.

2. *Labor market bias*—resulting from the fact that individual adjustments in work patterns made in response to experimental treatments are not large enough to reveal the effects of wages and work-hour contracts that would result in a national labor market in which many households adjusted their desired work time by a small amount. Browning[28] has investigated the

[27] Charles Metcalf, *Final Report,* vol. III.

[28] Edgar Browning, "Incentive and Disincentive Experimentation for Income Maintenance Policy Purposes: Note," *American Economic Review* 61 (1971): 709–712 and "Income Redistribution and the Negative Income Tax: A Theoretical Analysis" (Ph.D. diss., Princeton University, 1971).

theoretical effects of this labor market bias and Husby[29] has attempted some national program cost estimates on the basis of certain assumptions about the ability of national NIT recipients to exert an aggregate pressure on both wages and labor market practices, such as the rigid forty-hour work week.

3. *Aggregate expenditure bias*—resulting from the fact that a national NIT would involve substantial redistribution of national income and thereby affect the ability to finance other types of public expenditure programs that in turn have a bearing on the choice between income and leisure. This is essentially a federal level policy issue resting on the estimate of probable national cost that is missing as a product of the NIT. Browning[30] provides a theoretical discussion of the elements of the national debate.

4. *Hawthorne effects*—reflecting the possibility that experimental subjects may respond differently, because they are being watched and/or because they may have an explicit desire to influence the experimental outcome in a certain direction. The experimenters made careful and apparently successful efforts to minimize the intrusiveness of the field and reporting operations on the lives of the sample families. With a few exceptions, such as the zealousness of the press in tracking down and interviewing several families early in the experiment and some checking by state welfare agencies for double collections, there seems to have been little awareness of the presence of objectives of the experimental team. Indeed, this invisibleness of the experiment seems not only to have protected the results from Hawthorne distortions but to have extended to considerable unawareness of some of the treatment features themselves!

The theme of this chapter has been that we have learned a good deal from the New Jersey Experiment about the probable bounds of labor supply responses to an NIT although not nearly enough to fulfill the policy requirements for the evaluation of a national NIT. Difficulties in interpreting how rather different subsets of responses occur within the overall bounds stem partly from decisions made in the design and execution of the experiment itself and partly from certain inherent difficulties in using experiments necessarily constrained by time and budget to ascertain permanent program effects. Chapter 8 discusses the policy implications of the experiment in more detail.

---

[29] Ralph Husby, "Work Incentives and the Cost Effectiveness of Income Maintenance Programs," *Quarterly Review of Economics and Business* (1973): 7–13, and "Impact of a Negative Income Tax on Aggregate Demand and Supply," *Western Economic Journal* (1973): 111–117.

[30] Browning, "Incentive and Disincentive Experimentation."

Appendix to Chapter 6

Summary Characteristics of Analyses of Labor Supply Responses to the New Jersey Experiment

Analysis	*Regression(s)*	*Dependent Variables*	*Control Variables*	*Experimental Parameters*	*Sample*	*General Results*
Male heads	$X = C + LR$ $LR =$ $(a+bS_g+cS_r)\theta$ $+(d+eS_g+fS_r)\theta^2$	LFPR hours (H) employ (E) earnings (Y_e)	$S=f(Y,W,M)$ splines for: age, education, health, sites, family size, Y_o, H_o	splines: g—.75, r—.5, M, $time_c$, $time_e$	693 continuous families (Q's 8–13) of which: 346 male heads 134 controls 212 experimentals by race: W 155 B 117 PR 74 by site: T 30 P/P 79 JC 118 S 119 by income stratum: I. 90 II. 118 III. 138	W: —1.9H, +1.8% LFPR, + .4% E B: +3.2H, +2.4% LFPR, +6.7% E PR: —2.1H, —1.8% LFPR, —9.4% E

Wives	$X = C + LR$ $LR =$ $f(X,Z,L,T,TZ)+u$	LFPR (% Q's) hours (H) earnings (Y_e)	splines for: age, education, family size & composition, health interacts. of: site-race, treat.-child, male employ, male health H_o, Y_{oe}, Y_{ue}	g,r,P T(dummy) r′ (TZ)'s	693 continuous families (Q's 8–13) of which: 346 wives 134 controls 212 experimentals by race, site, and income as above of which worked: 51 controls 87 experimentals	W: −8% LFPR, −100H, −\$200Y_e B: ϕLFPR, ϕH, ϕY_e PR: ϕLFPR, ϕH, ϕY_e
Families	$X = C + LR$ $LR =$ $f(T,S_g,S_r,$ sites, $\hat{Y}/PL$, $S_r{*}\hat{Y}/PL, S_g{*}\hat{Y}/PL$, $T{*}\hat{Y}/PL$, health, health$*$T) f(site dums, $time_c$, $time_e$, health, time$*\hat{Y}$, time$*\hat{Y}/PL, S_g, S_r$, $S_{g'*}\hat{Y}/PL, S_r{*}Y/PL$)	Total fam. earnings/wk. total fam. hours/wk.	site (dum), time spline, $\hat{Y}_*$ time, $time_s$, health, age, education, family size, $\hat{Y}$, $\hat{Y}^2$, $\hat{H}$, $\hat{H}^2$	splines: g—.75 r—.5 P, time, T, (TZ)'s, (YZ)'s, $Y > Y_b$(dum) Y_*	693 continuous families minus two lowest plans (97) and (66) elim. from $\hat{Y}$ and $\hat{w}$ calcs.= 530: W 228 B 175 PR 127 by site and income not revealed	W: −10% H, −10% Y_e B: ϕH, ϕY_e PR: −9% H, −8% Y_e

NOTE: General results are calculated at the central plan (g=1.0, r=.5).

Summary
Regression Estimates of Control-Experimental Differentials in Labor Supply of Husbands, Wives, and Families, Quarters 3–10

	Labor Force Participation Rate	*Employment Rate*	*Hours Worked*	*Earnings (Weekly)*
Husbands				
Whites				
Absolute Difference (%)	—.3(—.3)	—2.3(—2.6)	—1.9(—5.6)	.1(.1)
Blacks				
Absolute Difference (%)	0(0)	.8(.9)	.7(2.3)	8.7(9.3)
Puerto Ricans				
Absolute Difference (%)	1.6(1.6)	—2.4(—2.7)	—.2(—.7)	5.9(6.4)
Wives				
Whites				
Absolute Difference (%)	—6.7[a](—32.2)	—5.9[a](—34.7)	—1.4(—30.6)	—3.1(—33.2)
Blacks				
Absolute Difference (%)	—.8(—3.6)	—.3(—1.5)	—.1(—2.2)	.8(7.8)
Puerto Ricans				
Absolute Difference (%)	—3.8(—31.8)	—5.2(—48.3)	—1.9(—55.4)	—4.1(—54.7)
Families				
Whites				
Absolute Difference (%)	—5.3[b](—9.1)	—6.1[b](—12.0)	—6.2[b](—13.4)	—10.1(—8.1)
Blacks				
Absolute Difference (%)	—1.6(—2.9)	—1.6(—3.3)	—2.2(—5.2)	4.1(3.6)
Puerto Ricans				
Absolute Difference (%)	2.4(5.0)	—1.0(—2.2)	—.4(—.9)	5.0(4.9)

[a] Significant at the .95 level.
[b] Significant at the .99 level.
SOURCE: U.S. Department of Health, Education, and Welfare, *Summary Report: New Jersey Graduated Work Incentive Experiment* (Washington, D.C.: December 1973), pp. 22–27.

Chapter 7

Non-Labor Supply Experimental Responses

INTRODUCTION

Although the central issue in the NIT Experiment was the labor supply response to experimental treatments, the experiment also covered a variety of additional possible responses, some seemingly very far removed from labor supply issues. The variety of subsidiary topics covered defies positive classification: hence the title of this chapter indicating that it covers the residual category formed by non-labor supply response measures.

The design of the experiment reflects the centrality of labor force response as the focus of the NIT Experiment. So does the composition of the research team with the main positions of authority and responsibility going to economists. Still there was some interest in the non-labor force response to NIT, enough for OEO to include such concerns in the definitions of the goals of the experiment. Correspondingly, there was enough interest on the part of non-economists for some at the University of Wisconsin and at Princeton to join the research teams at Mathematica and IRP respectively.

There are several good reasons for including such concerns in the NIT Experiment. Policy issues surrounding NIT do not end with questions about labor force response. Existing welfare programs were supposed to have a number of perverse incentives built into them, for example, a pro-natalist bias that arises out of the tying of benefits to family size and an incentive toward family dissolution arising out of the bias in eligibility requirements against intact families.[1]

There was also some concern among conservatives with what might be called the "color television" problem; an increase in the income of the poor would only mean expenditures on "frivolous and unnecessary luxuries."

On the liberal side, a common criticism of the existing welfare system was its alleged negative social psychological consequences for welfare clients. Welfare supposedly stigmatized and degraded its clients with means test for eligibility and constant supervision of client households, leading them to a lowered self-esteem and apathy.[2] Finally a new income maintenance plan might have some effects upon the jobs taken by low income persons either by making low paying jobs bearable or by subsidizing job searches. Each of these policy issues merited inquiry.

In a more comprehensive vein, there was both policy and social science concern over the supposed pathology of the poor. On almost any indicator of social pathology, the poor evidence greater incidence and prevalence rates. Crime, juvenile delinquency, mental illness, most organic diseases and disabling physical conditions, low levels of intellectual performances, family instability, and so on are all found more frequently among the poor. It has been characteristic of each new social welfare measure from the early days of the public health movement to the latest twist in social casework to claim for itself the ability to lower the levels of such indicators among the poor, at least "in the long run." When a negative income tax plan comes up on the agenda, it would most likely prove to be no exception. Advocates would claim for it miraculous curative properties while opponents would likely insist that the pathologies were root causes of poverty, conditions unlikely to be cured by income augmentation alone.

---

[1] This was particularly the case for AFDC programs which were initially restricted to female-headed families. Even under the modified AFDC-UP, eligibility was restricted to families in which the male parent was unemployed or underemployed (see Chapter 3).

[2] Oddly enough, very few raised the question whether any transfer payment plan, let alone the NIT ones tested out in this experiment, would have the same defects. It may not be necessary to have the same means test to be eligible for payments, but it is necessary to submit some statement of earnings and other income. The possibility of fraud and the likelihood that some fraud would be detected would mean that eventually any negative income tax scheme would resemble in its administration the existing welfare system. Indeed, it is difficult to see radical differences between welfare and the payments plan in these respects when we consider that a constant monitoring of income was involved in both along with investigations of possible fraud and so on. See Chapter 3 for a description of relevant administrative procedures employed in NIT.

SOCIOLOGICAL AND SOCIAL PSYCHOLOGICAL THEORY AND POVERTY

The policy questions have their counterpart in social science issues. Many of the supposed benefits or negative effects that might flow from a negative income tax program can be restated in terms of the controversy over the idea of a "culture of poverty." According to Oscar Lewis who coined the term,[3] poor people in an open society develop a culture that effectively prevents them from rising out of the condition of poverty. The hallmark of a culture or subculture of poverty is allegedly a value system that stresses, among other things, a short, rather than long-term time orientation, a preference for immediate sensory gratification as opposed to rewards stemming from achievement and status, and so on. Lewis lists seventy traits that characterize the culture of poverty. As a "subculture" the culture of poverty is "inherited" through early childhood socialization by each succeeding generation so that children of poor families can rarely rise above their origins. Its holding power over the poor is so strong that Lewis saw that little could be done for the poor short of mass psychiatric treatment.

The leading contending alternative to the "culture of poverty" advanced by other social scientists conceded that the poor resembled to a greater or lesser degree the description advanced by Lewis, but stressed that these characteristics arose continually in response to the conditions of poverty and were not passed on from generation to generation as a subculture. Rather, improving the conditions of the poor would lead to a disappearance of the signs of personal and social disorganization that everyone agreed existed among the poor. For some who held this view, an income strategy was an appropriate remedy; for others, a job strategy was held to be the more effective nostrum.

With the exception of those who held to the conception of a "culture of poverty," sociologists and social psychologists dealing with poverty all had some expectations that a negative income tax would have *some* non-labor force effects. Exactly what sorts of effects, how strong such effects would be, and what was the time span of exposure to such a program that would be required for effects to manifest themselves were all questions to which the rudimentary social science theory could provide no answers.

Although static equilibrium theory was silent on many points concerning the size of the expected labor force responses to a negative income tax plan, it did at least predict both the existence and direction of the response. In contrast, sociology and social psychology provided theories that were

---

[3] Oscar Lewis, *La Vida* (New York: Random House, 1965).

vaguely formulated and provided contradictory predictions: From the "culture of poverty" hypothesis one would predict, if anything, that there would be no response either in labor force or in other terms. From the competing theory, one might also predict no response depending on how long a run was thought to be necessary to reverse the effects of poverty.[4] The extent to which this is so is demonstrated in almost all of the papers that arose out of a two-year long monthly conference on poverty run by the American Academy of Arts and Sciences.[5]

Previous empirical researches on the characteristics of the poor were not of very much help. While the literature contained many descriptions of the quality of life among the poor and of relevant characteristics, it tended to be dominated by qualitative rather than quantitative researches. Well-designed quantitative studies of the poor have only come into the literature in the last few years. At the time of the design of the New Jersey-Pennsylvania Experiment, definitive research on the poor was quite slight in volume.[6] Even more important, most of the statements that had appeared in the literature concerning the characteristics of the poor were based upon studies that were badly flawed in one way or another. For example, one of the alleged main characteristics of the poor, repeated in citation after citation, was that poor people lacked the ability to defer gratification. The basic reference from which the citation was taken was a small study of high school students who were asked, in effect, whether they would save or spend a small sum of money (five dollars) if given to them. In the original study, the differences between poorer and richer students were not very great (although statistically significant), nor did the study take into account what were the differences in cash on hand between poorer and richer students.[7]

---

[4] This discussion may leave the reader with the impression that the culture of poverty "theory" dominates the sociologists' and social psychologists' views on poverty. We would hazard the guess that most reject the theory—certainly most who worked on the income maintenance experiment did so. The prominence given to this formulation is more a function of its monopoly position than of its persuasiveness: It is virtually the only contender for the position of a "theory" of poverty.

[5] Daniel P. Moynihan, ed. *On Understanding Poverty* (New York: Basic Books, 1968).

[6] Two contemporary literature reviews bear out this point: Zahava D. Blum and Peter H. Rossi, "Social Science Images of the Poor" in Moynihan, ibid., and Vernon Allen, "Personality Correlates of Poverty," *Psychological Factors in Poverty,* ed. Vernon Allen (Chicago: Markham Publishing Co., 1970). It should be noted that Vernon Allen was one of the social psychologists at the University of Wisconsin who played an important role in the experiment, contributing many ideas concerning the non-labor supply response measures to be included in quarterly research interviews. It is difficult to reconcile his reviews of the literature indicating that very little was known concerning personality correlates of poverty with the kinds of measures included in the quarterly interviews.

[7] The obstinate persistence of research findings of this sort against the contradictions of better research can be seen most flagrantly in Edward A. Banfield's *The Un-*

Another problem with the literature was the absence of a clear definition of who were the poor and vague indexes of association. Thus, findings that amounted to correlations of .05 to .20 on samples that largely missed households below the poverty line were magnified into characteristics that sharply differentiated between the relatively affluent and the poor.

In short, empirical social research of any minimum substance that could illuminate the characteristics of poor individuals or households was simply missing. In its absence, qualitative accounts of little probity tended to dominate the image of the poor in social science literature. It was an image that depicted the poor as impulsive, lacking in foresight and ambition, alienated, anomic, and possessed of a fragile ability to sustain family relationships or participate in the larger society.

The weakness of sociological and social psychological theory coupled with the absence of firmly based empirical knowledge about poverty meant that the attention of the sociologists and social psychologists went to issues that were agitating the conventional wisdom of conservative policymakers. The result is the hodgepodge of topics that will be discussed in the remainder of this chapter.

AN OVERVIEW OF THE NON-LABOR SUPPLY FINDINGS

This section of this chapter provides a summary of the findings contained in the diverse analyses of non-labor force effects. Although we have stressed the roles played by sociologists and social psychologists in the opening section of this chapter, some of the topics covered fall clearly within the substantive domain of economists—for example, consumption behavior. Others are in the overlap areas between economics and sociology—for example, job turnover and school attendance. The remainder lie clearly in areas that have been dominated by sociologists and social psychologists—organizational membership, family cohesion, and such attitudinal areas as anomie and self-esteem.[8]

In each of the sections that follow we will take up what appears to be a separate topic of substantive concern. We will present first a description and

---

heavenly City (Boston: Little, Brown Co., 1970), who raised the alleged characteristic of short-range time perspectives and inability to defer gratification to the status of *the* distinguishing features of the urban poor. See P. H. Rossi, "The City as Purgatory," *Social Science Quarterly* 51 (1972): 4.

[8] It is difficult to do complete justice to the many papers reviewed in this chapter, especially since many appear to be first or intermediate attempts at analysis. The final forms in which these analyses might appear can be somewhat different than described here. However, it seems unlikely that the findings as described here will change drastically: There may be needles in those haystacks, but there are not likely to be any overlooked crowbars.

critique of the data base employed, second, a review of the analytical procedures used, and finally a summary of the main findings along with an assessment of the extent to which those findings may be taken as relatively firm.

Consumption Behavior[9]

Consumption behavior has both a policy and a theoretical relevance. On the policy side, the issue is how "sensibly" would the payments be used? According to fears of the opponents of NIT (and of other transfer payment schemes), the improvident nature of the poor would lead them to use the payments for "unnecessary" purchases: liquor rather than food, color television sets rather than washing machines; luxury cars rather than "reasonable, decent" used cars.

On the social science theory side, the issue was whether families would regard payments as additions to "permanent income" in which case payments would not be expected to affect the distribution of income purchase categories or "transitory income" (windfalls) in which case one might expect some alteration in the pattern of expenditures.

With the exception of health services (to be treated separately later), the three papers dealing with consumption behavior have all been written by economists. Wooldridge addressed herself almost entirely to experimental effects on housing consumption. Metcalf attempted the difficult task of discerning what might be the effects of a permanent negative income tax plan on a wider variety of consumption behaviors. Nicholson's paper deals with the assessment of experimental effects on the same broad spectrum of consumption, being differentiated from Metcalf's work primarily by being unconcerned with estimating the effects of a permanent plan.[10]

The Data Series

The data upon which analyses are based are obtained from a subset of the quarterly interviews. On some quarterly interviews housewives were asked to estimate their expenditures on food for preparation of home-cooked meals, on food obtained outside the home, and on purchases of clothing. At the pre-enrollment interview, questions were asked about the possession of various appliances, automobiles and trucks, insurance policies, assets in savings, cash on hand, and information on mortgage holdings. All three authors complain in their papers about the inadequacy of the data

---

[9] This section is based on Judith Wooldridge, Charles Metcalf, and Walter Nicholson, *Final Report,* vol. III.

[10] In practice, this meant that Metcalf used pre-enrollment income and Nicholson contemporaneous income measures in their specifications of experimental effects.

base. For example, the pre-enrollment checklist of possessions held did not ask for prices or time of acquisition; the items on mortgage holdings do not clearly differentiate between current mortgage balance and original mortgage amount. No questions were asked about amounts spent for a variety of services including services, such as utilities, that are connected with housing.

The measurement of household stocks of consumer goods and their movements into and out of households is not an easy task to perform with high accuracy. Furthermore, to do so would involve devoting considerable research resources to this topic, an allocation that would mean that other areas would be slighted. Whether or not the research staff made the correct decisions in allocating as much effort as they did to this topic is a matter that is easy to judge in hindsight and difficult to foresee. Given the fact that some important experimental effects were found with respect to consumer behavior, we can wish that more effort had been devoted to the topic. This criticism is most properly seen as the starting point for more attention in other experimental studies of NIT, rather than as a fatal flaw of judgment in the NIT research group.

The most clearly defined variable concerns home ownership and monthly rental. For the rest, researchers have to rely on respondent estimates (for example, for food expenditures) or have to impute the acquisition of durable items and automobiles by comparing and justifying inventories made at different points in time.

There are several obvious deficiencies in the consumption data series: Only certain categories of consumption were covered; heavy reliance was placed on respondent estimates; the purchase prices and depreciated values of possessions had to be estimated at most points in time; and no attempt was made until the follow-up post-experiment interview to determine whether families treated payments separately in their budgeting or lumped payments with other sources of income.[11]

Analyses

Although the base number of families used varies somewhat from paper to paper, depending on the number of cases that have to be left out because of missing information, all use that set of families that were continuously in the experiment for the total period in question.

Data are analyzed in all three papers using multiple regression techniques with some additional work in Wooldridge's paper using probit analysis. The differences among the papers lie mainly in the dependent variables and in

[11] No analyses have yet been made (that were available to us) of the post-experimental interviews dealing with this topic.

the definition of control variables to be employed. Thus Wooldridge confines her analysis entirely to the purchase of housing, the payment of rent in private housing, and moves from public housing. In an effort to obtain estimates of effects on consumption that are free from labor force experimental effects, Metcalf employs pre-enrollment earnings and corresponding payments as a measure of permanent income and experimental effects. In contrast, Nicholson uses actual income disaggregated into earnings, other income, and payments.

Findings

Perhaps the most dramatic experimental effects were shown in Wooldridge's paper. Families in the experimental group were more likely to purchase a home during the experimental period, renters increased the amount of rent they paid (and presumably achieved better housing thereby), and experimentals living in public housing at the time of enrollment were slightly more likely to move out of public housing. Even more startling was the fact that experimental families that were not receiving payments (that is, were above the break-even levels) showed experimental effects, indicating that being on the experiment possibly gave them the security to venture more of their income in housing or made lending institutions more willing to provide mortgage money.

Unfortunately the amounts of money spent for housing for homeowners and those in public housing are difficult to estimate with the best of data; without these data, homeowner costs and housing costs for households in public housing are impossible to estimate. Hence, although we do know that renters in the private market ended up spending more money on housing if they were in the experimental group, we do not know whether the same can be said with certainty for the other two groups.

It should be borne in mind that the households participating in the experiment tended to be younger, have a lower proportion of homeowners, and have larger families than is characteristic of households in the tracts from which they were selected. Hence, these are households starting out initially with a depressed rate of home ownership at a point in their life cycles at which families ordinarily acquire homes. It may well be the case that experimental families accelerated their home buying in response to the fact of participation in the experiment. It is important to note that this is an important finding, one that shows that NIT can have an important effect on the level of living of poor and near-poor households. Accelerating home purchase behavior means that the experimental households can indulge more readily their preferences for owned housing, presumably representing an increase in housing quality for a longer period of their household existence than control families.

The experimental effects on other types of consumption are not as clear or dramatic. Both Metcalf and Nicholson find that experimental families are more likely to acquire durable goods, home production appliances particularly (for example, washing machines, refrigerators). But, other forms of consumption (for example, food, other durables, and clothing) show inconsistent patterns; for example, black households were less likely to increase their food consumption expenditures than whites according to Nicholson's analysis, but Metcalf could not substantiate such a finding in his analysis.[12]

The evaluation of these findings hinges upon two issues. First, since the data bases are variable in quality, some of the findings are less plausible than others. A home purchase seems a much "harder" fact than, for example, housewives' estimates of amount spent on food consumption outside the home, so it is more likely that the home purchase behavior is "real." A second issue centers around whether these findings are in some sense artifacts to be found only in experiments. Here the main problem seems to be whether under a permanent negative income tax plan similar behavior can be expected. Despite Metcalf's heroic attempts to solve this problem with a theoretical model of the relationship between short-run experiments and long-range programs, the issue still remains an open one.

The findings concerning housing expenditures and durable purchases are among the firmest positive experimental effects to be found in the entire set of papers coming from the experiment. Assuming that such effects are both firm and characteristic of behavior under permanent plans, the policy implications are considerable. They indicate that a general income strategy may improve the housing situations and the material level of living of the poor substantially.[13]

Family Composition and Family Relationships

The family life of the poor has been brought into the limelight of public policy discussions by the considerable growth in one of the major existing social welfare programs, Aid to Dependent Children (ADC). Authorized in the original Social Security legislation of the 1930s, ADC was a categorical program of aid to fatherless family units, originally envisioned primarily

[12] It is interesting to note that not one of the authors directly addressed himself or herself to the frivolous consumption problem.

[13] Assuming no compensating price effects that would simply raise the price of low-cost housing without material improvement.

for the support of orphans and children whose mothers had been widowed, deserted or divorced. The growth of the number of female-headed households in the Post-World War II period made this program one of the major welfare programs in terms of funds expended and coverage.

It is not at all clear why the postwar period experienced such a burgeoning of ADC. At least part of the reason was a considerable increase in the efficiency of welfare departments in obtaining better and more complete coverage of the eligible population. Some claimed that the program offered a perverse incentive to family dissolution by restricting eligibility to fatherless households although relaxation of this restriction in the middle 1960s did not seem to halt the steady increase in fatherless households.

The issue of the perverse trends among poor families was injected into the politics of race relations by Daniel Patrick Moynihan's analysis of trends in family composition among blacks, a publication that made its author famous and infamous.[14] Moynihan's analysis of postwar trends among black families suggested that the fragility of black families was an inheritance from slavery days augmented by the job and income insecurities of urban living.

In contrast to some of the other areas of behavior discussed in this chapter there was no dearth of hard data on the characteristics of the poor in these respects. The incidence rates of divorce, desertion, and separation were clearly inversely related to household income, occupational level, and educational attainment. So were prevalence rates of incomplete households. In addition, fertility data also have shown an inverse relationship to socioeconomic levels although the variance associated with socioeconomic status had been declining in recent decades.

It could be argued that a negative income tax program would have some impact upon these trends. On the one hand, since payments were not tied to qualitative aspects of family composition, the perverse incentives of some welfare programs would not operate.[15] Hence, participation in the plan could lessen the incidence of family dissolution. On the other hand,

---

[14] Daniel P. Moynihan, *The Negro Family: The Case for National Action* (Washington, D.C.: Government Printing Office, 1965).

[15] Of course, both New Jersey and Pennsylvania were states in which welfare eligibility was not tied to family composition. New Jersey at the start of the experiment was operating its welfare program under old rules that rendered intact families ineligible, a rule that was relaxed shortly after the experiment got under way.

The rules under which experimental payments were divided in cases of household dissolution were set up to provide a continuity of support for individuals but did not recognize a reorganized household as eligible for payments on the same basis as other families of similar composition. Thus a husband separating from his wife would take some part of the payments with him, but if he or his wife remarried, the newly constituted household would not be recognized as such for the purpose of payments.

the plan had a possible natalist bias since the addition of children[16] to a household moved its break-even point and payments upward and provided an incentive to skew child-rearing into the experimental period when the wife's work in the home as a housewife was partly subsidized.

The design of the New Jersey-Pennsylvania Negative Income Tax experiment, however, did not provide a good test of either possibility. Eligibility requirements stipulated that households be intact and were tied to household size. Newly formed households, by virtue of small size, were not likely to be eligible; hence, households most subject to dissolution under "normal" circumstances were underrepresented. The households most likely to be eligible were therefore households that survived the early period of marital instability and had grown large enough to be poor but were not yet old enough to undergo contraction as children left.

It can be argued that the rules of eligibility provided a set of households that were more stable than a more ecumenical selection would have provided and were also households that had completed their fertility.

However, the most important reason that NIT was not a good test of the pro-natalist incentives of a negative income tax plan was its short duration. An additional child is a financial responsibility for far longer than a three-year period, and it would not take much in the way of sophisticated computation to show that the payment increments for an additional child over the three-year period (actually it could only be a maximum of twenty-six months assuming that pregnancy was started as soon as a household was enrolled in a treatment group) would pale into insignificance when compared with the long-term fiscal liabilities involved. A permanent plan, depending on its specific features, could therefore have a much more important effect on fertility.

Hence, the results of the experiment are likely to be serious underestimates of the long-term effects of a permanent negative income tax plan. The virtue of the findings may be that if they were postive (i.e., NIT treatments increase fertility), then a permanent plan could be expected to make an even stronger impact.

Data Bases

Household composition changes were among the best measured variables. Each quarterly interview reviewed household membership noting additions

---

[16] NIT payments increased for each additional child up to a total of six children. Given that the participating families at pre-enrollment had an average size of six, typically including four children, the potential effect of the experiment could not have been as pro-natalist as might have been the case for families of smaller size.

and subtractions. One of the quarterly interviews with housewives asked about pregnancies and the outcome of terminated pregnancies.

On the more qualitative aspects of family life, the data bases are less extensive. A single item asked at pre-enrollment and in the fifth quarterly interview was designed to measure "husband and wife togetherness." A four-item "family togetherness" scale was administered also at pre-enrollment, and the fifth quarterly interview was constructed of such items as how often parents played with their children, took their children places, how often the family sat down to meals together, and also included the husband-wife togetherness item. Finally, a "family leisure" scale measured whether family members went to the park or to the zoo,[17] a restaurant, a movie, or a bar within two weeks prior to interviewing. The last scale was administered at the third, seventh, and eleventh quarters.

These scales hardly exhaust the measurement of family relationships. There is certainly more to family life than "doing things" together, even though "things" is a term vague enough to cover patchwork quilting or bizarre sex practices. The considerable research tradition of family sociology is completely unrepresented in either the items used or in the bibliography of the paper in which these data were analyzed. Granted that family sociology is not a field that has attracted the best of empirically oriented sociologists, still a great deal more is known about family cohesion than is represented in these items.

Analyses[18]

Two of the papers dealing with these issues employ familiar multiple regression techniques. Cain's paper on fertility regresses pregnancy and/or newborn children on a set of demographic variables and a set of experimental variables for second, sixth, and tenth quarterly interview data. Ladinsky and Wells do much the same with respect to the measures of family integration.

The Knudsen, Scott, and Shore paper stands out from among all the papers in the entire set by employing a very different mode of analysis. Having characterized each family unit as in one or another of a variety of household composition states (for example, nuclear family, extended family,

---

[17] It should be noted that none of the cities used as "test bores" had municipal zoos. Questions used were sometimes copied slavishly from other sources without considering modifications for the particular circumstances of the sample families being studied. Similarly the items on "eating out" might have been modified in the light of the very low incomes of the NIT families.

[18] Jon Helge Knudsen, Robert A. Scott, and Arnold A. Shore, *Final Report,* vol. III; Jack Ladinsky and Anna Wells, *Final Report,* vol. III; and Glen G. Cain, *Final Report,* vol III.

female-headed family with children, etc.), they undertake a Markov chain analysis contrasting experimental and control families by the transition probabilities computed to account for changes from one household state to another over various time periods. Households are disaggregated into subclasses on the basis of demographic characteristics (for example, race, educational attainment, pre-enrollment income, husband's age, generosity of plan, etc.).

It is difficult to discern what is going on in the Markov chain analysis presented in the Knudsen and other papers. The parameters computed have little directly interpretable meaning, being ratios of transition probabilities, and no tests of statistical signficance are presented (although computed)—a deficiency that makes it hard to know when to pay attention to a finding. But, even more important, the necessity to form subclasses by the polytomization of continuous variables (for example, age of husband is divided into above and below age 35) means that much information is thrown away and few stratifying classes can be used without running out of cases. Hence, the effects shown are not the usual ones that are net of a more or less uniformly employed set of background variables but are only net of some subset treated crudely.

Findings

In all three papers on family composition no significant and consistent experimental effects were found. Experimental treatments neither increased nor decreased fertility; nor did they affect family state transition probabilities; nor was family togetherness increased or decreased. Whatever variance was explained is accounted for mainly by interindividual differences rather than as treatment effects.

Further and more sophisticated analyses of these data—especially those relating to family composition changes—may bring to light some experimental effect, although the likelihood of their doing so is quite small. Especially unlikely are experimental effects on "family togetherness" measures, variables whose measurement leaves so much to be desired.[19]

---

[19] It is difficult to judge whether the levels measured (that is, fertility, family togetherness, probability of family composition change, etc.) are particularly high or low in comparison with comparable groups. Ladinsky and Wells express surprise that these couples seem to be high on togetherness. Knudsen and others never present marginal frequencies on amount of family composition changes, nor does Cain compare his fertility data with those of some possible comparable group not in the experiment. If the experimental design did bias selection toward more large, stable families, Ladinsky's and Wells' findings are consistent with the interpretation, and we should also expect to find lower than expected fertility and composition change rates. The expectations with respect to fertility are based on the assumption that large families are more likely to be families that have reached their maximum fertility.

Educational Efforts of Adolescents

In the NIT Experiment, payments are tied to total family income and to household size. Hence, the labor force participation of young people may be expected to be affected by experimental treatments. From one point of view, young people, whose wage rates are low, may be especially affected by tax rates making leisure more attractive, assuming that their earned income is pooled with other sources of household income. From another point of view, youngsters have the option of remaining or continuing in school, a "leisure" activity not immediately productive of income but which has some impact on future earnings. Experimental treatments should therefore make staying in school or resuming schooling more attractive to those youngsters in families receiving experimental treatments.

Sample selection and experimental design should provide a larger-than-usual proportion of adolescents in the experiment. The bias toward large households implies a higher probability of older children in the household. Indeed, it appears to be the case that somewhere around 20 percent of the households had at least one adolescent between 16 and 18.[20] It is not clear what the impact of this selection is, but if we take seriously the findings in several researches that the number of siblings has a steady, although minor, depressing effect on educational attainment,[21] then this is a group that is especially likely to discontinue its schooling early.

Although the legally defined age at which a person may leave school without being declared a truant usually is 16, in fact, most young people remain in school beyond that point. A majority of most subgroups in the United States today completes high school, and a large minority goes on to some kind of post-secondary education. Hence, although there is a sharp drop in school attendance at age 18 (when the largest proportion finishes high school), significant degrees of school attendance persist until the early twenties.

Given this pattern of school attendance, the critical years to observe for experimental effects encompass the age period from 16 through at least 21. In the first quarter of the experiment, 16 percent of the 16 to 18-year-olds are neither working nor in school, another 20 percent are working, and the remaining 64 percent are in school. In short, nearly two-thirds are continuing their educational effort during this age interval, presumably moving into the labor force beyond age 18.

This pattern of school attendance is emphasized here because the chap-

---

[20] This statistic is calculated from the paper on which this subsection is based and may be off base if many of the households had more than one adolescent in this age range.

[21] James S. Coleman, Zahava D. Blum, and Peter H. Rossi, "Intra-Generational Occupational Mobility" (Unpublished manuscript).

ter[22] upon which this subsection comments is based upon an analysis only of 16 to 18-year-olds, a group whose responses can be expected to be less sensitive to choices than the 18 to 21-year-old group. Hence, the analysis presented is a conservative estimate of the effect of experimental treatments upon the labor force participation and school enrollment of young persons.

Data Base

School attendance of young persons in the household is probably underestimated because questions on the quarterly interviews directed at adults over 16 in the household did not specifically allow for school enrollment as a full-time activity.[23] School attendance had to be volunteered as a special response category, and hence, some respondents may not have realized that going to school is an acceptable alternative response.

In his paper, Mallar chooses to deal only with the age range 16 to 18, a restriction that most likely leads to conservative estimates of experimental effects. Data are from the first, fifth, and ninth quarters since these are the only quarterly interviews occurring during the school year in each site.

Analysis

Mallar assumes that the young people make two decisions: First, they decide whether they will, on the one hand, choose leisure or, on the other hand, choose work or school;[24] and, second, once they have decided that they will either go to school or work, they then decide between those two last activities. This decision model leads him to present two forms of analysis: One attempts to discern experimental effects on the first decision; the other is concerned with the second decision. The data are analyzed separately for each of three quarters by ordinary least squares as well as by probit analysis.

Findings

Although experimental effects can be discerned for some subgroups at some quarters, by and large, no clear-cut patterns emerge either for non-

---

[22] Charles Mallar, *Final Report*, vol. I. Mallar has indicated that subsequent analysis has extended the age range beyond 18 with the expected result of strong experimental effects.

[23] In each quarterly interview, all adults 16 and over were asked a series of questions mainly centered around labor force participation. The alternatives read to the respondent as answers to the question, "What were you doing last (week, month)?" did not include "going to school." Respondents had to volunteer school attendance as an answer. Three of the quarterly interviews (1, 5 and 9) asked specifically about school attendance for children 18 or under, data which form Mallar's chapter.

[24] Apparently, Mallar grouped working and going to school together because they are similar activities (i.e., work) as opposed to opting for non-work (i.e., leisure).

labor force participation or school enrollment. A possible slight effect appears for older young men (18) who are slightly more likely to stay in school. In short, experimental treatments do not lead young people to drop out of the labor force nor do they bolster the retention ability of schools.

Again, it is difficult to interpret the findings. There are good reasons to suspect that analysis is conservatively biased and possibly applied to the wrong age group. Certainly no drastic effects are perceived for young people who would ordinarily be in school.

Job Turnover, Duration of Unemployment, and Job Characteristics

The experimental effects on the earnings and work effort aspects of labor force supply are treated in earlier chapters in this volume. There are other aspects of work where some effects can be expected. In particular, experimental effects might be discerned in job turnover, with guarantees lessening the risks of temporary unemployment and perhaps subsidizing more productive job searches. In addition, there are qualitative aspects of the occupations and jobs involved. Some jobs are more satisfying or provide more prestige than others that yield the same earnings.

The job turnover among participants in the experiment was quite high: At least 47 percent of the male household heads changed employers in the two-year span between pre-enrollment and the eighth quarterly interview.[25] Compared to the five-year proportion change shown in the 1970 Census for the New York-Newark SMSA, 38 percent, the experimental turnover rate of 47 percent is a very high rate of job turnover.[26]

Data Bases

At pre-enrollment and each subsequent quarter the job title and employer for each adult 16 or over were ascertained. Respondents were also questioned about periods of unemployment in the three-month period covered by each quarter. In Spilerman's paper[27] job turnover is measured by comparing employer at pre-enrollment with employer at eighth quarterly. No explanation is given for preferring this definition over alternatives; for example, all job transitions for all quarterly periods might have been used.

In addition, Spilerman used outside data sources to characterize the oc-

---

[25] This proportion refers to net change arrived at by comparing employers at the two periods and noting whether they were the same or different. If a person had changed employers several times in that period, the additional changes were not counted. Hence, 47 percent turnover is a conservative estimate.

[26] It should also be noted that their earnings are considerably below the average for persons in the same occupations in the New York-Newark Combined SMSA, suggesting that participants may be holding marginal jobs in marginal occupations and for these reasons subject to greater job instability.

[27] Seymour Spilerman and Richard E. Miller, *Final Report,* vol. I.

cupations held at both times. Data from Parnes' longitudinal study of males were used to construct Duncan occupational status scores[28] and aggregate measures of job satisfaction in two dimensions—job content and financial rewards—for each occupational title. The 1970 Census one-in-a-thousand tape yielded average earnings for each occupational title for jobholders in the New York-Newark Combined SMSA, a calculation that would provide "expected" earnings for persons in each Census occupation class in roughly the same geographical region as participants in the sample.

The two outside-the-experiment data sets provided measures that were independent of the data set generated by the experiment and, hence, variables that represent what Spilerman called the "expected" characteristics of occupations held by participants. Comparing participants with "expected" variables produced some surprising results. The most striking contrast is between participants' earnings and the "expected" earnings for persons holding those occupational titles. The Census average earnings for persons in those occupations is $7,573, while experiment participants' earnings were only $4,001 (or about 53 percent as large). Although participants may be younger than their fellow workers, the age difference and associated age-related earnings differentials cannot be large enough to account for this great difference in earnings. Not only are participants on the bottom of the occupational structure in terms of the job titles they held, but even for those poor jobs they were being paid considerably less than was customary at the time.[29] Obviously, participants in the sample were very marginal indeed.

Analysis

Regressions were run with job turnover, weeks unemployed, Duncan occupational status score, "expected" earnings, and "expected" job satisfaction levels as dependent variables. Experimental treatments were expressed in the regressions both in the spline formulation and as "benefits" defined as payments anticipated on the basis of the previous year's earnings (and in the case of unemployment as previous year's wife's earnings).

Findings

Spilerman finds some of the few relatively strong occupational effects that have been yet uncovered in the reports. He finds that the more generous the

---

[28] See Otis Dudley Duncan in Albert Reiss and Paul K. Hatt, *Occupational and Social Status* (New York: The Free Press, 1962).

[29] Of course, labor market differentials are also at work. Trenton, New Jersey and Scranton, Pennsylvania, are outside the New York, Newark Combined SMSA and even within that SMSA, workers in New York City count more toward these SMSA averages than workers in the New Jersey experimental sites. However, it seems highly unlikely that such area differences can account for the noted discrepancy.

plan experienced, the less the probability of job turnover. Further under generous NIT plans, occupations that have poor "expected" job characteristics (earnings, occupational status, and job satisfaction) tend especially to retain their employees, indicating that NIT apparently acts as a wage subsidy permitting individuals to remain in low paying jobs.

Regressing duration of unemployment, Spilerman finds a slight tendency for persons in low earning occupations on generous support plans to have a shorter period of unemployment if they change jobs. He argues that this finding is also consistent with a wage subsidy effect.

The experimental treatment effects on "expected" job characteristics are complicated and not entirely clear.[30] However, Spilerman claims that he discerns two tendencies. First, younger persons tend to move to better jobs, the more generous the treatment given to them. Second, older persons tend to stay on in their jobs, the more generous the experimental treatment. Perhaps young persons were using the payments to subsidize job shifting to improve their status and earnings while older persons used payments to fill out the deficiencies in their earnings. Spilerman's paper points in some potentially quite productive directions. His findings concerning job turnover and its functions for young and old workers are quite intriguing. However, the full data set has been far from exhausted. There are many more job changes that can be analyzed, and there are other job characteristics that might be looked into. His interpretations of the findings will be more plausible if they hold up under replication in the general set of job changes provided by the data.

Health

Health was viewed in the experiment from two perspectives: the impact of the health status of household members on their labor force efforts under experimental treatments and the impact of experimental treatments on health status. From the first perspective, leisure might be regarded as a more desirable good by those who are suffering from ill health, and the experimental treatments may thus decrease their work effort. From the second perspective, health may be affected by the changes of life afforded by experimental treatments, and health care may be regarded as another item of consumption.[31]

---

[30] For example, comparisons between pre-enrollment and eighth quarterly "expected" earnings show that whites are reducing "expected" earnings while blacks are doing just the opposite. However, when analysis is restricted just to those persons present at both pre-enrollment and eighth quarter, the results are just the opposite. Either differential attrition is causing the switch or differences in the specification in the two analyses are at the heart of the difference. Spilerman prefers the first explanation.

[31] Although asked for in some of the quarterly interviews, money spent on health care, net of insurance repayments, was not used in the analyses reviewed here.

In the first case, the health status of an individual is a variable that changes the price of leisure and/or work. In the second case, health care expenditures are conceived of as a resultant similar to the consumption of housing and durables.

Data Bases

The data used in both analyses[32] come from questions adapted from National Health Survey questionnaires asking (retrospectively over the previous period) about chronic conditions, number of days lost from work, number of days spent in hospital, number of physician visits, etc.

For the analysis of the impact of health conditions on labor effort a respondent was characterized as unhealthy if he or she claimed at least two chronic conditions and/or was absent from work for health reasons at least seven days in a year. Under this definition 32 percent of the male household heads were classified as unhealthy. It should be noted that this definition is contaminated by incorporating within itself labor force effort in the form of days lost from work.[33] While this contamination may not be serious in the analysis of male household heads, it does become quite serious in the analysis of spouse's work effort. Since, on the average, wives worked about four weeks in each year, using days lost from work as part of the definition of unhealthy leads to the anomalous finding that unhealthy wives work more than healthy wives.

Data on health and health care consist of simple counts of such indications as number of reported chronic conditions, days lost from work, and physician visits.

Analysis

For each of the three years of the experiment, earnings, number of hours worked, and hourly wages were regressed on the health parameters and a set of usual background factors.

The experimental effects on health were studied by regressing the health parameter on each of the indexes referred to previously and on the background factors.

---

[32] David Elesh and Myron J. Lefcowitz, *Final Report,* vols. I and III.

[33] Since the definition of ill health allowed individuals to be classified as unhealthy by either claiming chronic conditions or reporting being absent from work seven or more days or both, it is not clear to which extent work effort and the definition of ill health are overlapping. The authors report a correlation (gamma of .575) between the number of chronic conditions reported and the number of days lost from work, but this index does not provide a specific enough measure of the degree of overlap between the two components of the definition. Obviously, the seriousness of the contamination depends on the degree of overlap.

Findings

There is a decided effect of being healthy or unhealthy on work effort. Healthier persons earn more and work more hours than unhealthy persons. Three major experimental effects were found. First, the experimental effects were strongest during the first year of the experiment. Second, the lower the guarantee, the more the difference in earnings between healthy and unhealthy household heads. Third, the higher the tax rate, the smaller the earnings difference between healthy and unhealthy household heads. Thus, the less generous the guarantee, the more healthy persons and unhealthy persons diverge in the labor supply and work effort, but the less generous the tax rate, the more healthy and unhealthy persons converge.

It is difficult to make any sense out of these findings. It is hard to think of mechanisms—economic, sociological or psychological—that would lead unhealthy individuals to work as much as healthy individuals under these two sets of conflicting circumstances.

The findings with respect to experimental effects on health status and health care utilization can be summed up in one word: nothing. There are no significant experimental treatment effects on any of the indexes for household heads, their spouses, or for children.

The analyses and resultant findings in these two papers leave much to be desired. One of the major problems is to define health conditions that are uncontaminated by work effort. It would seem that had the authors chosen to use the number of chronic conditions as the definition of health, they would have been much better off when it came to the interpretation of effects.

Social Psychological Variables

Perhaps the unique sociological and social psychological contribution to the data of the experiment was a set of scales designed to measure variables of a more "purely" sociological and social psychological type. Some of the measures refer to social bonds between the respondent and other people, others refer mainly to states of morale, and still others are counts of common psychosomatic symptoms.

Nothing seems more firmly established in the nearly half century of field surveys than the ever present but modest correlations between measures of socioeconomic status (income, occupation status, educational attainment) and a very large number of such sociological and social psychological measures. The higher the social status of the individual, the more he reports he is happy, feels efficacious vis-à-vis the political system, has fewer psychosomatic symptoms, worries less, has higher self-esteem, experiences less anomie,[34] has a higher sense of being in control of his fate and destiny, is

[34] A feeling that norms and standards are in a great state of flux is characterized as anomie.

more satisfied with his job, income, and life in general, has more friends, belongs to more organizations, and even sees more of his relatives.

The literature upon which this generalization is based often does no more than show that poorer people are worse off in one or more of these respects than the more affluent. The size of the relationship and its ability to withstand testing for spuriousness is often not shown in detail. The zero order correlations involved appear to be .2 to .3 computed over a fairly wide range of socioeconomic status. Of course, the relationship would be considerably lowered were one to compute over a restricted range of socioeconomic status, either on the high or low side of the socioeconomic status distribution. There is, therefore, very little reason to expect that, within the narrow range of socioeconomic status represented among families selected for eligibility under the experiment, relationships of these variables to socioeconomic status are likely to hover around zero. As a corollary, it is also unlikely that shifting families around within this range by experimental treatments would produce noticeable effects.

Even more important, these variables are supposed to be measuring relatively steady states of individuals. Psychosomatic symptoms, for example, are supposed to reflect psychic conditions of neurosis or even psychosis that are supposed to be characteristics difficult to change and not subject to easy manipulation through any sort of therapy. To expect that experimental treatments would affect such states is to violate such a view of what these measures are supposed to represent.[35]

In the three papers considered in this subsection, two regard these variables as possibly being affected by experimental treatments while one considers the social psychological variables as mediating between experimental treatments and labor force response.[36]

Data Bases

The data are derived mainly from short scales posed to male household heads in the form of attitudinal questions. Since is is difficult to give a description that captures the flavor of such questions, the following selection may provide enough examples.

> How much do you worry about the possibility of losing your job? Do you worry a lot, a little, or not at all?
>
> I feel that I have a number of good qualities. (Agree strongly, agree, disagree, or disagree strongly?)

---

[35] Of course, empirical evidence on the correlations across quarterly interviews indicates that they are far from steady states. For example, Ladinsky and Wells report interquarterly correlations ranging from .02 to .203 for measures of sociability. Similar low correlations are reported by Middleton.

[36] Jack Ladinsky and Anna Wells, *Final Report,* vol. III; Russell Middleton and Vernon L. Allen, *Final Report,* vol III; and Sonia Wright, *Final Report,* vol. I.

Have you felt irritable, nervous or fidgety (in the last month)? (Often, a few times, once or twice, or never?)

What is lacking in the world today is the old kind of friendship that lasted for a lifetime. (Agree or disagree?)

How frequently do you see relatives? (Nearly every day, once a week, every couple of weeks, monthly, or less?)

The scales have mostly been borrowed from those used by other investigators and have some standing in the social psychological literature. Indeed, some have been found to be of considerable practical use; for example, the psychosomatic symptom list was developed during World War II as a screening device to detect soldiers who were likely to break down under battlefield conditions and has been used in at least one major epidemiological study of mental health. Some of the scales were further refined by Middleton and Wright by factor analyzing items from a number of different scales, using as final scales only those that showed up as clearly distinctly different from others in the final rotated factor matrix.

Used with the participant population, most of these scales had very low inter-interview reliability, with correlation of about 0.20 (according to Middleton). Reliability measures constructed on the basis of internal consistency among items belonging to each scale also yielded low coefficients.

It is difficult to take these measures very seriously especially when used with a very poor population of low educational attainment.[37] Often the scales were shorter versions of the scales developed by their originators. Answer categories were crude. Face validity, although viewed as sufficient by Middleton, seems to us to be less than obvious.

Analysis

Scale scores used were simple summations of answers to items in each scale. More sophisticated scoring schemes correlate very highly with the procedure used, according to Middleton.

Each of the papers used a slightly different approach. Perhaps the most elaborate was that used by Middleton who first factor analyzed the items, "purifying" scales. Then experimental variables and background factors were regressed on the purified scale scores. Middleton also attempted several path analyses, the most elaborate of which used canonical correlation techniques to compute path coefficients for "unmeasured" variables.

Sonia Wright's paper also started out with a factor analysis of items, using the purified scales as regressors on labor force measures along with experimental parameters and background factors.

---

[37] Average educational attainment for male household heads participating was around ten years, indicating that the typical participant was a high school dropout.

Ladinsky and Wells simply regressed their scale scores on experimental parameters and background factors.

Findings

All three papers found that these variables had no discernible consistent effect on earnings and work effort. They were also unaffected by experimental treatments. Middleton ends his paper on a slightly upbeat note, stating that the results of his analysis indicated that experimental treatments neither improved those who were subjected to them nor worsened their social psychological states.

It is difficult to take these analyses seriously. The measures used are simply bad measures of anything as indicated by their low internal consistency reliabilities and low inter-interview correlations. It is also clear that there was no particular reason to expect that the experimental treatments would affect such outcomes, even if measured well, since there is little evidence from previous literature that such variables are very sensitive to income differentials in a narrow range of incomes. Finally, although such concepts as self-esteem and anomie have some intuitive appeal, it is doubtful that they are tapped by the measurement devices used here.

SOME CONCLUSIONS CONCERNING NON-LABOR SUPPLY RESPONSES

Perhaps the most disappointing aspect of the analyses reviewed in this chapter has been the quality of the data bases used. Consumption behavior, although a topic that might be thought of as a central one to a study of NIT, could only be analyzed by employing a set of heroic assumptions concerning the values of consumer durables. Despite the fact that work effort was also a central issue in NIT, little effort went into the measurement of characteristics of jobs other than earnings and hours worked.[38] Spilerman's analysis at least hints that there are other occupational effects that might profitably be pursued, especially since what he found has some implications for macro-level NIT effects. Although the measurement of health is not easy, there was no reason to confound the measurement with its possible effects: The amalgamation of health complaints with days lost from work seriously undermines the use of those data in any study of earnings or work effort. The

[38] Inspection of the core questionnaires indicates that a great deal of effort went into the measurement of topics that so far have been unanalyzed, as for example, journey to work, reasons for unemployment, and reasons for shifts in family composition. Such seemingly critical issues (to these authors, anyhow) as whether overtime was offered to workers, whether such overtime was optional, or what were the specific wage rates were almost completely neglected.

social psychological measures appear to have been borrowed with indiscriminate taste from among precisely those instruments that have been subject to the most criticism. Such scales have made very little sense when employed in other investigations and make even less sense when applied to the NIT sample.

The impact of data quality is shown on the effects uncovered. The strongest effects are shown for those items that were best measured—home ownership, acquisition of consumer durables, and job turnover. The inconsistent experimental effects that hovered around zero were found for the social psychological variables.

Chapter 8

The External and Internal "Politics" of the Experiment

INTRODUCTION

All large-scale, policy oriented research projects are conducted within a political context, and all research operations create their own internal political systems. The context for a research project includes the organizations within which the project is embedded, the relations with sponsors and sources of funds, audiences that are willing or not willing to learn of results, and sometimes even the subjects of the research or their organized representatives. For large-scale, policy oriented research sponsored by a controversial government agency, these elements of context impinge with particular force. The NIT project was no exception: There were several instances when the project moved perilously close to the kitchen fire even though the support of its sponsor, OEO, was strong and unwavering. The nature of these events and how they were successfully handled are integral parts of the lessons to be learned from NIT.

Large-scale research projects require correspondingly large staffs, coordination among a wide variety of roles, and a set of rules for making decisions that are binding on participants. Whatever the level of support, resources available to a project are always scarce relative to needs necessitating some means for adjudicating among competing interests. NIT was obviously a large project. Its organizational problems were complicated by being divided between two organizations, IRP and Mathematica. The division of labor meant that subgroups doing diverse activities arose. A field organization that conducted interviews and an administrative unit that computed and made payments to eligible families were housed at Mathematica's offices in Princeton. In Madison, IRP staff members and University of Wisconsin faculty served as project designers and analysts, a function shared with some of Mathematica's staff and part-time consultants from Princeton University. Despite the generous funding provided by OEO, resources were still limited, and decisions had to be made whether particular demands for data could be reconciled with competing demands and available resources.

Finally, the research staff came from heterogeneous backgrounds and diverse disciplines: the major division being between economists and sociologists.[1] The problems arising out of the internal politics of the NIT are also germane to a consideration of the lessons to be learned from this research project.

PRESSURES FOR EARLY DISCLOSURE OF FINDINGS[2]

The NIT Experiment was designed to run for three years. Although there were plans for interim reports to OEO, there were no set plans for widespread public release of early findings. Rather the plan was to provide findings for public release in the form of a final report to be issued sometime after the experiment had run its planned course. To be sure, close running tabs would be kept on the NIT families but more as an administrative monitoring than for the purpose of providing interim information on findings. This long-term perspective was consistent with the expectation that it was the policymaking needs of some years beyond the completion of the experiment that were being served: Few expected that some form of NIT would be placed on the political agenda during the course of the experiment itself.

Yet the political atmosphere that led to approval of the experiment itself was also a climate that was inclined to look upon the idea of negative income tax plans as at least conceivable, if not desirable. Hence, within a few

---

[1] These terms were used freely to designate the major disciplinary split within the project, yet the "sociologists" included a few social psychologists while the economists included a political scientist, David Kershaw.

[2] For a more detailed exposition of these events and an analysis of the impact of the NIT Experiment on the formulation of FAP and the decision making process within Congress and the executive branch, see Margaret Boeckmann, "The Contribution of Social Research to Social Policy: A Study of the New Jersey Income Maintenance Experiment and the Family Assistance Plan" (Ph.D. diss., The Johns Hopkins University, 1973). Dr. Boeckmann's dissertation research was supported by a Russell Sage Foundation project. This section is based largely on the extensive discussion of the relationships between the NIT Experiment and Congress during congressional consideration of FAP contained in Chapter 4.

months after the NIT Experiment was started, the new Nixon administration began to think of an overhaul of the existing welfare system. The general idea of a negative income tax program as a replacement for all or a part of the existing welfare system had been hovering on the margins of the federal government's policy agenda for some years. As early as 1965 the Council of Economic Advisors undertook a study of negative income tax plans recommending in 1966 that a more extended study be made of this promising idea. Early in 1968, President Johnson appointed a commission to study income maintenance, the commission to report within two years of establishment. In the summer of 1968 hearings on income maintenance programs were initiated by the Joint Economic Committee of the Congress.

All of these events had taken place before the first payment was made to the first families enrolled in Trenton, New Jersey. At the same time as the debate over the design of the experiment was going on, the new Nixon administration with Daniel Patrick Moynihan on board began to explore the possibilities of welfare reform with negative income tax plans receiving particular attention. By the middle of April 1969, the president had delivered in a message to Congress a plan for reform that hopefully would correct some of the deficiencies of the then current welfare system.

Within the White House staff, two different approaches were being debated: Daniel Moynihan and George Schultz were leaning toward a plan that would have a high guarantee and strong work incentives, while the president's economic advisor, Arthur Burns, stressed a much lower guarantee and work requirements. By the end of the summer of 1969, a compromise Family Assistance Plan (FAP) was devised and by the beginning of October, legislation embodying FAP was introduced into Congress. In short, the NIT Experiment had been barely underway for a year and had yet to complete enrollment of families in Scranton, Pennsylvania, when legislation embodying some of the ideas of a negative income tax proposal was introduced into Congress.

It is not at all clear how much the NIT Experiment influenced the FAP legislation at this stage. Certainly the technical staff of OEO and HEW who had participated in the formulation and approval of the NIT Experiment were involved as consultants to the various participants in the process. Moynihan was certainly aware of the experiment, as later events were to prove. Perhaps the clearest point of contact between the experiment and the groups that were arguing over policy formulation was over the administration of an income maintenance plan: In setting up the NIT Experiment much thought had gone into the question of an appropriate accounting period, and information on this score was fed into the early discussions in the executive branch that led to formation of FAP.

As the FAP legislation in 1969 came before the House Ways and Means

Committee, Harold Watts offered to ranking Minority member Congressman John W. Byrnes (Wisconsin) to testify on FAP, an offer that the Ways and Means Committee took up in November 1969. Watts's testimony in an open meeting of the committee was in favor of the FAP legislation, pointed out the general similarity between the design of the experiment and the drafting of the FAP legislation, and made some suggestions concerning the accounting period to be employed.

The Ways and Means Committee requested that the NIT Experiment staff testify again in January 1970 but this time behind closed doors. Watts, Kershaw, and Bawden[3] testified in this session. The testimony given in this session also emphasized the administrative aspects of the NIT Experiment experience. Kershaw testified in fairly vague terms on his impressions of the results of the NIT Experiment thus far, indicating that he could not discern any meaningful trend in work response.

Around the same time as the NIT principals were testifying, a "leak" appeared in the *New York Times* to the effect that the Ways and Means Committee staff had uncovered a "secret study" that projected a very heavy work disincentive response to FAP and possibly an incentive for breaking up families. In response to this rumor, the administration began to press for some harder data from the NIT Experiment. Moynihan is reputed to have expressed his displeasure in no uncertain terms to John Wilson, then director of Research, Plans, Programs, and Evaluation at OEO, that the NIT Experiment had been going for more than a year and that some hard results ought to be available. At the same time, Kershaw had communicated to OEO that he thought it would be possible to put together some data on the first 500 or so families that had been enrolled initially. Wilson gave the go-ahead signal to Kershaw and within the short space of a few weeks, Kershaw and Watts *hand-tallied*[4] some of the data from 509 of the first-year enrolled families.

The hand-tallied results were incorporated into a report written by Watts and Kershaw entitled "Preliminary Results of the New Jersey Work Incentive Experiment." The results purportedly showed that there was no discernible work disincentive nor were there any severe changes in consumption patterns among experimental families that were receiving payments. Wilson discussed the preliminary results in a cabinet meeting, President Nixon incorporated the generally optimistic findings into a speech he gave at a

[3] Lee Bawden was the principal investigator of the Rural Income Maintenance Experiment being conducted by the Institute for Research on Poverty in two rural sites, one in Wisconsin and the other in North Carolina.

[4] Hand-tallies were necessary because the data, although available on tape, had been formatted in so awkward a form that it was not possible to be retrieved in a useful fashion. Indeed one of the major problems that had to be overcome before final reports were produced was to reformat the computer software system.

governors' conference, and the "preliminary report" was released to the public in the middle of February. It should be noted that the preliminary report contained statements to indicate that the findings were partial, tentative, and subject to change when data from other sites would be available and when a longer time experience with the experiment was assessed.

Thus within less than eighteen months of the beginning of the experiment, some of its results were beginning to filter into the policymaking process. However, it should be clear from this account that the infiltration was far from optimum. First, although the first year's experiences of the initial group of families were of some interest, it was not at all clear that these data were of sufficient quality and generality to warrant much attention. The New Jersey cities were the first sites at which families were selected: The early data series on income, work effort, and consumption patterns were early recognized as bearing significant defects; and hand-tallying was a far from reliable mode of data processing although a subsequent check by the General Accounting Office (GAO) found that the data had been coded and tallied correctly. In addition, the initial group of families was drawn disproportionately from among blacks and Puerto Ricans, groups from whom it would be hard to draw generalizations about the total impact of FAP on the working poor.

Second, although FAP had some kinship to the NIT Experiment, there were also some very critical differences. FAP was designed to supplement the existing welfare system by providing payments to the working poor while the NIT plan was intended as a replacement. NIT had no built-in work requirements while FAP contained both manpower retraining features and a work availability requirement that led to its being called "work-fare." The level of guaranteed support in FAP was identical to that of the least generous plan being tested in NIT. It should be noted that these differences did not invalidate an extrapolation of NIT to FAP: First, NIT did turn out to be in competition with the existing welfare systems of New Jersey and Pennsylvania; second, few expected that the work requirements of FAP could be effectively implemented; finally, the FAP plan was one that was at the lower limits of the policy space of the experiment, even though as a treatment, the lowest plan was so far inferior to the local welfare plans that few eligible families assigned to that plan elected for NIT payments.

Third, and most important to the present discussion, the testimony of NIT personnel and the release of preliminary results were interpreted as partisan behavior of the experimenters. Watts's early testimony was certainly volunteered in an effort to be helpful to the FAP proposal. All of the testimony presented was offered at the request of the administration or administration supporters.

The testimony also brought the NIT Experiment to the attention of the mass media. Television reporters asked for access to experimental families, requests which were consistently turned down.

The most important immediate consequence of entry into the public attention was a decision by the GAO to audit the experiment. GAO officials sensed that the preliminary report might play an important role in the then upcoming Senate Finance Committee Hearings, wondered how preliminary and tentative were the findings, and decided to audit the experiment.[5]

They asked for access to the raw data series in order to evaluate the data series, including names of participating families (possibly to check directly with them whether data on families were correct). Kershaw resisted giving complete access to GAO investigators, the critical point being information that would reveal the identity of participating families. Accepting this compromise, GAO investigators sampled some of the data and issued a report. GAO investigators emphasized the tentative character of the preliminary findings, expressed some satisfaction with data quality and the tabulation of findings, and endorsed the continuation of the experiment as a valuable aid to the policy formation process.

Despite the GAO report's generally favorable findings, the impact of the GAO investigation was, ironically, to undermine the credibility of the *Preliminary Report.* Representatives on the Ways and Means Committee interviewed in 1972 remembered the testimony of the NIT personnel adding a qualifying phrase to the effect that they also remembered something was wrong with their data that the GAO had to look into. The sting of the GAO investigation was not modified by Watts's issuance of a later report entitled "Adjusted and Extended Preliminary Results from the Urban Graduated Work Incentive Experiment."

By the time that the FAP legislation came up for hearings in the Senate Finance Committee, the NIT Experiment and its personnel had taken on a decided partisan look in the minds of those who were opposed to the FAP legislation. When Watts testified before the Senate Finance Committee, Senator John J. Williams (Delaware) dismissed his testimony by asking only one question: whether Watts's salary was being paid by OEO.

Senator Williams also struck hard at the NIT Experiment by demanding of OEO that the agency produce a list of the names and addresses of participating families suggesting that funding for the experiment would be cut off if compliance was not forthcoming. Senator Williams' request created considerable consternation among NIT staff and OEO since congressional subpoena power could have compelled disclosure if the senator had been willing to push the issue that far. Apparently feeling that his objections to

---

[5] Under a 1967 amendment to the poverty act, the GAO was assigned the responsibility to audit the performance of all OEO programs.

FAP had gone far enough, Senator Williams did not push his request for access to "raw data," when OEO refused to honor his request on the grounds that the data were collected under promises of confidentiality.

The 1969–1970 version of FAP legislation did not pass through Congress, achieving approval of the House but falling short of necessary support in the Senate.

A second version of FAP was introduced into the next session of Congress in the fall of 1970. NIT personnel volunteered to introduce some new data into congressional hearings on this second go-around, but OEO officials were more cautious. Besides, the new tabulations made by Harold Watts showed a slight work disincentive. OEO officials argued that the release of such preliminary data might do some harm to the FAP legislation.

OEO eventually gave permission to Watts and Kershaw to send additional findings to the House and Senate. Not much attention was paid to their findings partially because the issues that engaged the attention of congressmen were no longer ones of work disincentives but of the effects of overlapping welfare programs to which the NIT Experiment could make little contribution. But, some of the lack of attention to the NIT results was a matter of discounting what had come to be regarded as a partisan and somewhat shaky source of information. In the recollections of congressmen interviewed later, the impact of the GAO report on the previous (1970) preliminary report was considerable.[6]

A hindsightful analysis of the NIT experiences in trying to be relevant to the decision making process reveals the dangers that are involved. First, it is apparently easy to become identified as a partisan if one pursues the apparently contradictory roles of advocate of a plan and the bearer of scientific findings. Reasonable questions raised about the findings tend to accentuate the perception of one's role as advocate. Second, it is difficult to resist the pressures of the sponsor. OEO was very much part of the executive branch: The public release of the preliminary report by OEO was correctly seen by

---

[6] The discounting of the NIT Experiment's results is aptly illustrated in the following excerpt from a personal interview (reported in Boeckmann, "The Contribution of Social Research," p. 196) with Geoffrey Patterson, legislative aide to Senator Abraham Ribicoff:

> I guess that in 1970 there had been some discrediting of the experiment. That the size of the sample was small. That they had reported findings too early. I remember that when I had suggested to the senator that we use it in a statement to support our idea that by providing a FAP type approach that you would actually be encouraging people to work, he said, "No let's not emphasize that experiment because of its controversial nature." And I know that the Finance Committee had been attacking it. And whenever you are using data to support your position, you always try to come up with the strongest data possible you can, and if that information has already been attacked fairly strongly, you decide well, we will drop that and go on to something that we have a great deal of confidence in.

Congress as a partisan move. It should also be noted that the NIT staff willingly volunteered to assemble the preliminary report, a move that they were later to regret, at least partially.[7]

Finally, the incident with Senator Williams firmly brought to mind on how fragile a base are erected researcher promises to respondents of confidentiality. Until there is some statutory foundation on which the promise of confidentiality can be based, confidentiality cannot be guaranteed. Had Senator Williams wished to pursue the matter and had he the support of his colleagues, the raw data of the NIT Experiment could have been subpoenaed. Possibly NIT personnel and OEO would have chosen to fight such a subpoena through the courts; even so the outcome would have been in doubt.

THE MERCER COUNTY PROSECUTOR AND THE NIT EXPERIMENT

Threats to the promises of confidentiality extended to participating families arose from local sources as well. As the experiment began to achieve some publicity in the latter part of 1969, the county prosecutor of Mercer County (in which Trenton is located) began to inquire into the possibility that some of the participating families may have been accepting payments from both the experiment and public welfare. NIT payments not reported to welfare authorities constituted evidence of neglect, if not intentional fraud, on the part of participating families.[8]

Almost any system of confidentiality can be broken if enough attention is given to the problem. The county prosecutor managed to determine the names of a few families in Trenton who were on the welfare rolls and also participating in the experiment and in late 1969 issued a subpoena to Mathematica to produce the records of payments to about a dozen participating families.

---

[7] Watts has expressed the view that he did not feel it would have been socially responsible to withhold interim information useful in the policy debate, stating "The one principle I did regard as important was to assure equal accessibility to the partial and preliminary findings to all participants in the policy process—not just the immediate sponsors of the project." (Personal communication, July 1975.)

[8] Families receiving welfare payments were supposed to report immediately all change in income that might affect such payments. This is a rule that is not very rigorously enforced, as most studies of the administration of public welfare show. The discretion that is allowed caseworkers in most welfare systems is often exercised in overlooking earnings from casual and intermittent employment, employment of secondary wage earners (teenagers), and so on. A thorough investigation of almost any welfare roll will bring to light instances in which some families are receiving at any one time more than they are due under current rules and regulations. Thus a "cheap shot" for any state's attorney would be to institute an investigation into "welfare fraud."

It should be noted that when the experiment first started it would have been legally impossible for participating families that remained intact to have been eligible for AFDC in New Jersey since payments could only be made to households in which there were no work-eligible males. When the New Jersey welfare law was changed early in 1969 extending coverage to families with an unemployed male parent present (AFDC-UP), some of the families participating in the experiment became eligible for welfare payments. Families initially enrolled in Trenton were told that they could receive payments from both although they were advised that they had to report welfare payments as income on their monthly report forms and that they were legally obligated to report experimental payments to welfare authorities.[9] Families enrolled in other sites that were solicited after AFDC-UP had been enacted in New Jersey were told that they had to choose between welfare and NIT payments and could not receive both.

Mathematica's response to the county prosecutor's subpoena was to give the prosecutor a summary of the payments made to the families about whom information was requested but to resist opening the records of all families to the prosecutor's office. In a move to quash the subpoena, Mathematica argued that to open the records was to violate the pledge of confidentiality made to participating families, that the experiment served a useful purpose, and that whatever apparent fraud had been committed may have arisen out of the understandable confusion in participating families' minds between the two systems of payments. Mathematica's arguments were backed by statements from OEO officials about the importance of the experiment and careful applications of pressure on the county prosecutor from a variety of sources.

For a period of nearly a year the county prosecutor's office persisted in its attempts to subpoena Mathematica's records on participating Trenton families. Mathematica countered by handing over summaries of NIT payments made to families about whom specific requests were made but continued to resist turning over more complete records. At several points, David Kershaw indicated his willingness to go to jail rather than break Mathematica's pledges of confidentiality.

A compromise was eventually reached in which the NIT Experiment assumed the liability for whatever overpayments were made by the Mercer County welfare department, a sum that totaled approximately $20,000 for the eighteen-month period that the fourteen families were receiving dual

---

[9] This decision was made in order to maintain faith in the original agreements made with enrolling families in Trenton. Since there was initially no problem of overlap with AFDC, no mention was made in the enrollment process of the possibility of conflicts with welfare. Hence, NIT administrators felt that it would be more in line with the original understandings undertaken with Trenton families to allow participation jointly in welfare and the experiment.

payments. In addition, quarterly checks were instituted with the welfare departments at all the sites in which participating families' names were checked against the welfare rolls. The rules were then changed for Trenton families to prohibit dual participation.

As in the case of Senator Williams' request for raw data, the subpoena power of the Mercer County prosecutor was never put to the ultimate test.[10] The subpoena was never quashed, it was withdrawn when the compromise involving repayment was reached. Hence, the issue whether pledges of confidentiality would be upheld by the courts as sufficient reason for withholding detailed information on participating families was never tested.

This incident was to prompt HEW to ask the National Academy of Sciences/National Research Council Committee on Federal Evaluation Research to conduct a study of the problem of confidentiality to research evaluating social programs. The committee with the aid of legal scholars has drawn up a suggested federal statute extending to evaluation research the same protections extended to members of the press concerning the materials obtained in confidence from informants. Whether this legislation is ever to be presented to Congress is largely a matter of conjecture.[11]

CONCERNING SOME EXTERNAL POLITICAL PROBLEMS OF CRITICAL SOCIAL POLICY RESEARCH

The vast bulk of social research has proceeded over the past fifty years without serious challenges to the informal pledges of confidentiality extended routinely by social researchers to their respondents. Much of the research, however, has only been remotely related to social policy, and little has had as close a connection with ongoing policy formation as in the case of NIT and the consideration of FAP in Congress. An additional vulnerability of the NIT field experiment is that it involved the possibility that participating families by virtue of their participation could be involved in seeming fraud.

Two lessons may be drawn from the NIT Experiment: First, it is important to build up and retain an image of impartiality as opposed to an image of partisanship. The attempt on the part of NIT researchers to act in the dual (and somewhat contradictory) role both of advocates of FAP and

---

[10] A very similar case involving the county prosecutor of Bergen County who wished to examine records for participating families in Jersey City was also solved by a similar compromise. The amount of overpayment in Jersey City was considerably smaller since rules prohibiting dual payment had been in effect from enrollment on and families apparently understood the rules.

[11] National Research Council, *Protecting Individual Privacy in Evaluation Research* (Washington, D.C.: National Academy of Sciences, 1975).

as the bearers of empirical data relevant to critical policy questions did little to build confidence in the outcome of the experiment. The experiment was perceived as flawed, and the experimenters as just another set of administration partisans.

Second, the legal foundations on which social researchers promise confidentiality are very insecure. Up to this point, the researchers have met the issue by finding a compromise that avoids bringing the issue to a clear resolution in the courts, a solution that only postpones the inevitable possibly in the hope that customary procedures will achieve some recognition in the courts.[12] It does appear as if some policymakers intuitively understand this vulnerability and use threats to subpoena raw data as means of placing pressures upon social researchers. It should be borne in mind that it is not at all clear how Senator Williams could have used access to raw data as means to his goal of discrediting the FAP proposal. Giving publicity to specific participating families might undermine the conduct of the experiment but would not be useful directly to Williams' cause. Similarly the indictment of a few families in Trenton for welfare fraud would certainly have made participating families in Trenton and in other New Jersey sites uneasy enough to drop out of the experiment, but it is hard to envisage that the welfare department in Mercer County would be materially improved by the county prosecutor's move although it is easy to see that the prosecutor could make some personal mileage out of his move.[13]

Finally, a comment must be made on the curious conjunction between the start of the experiment and the arrival of some sort of NIT proposal at the top of the political agenda. It is apparent that the political conditions that make it possible to conduct field experiments are the *same* political conditions that make it likely that a related proposal will appear on the agenda. Hence, the NIT Experiment, which was seen by the OEO administrators and NIT personnel as providing results relevant for a distant future, turned out to be badly timed for consideration as relevant to the FAP proposal. That this is not a circumstance that is unique to NIT can be seen from similar examples in other areas. For instance, at the same time that the current (Ford) administration is considering submitting a bill that would set up a national health insurance plan, HEW has just launched a long-term field experiment testing the impact of such insurance on the consumption of medical care. It is now quite clear that the results of the experi-

---

[12] There has also been some concern with insuring that data files are confidential by stripping identifying information from such files. This move assumes that if the data are subpoenaed and such moves are upheld by the courts, the data do not contain enough detail to constitute an unwilling breaking of confidentiality pledges.

[13] Something may be gained by the state's attorney in the way of favorable publicity as a prosecutor who is hard on "welfare cheaters."

ment, designed to provide information relevant to the design of a national health insurance plan, will not be anywhere near ready when a plan will be presented to Congress. Another set of examples are the current housing voucher experiments. There has been enough discussion of housing vouchers in the Nixon and Ford administrations to make one suspect that this too will appear in the form of proposed legislation long before results from the experiments are in.

This mistiming of field experiments on prospective social policies suggests that long-term field experiments conducted under the sponsorship of policymakers may turn out to be prematurely obsolescent. Instead, it may be necessary to consider other ways of sponsoring field experiments, which would be further removed from policymakers and the immediacy of their concerns.

INTERNAL POLITICS: CONFLICT WITHIN THE NIT EXPERIMENT

Mounting a field experiment of the size and duration of the NIT under the best of circumstances requires enormous skill, patience, and ability. This task was handled admirably by Watts and Kershaw for the NIT under conditions that could have had far more serious consequences for the integrity of the research output than those described. This achievement is made the more impressive in our opinion by the fact that a great deal of latitude was allowed for internal debate among the researchers themselves, and in one instance, the design controversy cited in Chapter 2, this debate threatened to stalemate the project.

The internal tensions of research projects are not often reported as part of the project documentation possibly because, for participants, the importance of such debates recedes rapidly with time and the inevitable focus on final results. We believe that several interesting and important lessons of value to future experimenters can be learned from examining the interorganization and interdisciplinary relations of the NIT. Some of these arrangements were choices of the funding agency, some were decisions on the part of the project directors, and some simply emerged from the "sociometry" of the individuals and disciplines involved.

The initiative for the development of the NIT Experiment was shared among a number of organizations and individuals. It was Heather Ross who submitted a proposal to OEO to undertake a field experiment in the Washington, D.C., area. Guy and Alice Orcutt reacted to that proposal by writing a paper endorsing the general idea and suggesting a set of ways in which the field experiment could be designed. Discussions took place among the staff of the research and planning unit of OEO. Finally, Mathematica submitted the proposal that was eventually considered.

Although individuals at the Institute for Research on Poverty had been involved in the discussion of field experimentation on NIT, IRP was not originally a partner in the proposal with Mathematica. Rather the entry of IRP into the picture as a partner with Mathematica followed a decision by OEO officials that it would be better that the responsibility for the experiment be handled by a university. (See Chapter 1.) Since IRP was a creature of OEO, designed to act as a basic research unit and "think tank" for that agency, OEO had a legitimate claim on its participation in the experiment.

With the entry of IRP as the prime contractor and Mathematica as a subcontractor, a division of labor was set up in which IRP staff members were to take design and analysis responsibilities while Mathematica staff members were to serve primarily as administrators of the payment plan and in charge of the extensive field operations involved. The division of labor was never absolute: Mathematica staff, particularly consultants Albert Rees and William Baumol, as well as David Kershaw and Heather Ross (who joined Mathematica's staff when their proposal to OEO was written), also intended to play roles in the design and analysis phases. IRP staff members also stepped outside their allotted roles and played parts in the design of the administration of the payment plan and gave technical advice on the field operations.

The design controversy discussed in detail in Chapter 2 was grounded in very real differences in the theoretical modeling of the work response phenomenon and in corresponding differences in analytical approaches. It can also be looked upon as an inter-organization struggle heightened by the geographical distance between Madison, Wisconsin, and Princeton, New Jersey.[14] The organizational question was whether IRP was to have the preponderant weight on design and analytical issues or whether Mathematica and its consultants were to prevail. The bitterness expressed in the various memoranda that were traded between the two locations expressed more than a neutrally charged intellectual disagreement over experimental design.

The settlement of the controversy by the Tobin compromise was one that largely favored the views of the Wisconsin group. The design is far from the

[14] Geographical distances of much smaller magnitude play a role in the following way: Those who meet and talk with each other frequently develop a sense of solidarity and intellectual camaraderie that often bolsters strongly a particular viewpoint. The Wisconsin economists meeting together at IRP daily apparently developed a viewpoint that was at variance with that developed at Mathematica among its staff and consultants.

classical randomized experiment and much closer to the allocation scheme computed by the Watts-Conlisk model.

Once the Tobin compromise was adopted, the division of labor between IRP and Mathematica jelled, with Rees and Baumol receding somewhat in importance in the design of the experiment. Although Rees was to write an overall summary to the final report and Baumol to write a summary to precede the administrative volumes edited by Kershaw, neither wrote any substantive chapters in the interior of the report. The heat of the design controversy had completely receded when we interviewed staff members in 1972 and 1973.

Running a research project of the complexity of the NIT Experiment for the relatively long period of time involved is by no means an easy task. The naturally high turnover of personnel in academia and research organizations often means that those responsible for critical decisions at the beginning of the project are not around either to suffer the disabilities incurred by wrong decisions or collect the rewards of correct ones. The NIT Experiment is rather unusual in that a relatively larger proportion of the original group of researchers were around to participate in the final rounds of analysis.

The continuity of personnel, especially among the principal investigators, meant also that the people involved had long worked out their relationships for most of the period of the project. Interviewing staff members at Mathematica and IRP, we found, for most of the economists on the staffs in both places, a strong regard and respect for each other's abilities and personalities. The style of administration set by Harold Watts in Wisconsin was a relatively relaxed one: Staff members at IRP worked hard and produced a very impressive amount of analysis without any sign that they did so under great pressure from Harold Watts. We did not penetrate Mathematica's staff as much and, hence, have a less well formed strong impression of the internal organization of that location.

Because of the dominance of economic objectives in the experiment, the sociologists, located mainly at Wisconsin, apparently came to feel somewhat alienated from the major thrust of the experiment. Early in the drafting of the basic contract with IRP and Mathematica, OEO officials insisted on the inclusion of other social science disciplines besides economics. Substantial issues of a non-economic sort were anticipated to be involved in the policy debate that was expected to arise around NIT when proposed, some of which we discussed in Chapter 7.

The sociologists and social psychologists involved in the experiment were drawn primarily from among University of Wisconsin departments although there was some participation in the experiment among Princeton sociologists as well. How individuals were recruited is not at all clear from the interviews we conducted with staff members. Some had been members of the staff of

IRP at the time the experiment was started. Others were attracted to the experiment's staff by invitation.

Whatever the process of recruitment, it was abundantly clear in the interviews we conducted with both sociologists and economists that the sociologists and the social psychologists occupied a peripheral position throughout the experiment. The economists dominated the design process.[15] Sociologists and social psychologists participated in the design of instruments and had some hand in the conduct of field operations although they were to complain in our interviews with them that their role in these operations was also a peripheral one. The main part allotted to them, as they saw it, was that of developing measures of non-labor force responses and only a minor role in the total design of the experiment. As a consequence the activities of this group tended to be regarded both by themselves and by other participants in the NIT as constituting a secondary activity of relatively low priority.

There were good reasons for regarding the interests of sociologists as peripheral. Indeed, since the experiment was designed mainly to measure work responses of participating families, effects of NIT on such areas of household behavior as family stability, attitudinal stances, and the like could not be estimated with maximum efficiency. But there was more to the marginal position of these social scientists than could be explained on that basis alone.

According to the sociologists,[16] the economists who ran the experiment had a very low regard for both their interests and skills. Indeed, as our interviews with the leading economists indicated, they would have preferred *not* to have *any* sociologists or social psychologists involved in the experiment. Although there was agreement that some of the household responses in which sociologists were interested were of some importance (e.g., health status and work satisfaction), others were regarded as bordering on the ridiculous (e.g., anomie, alienation, and "family togetherness").

It is difficult to assess the impact on the conduct and content of the NIT Experiment of the peripheral position in which sociologists and social

---

[15] In Chapter 2, we provided a quotation from a memorandum from Albert Rees presenting an argument for the analysis of variance model that the model would be better able to accommodate the interests of sociologists than the Watts-Conlisk solution. This was an argument advanced on behalf of sociologists but was not one to which the sociologists had made any contribution.

[16] Sociologists and social psychologists were conspicuous by their absence in formulating policy concerning field operations as well. Although some of the sociologists and social psychologists were not experienced in large-scale sample survey operations, some were, and it should be emphasized, *none* of the economists nor any of the staff at Mathematica had such experience. It must be said that the field operations were conducted quite well, especially once families had been enrolled (see Chapter 3 for a description of rather large refusal and inaccessible rates in the initial approaches to families in the screening process).

psychologists were placed. In some respects, the low regard for this group expressed by the economists was well deserved: A proper reading of some of the subsections of Chapter 7 of this report would come to the conclusion that many of the variables added to the experiment by sociologists and social psychologists had neither strong theoretical rationale nor reasonable policy concerns to bolster their inclusion. Many such variables were very poorly measured and hence could not be expected to be sensitive to the experimental treatments. Yet, one may also raise the question whether the seemingly casual sloppiness of the sociologists and social psychologists was not to some extent a function of being located on the periphery of the experiment.

One must also raise the question why sociologists and social psychologists were not more prominently involved in the running of the field operations of the NIT Experiment. In part, this appears to have been so, because few of the particular sociologists and social psychologists involved had much experience with large-scale sample surveys. But, none of the economists nor any of the staff at Mathematica had any experience with these either. It is difficult to argue that any further participation by sociologists and social psychologists would have materially furthered the conduct of the field operations. It must be said that the field operations were conducted quite well, especially once families had been enrolled. The impression of the senior author is that the staff at Mathematica in conducting field operations often engaged in re-inventing the wheel although it must be admitted that the end result was a rather well-designed version.

There are some points at which the help of some sociologists could have been used profitably. The economists defined work response in a relatively narrow fashion: Concern was focused mainly on earnings and hours worked. Other aspects of employment were relatively neglected. For example, it was only after considerable argument initiated by Seymour Spilerman that the occupations of household members in the labor force were coded in detail: the initial code being a rough set of categories that failed to distinguish among the majority of occupations held by working members of participating households. The promising line of analysis conducted by Spilerman (and described in Chapter 7) would not have been possible if he did not insist in the face of considerable reluctance on a recoding of occupations held.

Other contributions to the definition of a larger view of work responses might have been possible. Little attention was paid to measuring the ability of workers to alter their hours of work, a contribution that might have made it possible to isolate a set of workers for whom the experimental treatments would have been particularly critical.

As it was, the sociologists and social psychologists were given a restricted license to hunt on their own, adding variables of interest to them but not brought in to full participation in the entire research operation.

THE POLITICS OF LARGE-SCALE POLICY RESEARCH

The purpose of this chapter was to provide accounts of some of the problems encountered by the NIT group in dealing with the policy world and in dealing with their internal organizational problems. Some of the problems of dealing with the policy world are highlighted quite strongly by the threats that were made against the integrity of the experiment by policymakers who saw the NIT Experiment as a partisan activity. The internal politics of the NIT Experiment group, on the other hand, are quite ordinary problems, familiar enough to anyone who has had the slightest experience with large-scale multiperson and multidisciplinary research. In addition, it is also abundantly clear that whatever energy was lost in such imbroglios, there was still plenty left over for the staffs of Mathematica and IRP clearly to succeed in carrying through a most difficult research project.

Chapter 9

An Overview Evaluation of the NIT Experiment

INTRODUCTION

The central purpose of this final chapter is to bring together the analyses made in the body of this volume to arrive at an overall evaluation of the NIT Experiment. We embark upon this enterprise with considerable ambivalence: As we noted in the opening chapter, there is much to admire in the boldness of the experimenters in venturing upon what history will undoubtedly regard as one of the major "firsts" in policy related empirical social research, in their unflagging devotion to carrying out a long-term research endeavor, and in the technical skills with which the resulting data were handled. Nothing we can say can detract from the considerable accomplishment that this experiment represents for social science research. Yet there is much to criticize as the preceding chapters have detailed. We trust that the very real admiration we hold for the accomplishments of the NIT experimenters will not be submerged in the minds of the readers by the equally real and important critical comments we have made in the body of this report.

It is easy enough to be a critic: All pieces of empirical research are more or less flawed. There are simply too many points at which mistakes can be made or unforeseen events intrude to permit perfection in either design or execution. We believe that critics have a responsibility to make two kinds of judgments about the criticisms they offer: First, it is necessary to make distinctions, if possible, between those mistakes that constitute serious flaws and those that are less serious defects. Admittedly, this is a matter of judgment, yet we do believe that some sort of weighting ought to be suggested by responsible critics as a guide to those who have not digested the enormous volume of memoranda, working papers, analyses, and final reports produced by the experiment. Second, it is only fair to distinguish between defects that arise from incorrect planning and other errors of judgment and those that arise out of events or processes that could not have been anticipated in advance. This is essentially a distinction between "bad judgment" and "bad luck," the former being a legitimate criticism and the latter calling for sympathetic commiseration.

We will try to differentiate among the criticisms offered in these terms. Of course, the application of these distinctions is largely a matter of judgment, as the reader may discern in his pattern of agreement or disagreement with the observations that follow. We invite the reader to disagree and come to his own assessment of the NIT Experiment.

As we have indicated throughout the previous chapters, the experimenters attempted to narrow the scope of their research problem by carefully restricting the dimensions of their problem focusing on the limited objective of detecting labor supply response for a select group, the urban-industrial-working poor in intact families. There is no doubt that all research must be reduced to manageable proportions by some choices of the type discussed. It also must be recognized that these choices have a direct and important bearing on the usefulness of results of policy oriented research to policy-makers, not simply in terms of preserving the integrity of the research results themselves but also in terms of shedding light on the pivotal issues of the political questions raised by a policy. When it came down to the congressional debate on FAP, it was evident that while the labor supply question interested some congressmen in a general way, concerns were addressed more to the total costs of a national program, an issue to which the experiment could not offer an answer even when complete. Other congressmen—those who turned out to be the most vigorous opponents of FAP—were also preoccupied with the morality of giving support to non-working males/females at all. Such misgivings were not allayed by evidence that work dropped only modestly in a particular group or any sample. That is, the experimenters established their experimental objective with an eye to testing a piece of established microtheory rather than with a close eye to the hot political questions, apparently counting on OEO to make application of the results in the policy arena.

It has been stressed by the researchers and it is fair to recognize that the NIT Experiment was never conceived by its staff as a prototype negative income tax program but rather as a piece of behavioral research designed to get some information on the "raw materials" of income-conditioned transfer programs. Economic theory predicted that the two most important determinants of work response were the guarantee (or benefit level) and the marginal tax rate, so that an experiment was constructed to see what the "pure" response would be to policy manipulations of these parameters. The choice of an NIT program as a vehicle for these tests was a matter of timely convenience; the estimated responses to the component parameters in theory could be applied as well to the construction of other types of transfer programs. A number of the criticisms cited amount to arguing that although correct for theory testing this may have been an unnecessarily precise approach from the immediate policy standpoint and that to answer some of the most urgent political questions about NIT *as a program* would have required a different approach. Some critics have suggested that a "demonstration" project would have been more appropriate, a viewpoint to which we do not subscribe. A prospective NIT evaluation should have been a program of experiments with universes sampled of particular political relevance.

While an evaluation of the NIT Experiment should hold its principals to the quality of design and execution of research relative to the specific labor supply question posed, a full appreciation of the impact of the NIT on policy and experimentation requires it to be seen against the full sweep of the "welfare problem" to which it was addressed. It is one of the apparent ironies of the experiment that while its motivation sprang from a strong concern with poverty and a desire on the part of both the experimenters and OEO to affect national welfare reform, its most substantial contributions may well be of a more scholarly sort in the areas of experimental design and work behavioral response.

We divide the following comments into those concerning the design and execution of the experiment itself and those relating to the impact of the NIT on national welfare reform efforts and, more generally, on social experimentation as a policy research technique. We find this division useful, because, while there are obvious connections, the NIT was addressed to a very particular question of labor supply whereas many of the relevant and important issues raised by congressional policymakers concerned other questions that were not and could not have been addressed by this experiment. Whether this should be counted as a defect in the experimental design is less clear than the fact that it became a defect of the results for policy use.

CONCERNING THE NIT DESIGN

As we noted in Chapter 2, the designers of the NIT were forced to make a number of decisions about the size, composition, and distribution of the sample, the geographic location of households, and the administrative procedures for carrying out the experiment, each of which necessarily had the effect of restricting the generality and usefulness of results. Given their time and budget constraints, there was no way to avoid making these choices, and the appropriate evaluation issue is the care and ingenuity with which these choices were analyzed as well as their impact on the final policy debate. As the previous chapters indicated, those design choices that lent themselves to formulation in terms of tradeoffs among alternative objectives and the efficient allocation of the budget were analyzed in the utmost detail and with great ingenuity; those that involved familiarity with survey technique and field procedures were settled more perfunctorily; and a few, such as the truncation of the sample by income and the ethnicity factor, simply escaped attention altogether.

First, the choice of the target population as work-eligible male-headed families was based on the logic that these units were likely to be most responsive to the disincentive effects of wage and tax rates and that the political resistance to an NIT focused primarily on the behavior of males rather than on female-headed families. We have found little evidence that either of these assumptions was questioned either at OEO or among the experimenters themselves despite the fact that by so restricting the sample they were eliminating the possibility of testing responses of a large percentage of the poor located in female-headed families. Rather, the intent was to try to identify the maximum work reduction effect of the most sensitive group and by this means to narrow the range of results that had been predicted from previous literature using cross-section data. It seems clear that the ultimate purpose for undertaking this effort in OEO's mind was to be able to make some rough estimates of national program costs for a variety of income-related transfer programs, but since this was not an explicit charge to the NIT itself, the damage done to this ultimate objective by intermediate design decisions aimed at a more restricted objective was not clearly perceived.[1] As it turned out during the debate on FAP many members of Congress showed an equal interest in female work patterns and insisted that female heads be included in work requirements of any reform bill. In all

[1] Note here particularly the point raised as part of the design controversy that those advocating the Watts-Conlisk model allocation had "shifted the objective to minimization of the national cost per family of the NIT due to reduced work effort." Watts has written that the national cost element was introduced "only as a means of inducing differential importance to precision in various parts of the response function" and not with the intent of being able to generate national program cost estimates. Our point is not that the NIT promised national cost estimates, which it did not, but that this was certainly the underlying interest that OEO had in the experiment, so that when the more important design problems flawed the results even for this "sensitivity sample," very little could be salvaged from the experiment to bolster the policy debate in the political arena where national impacts *were* the important question.

fairness, it should be pointed out that subsequent NIT experiments did cover more adequately such issues.

Second, the decision to plan the NIT as a series of "test bores" in a small number of urban sites rather than as a probability sample of some larger population of direct policy interest had the effect of exposing the results to site bias from special features of those particular labor markets.

The experimenters chose the test bore strategy for what they regarded as compelling administrative reasons[2] but having made this judgment apparently failed to follow through with further consideration of its implications for generalizability of results even to other portions of the national urban labor force. A careful analysis preceding this decision would have undoubtedly raised questions about how to sample households, so that inferences about urban poor families could be safely drawn. As it now stands, the four sites are a haphazard sample of convenience. Inter-site variances of some appreciable size raise questions whether this sample is a reasonable base from which to make estimates that would hold for the New York-New Jersey-Pennsylvania urban areas, let alone urban areas in the United States. To argue that the experiment was never intended to produce results generalizable to the nation is unconvincing, especially in light of the reasons given by OEO for funding the research, and it is at least implied in the choice of urban sites that information was sought that would be generalizable to major portions of the wage labor force employed in urban areas.[3]

No doubt this point is more problematical after the fact than it was when the experiment was being designed. This is because the final analyses revealed no substantial response to the two program parameters, the guarantee and the tax rates, around which the design had focused, so that there is a natural tendency to examine the sample for hints about the probable response of the national population to a NIT program. In asking what *can* be learned from the experiment one confronts directly the frustrations of an ungeneralizable sample representing no universe directly useful for the purposes with which the Congress, the administration, or those interested in welfare policy alternatives are concerned.

A third criticism hinges on an oversight, probably stemming from the

[2] A concern of accessibility and worry over relations with local welfare departments as well as the absence of an AFDC-UP plan in New Jersey were the main reasons for rejecting the alternative of a national or regional sampling frame. A check with any of the major sample survey organizations would have revealed that accessibility was not a serious problem. How serious were the problems of welfare department "permission" was a matter of judgment and hence may have been sufficient reason for making a decision to concentrate sampling in a few places.

[3] In the "bad luck" category is the fact that one of the major administrative reasons —absence of an AFDC-UP program—was eliminated during the experiment, so that little was gained in exchange for the "test bore" choice, not even freedom from welfare contamination.

casualness with which sites were chosen, that later turned out to be critical. No attention was paid in the initial design of the sample to the factor of ethnicity. If there had been no reason to suspect that there would be large ethnic differences, then such an omission might be viewed as "bad luck" rather than bad judgment. But there had been considerable attention given in previous literature to the question of whether the employment and earnings patterns of whites and blacks differed in some structurally determined ways or merely differed because of differences in employment-related characteristics, and certainly spoken and unspoken arguments in the political sphere made it plain that racial differences in work response would be an important part of the public policy debate.[4] Not as much attention had been paid to Puerto Ricans but there were sufficient and good a priori reasons to suspect that their work experiences might also differ from those of whites. When it became evident after some enrollment experience in the New Jersey sites that poor households found in the central parts of these cities were disproportionately black and Puerto Rican, a belated effort at increasing the number of white families in the sample by adding another site introduced a further uncontrolled factor of site-ethnicity confounding.[5]

A fourth observation centers on the sample allocation model and the considerations that went into the design controversy described in Chapter 2. It seems to us that the rejection of the ANOVA model was a correct strategy, especially since the secondary hypotheses to the testing of which such an allocation would have been crucial were so poorly formulated and so much more costly per observation than alternative allocations and since it seemed apparent that the Watts-Conlisk formulation could accommodate as complex relations as were likely to be detectable at the level of treatments being applied.

While some of the most interesting contributions to the technique of experimental design derive from this controversy, it appears that the controversy itself was costly to the NIT in terms of time delays and something of a case of misplaced emphasis in light of other more important design problems that emerged in the analysis and from the field experiences.

It also turned out that families in the control group and those in the experimental groups who were above the break-even point were not as in-

---

[4] For example, this question was taken up in considerable detail in Peter M. Blau and Otis D. Duncan, *The American Occupational Structure* (New York: John Wiley and Sons, 1967).

[5] There is some disagreement whether the confounding is large enough to render findings problematic in some way. Although multi-collinearity does not bias regression estimates, it does introduce larger error estimates. Hence, the confounding of site and ethnicity may not affect the sign of a response, but it may make a response of a given magnitude more difficult to detect with a given level of confidence. In short, site-ethnicity confounding reduces the efficiency of the sample.

expensive as projected since it became fairly expensive to motivate families to stay in the study so that the advantage of an allocation that stressed the differential costs of families eligible for payments as compared to those who were not was slighter than supposed.

A further oddity is the fact that despite the experiment's design as an explicit piece of NIT policy research, policy weights were assigned to specific plans within the policy space in a rather casual manner without any clear consultation with policymakers at OEO or in Congress. In consequence the allocation determined using the Watts-Conlisk model reflects primarily the researchers' a priori *notions* of the political importance of alternative plans. We regard this as a curiosity rather than a serious defect since it is not apparent that any consensus could have been elicited from the diffuse interests of congress and administration in any case, but the casualness with which these parameters were set stands in sharp contrast to the extended analysis and debate over other elements of the allocation model.

A fifth criticism of the NIT design is one in which "bad luck" is the real culprit. New Jersey was selected as a site partly because its welfare plan at that time did not cover intact families with able-bodied male breadwinners. The changes made to include such households, instituted by New Jersey within a few months of the start of the fieldwork in Trenton, could not have been anticipated easily. Such changes, however, did affect the nature of the experimental treatments, subjecting them to competition from welfare policy that changed the experiment to one that measured the effects of NIT on work response when added to generous AFDC-UP plans. As such, it was likely to underestimate the impact of NIT considered alone and also when used as a supplement to less generous AFDC-UP (or similar) plans. As we noted earlier, overlaying the experimental treatments with a competing AFDC-UP program made it much more difficult to determine in the final analyses whether the "treatment" was the nominal guarantee and tax rates, the difference between these and the competing AFDC rates, or some even more complex combination of rates with "kinks" at points where there occurred strong incentives to switch from one program to another.

A sixth observation is of an effect that escaped notice altogether until it became apparent from the final analyses. Defining the eligible population for the sample as intact families whose total income was less than 150 percent of the current poverty level resulted in a truncated sample, especially for whites, in which families tended to be larger than the poverty population in general, to have fewer wives in the labor force, to have lower than expected levels of homeownership, and so on.

Watts and his colleagues have suggested since that the sample might have been selected on the basis of the earnings of the major breadwinner with payments conditioned on total family income, a strategy that might well have rectified the low level of wives' labor force participation and some of the other sample peculiarities. Whatever the correct strategy might have been, it is clear that the implications of defining the target population were far-reaching and important. While the consequences of adopting standard poverty definitions established for another purpose were seriously debilitating to the results, the effect was so subtle that we doubt it would have been discerned before it emerged in the final analysis.

A final observation on the design centers on a neglect by the experimenters to think through a full conceptualization of what constitutes an experimental treatment. If we recognize an experimental treatment as *everything an experimenter does* to members of an experimental group that *he does not do* to members of a control group, we must recognize the possibility that part of the experimental response detected might in fact be attributable to different administrative experiences of the two groups. The experimenters attempted to minimize administrative contact with recipients by leaving the initiative to make contacts with field office personnel, and to seek explanations of the various treatments and plans or to raise reporting questions largely up to the families. Yet events occurred that made the administrative side of the experiment for those receiving payments grow larger and more intrusive than perhaps intended. The action of the Mercer County prosecutor led to a heightened concern with the possibility of fraud and the brief televised "exposé" by CBS may have raised anxieties in participating families that their responses were not as anonymous as they (and the researchers) would have wished. These are simply possibilities, and neither we nor the researchers have any evidence to establish or dismiss them as affecting, though unintended, facets of "treatment" in some sites. Clearly, such happenings were beyond the control of the experimenters but nevertheless may have had marginally differential effects on experimental and control groups in the New Jersey sites as well as differential effects between the New Jersey and the Pennsylvania sites. We have already noted one such administrative effect flowing from the relatively more experienced field staff that enrolled and administered the NIT in Scranton after nearly a year of learning by doing in New Jersey.

In a slightly different vein, we note that experimental payments should probably include the $260 per year in filing fees paid to retain experimental families in the sample. This sum represents the equivalent of a wage increase of about four dollars a week to an individual working a thirty-five to forty hour week or about a 4 percent boost in the average family's weekly income conditioned only on filing reports. While control families also received fees for mailing in monthly address cards and for participating in the quarterly interviews, the difference in payments for filing is considerable.

It seems possible that control families would have regarded these incentive payments quite differently from experimental families who received their filing fees as part of their payments checks and hence may have combined them in their minds with the work-conditioned transfer payments. Again, we have no evidence on this and do not regard it as a substantial problem in the NIT case. We merely note such possibilities here to draw the attention of future field experimenters to the fact that administrative features of the design can be as much a part of the experimental treatment as the formal design parameters and that in some cases it may prove to be as interesting to experiment with alternative administrative methods as with other program characteristics.

CONCERNING THE IMPACT ON EXPERIMENTATION TECHNIQUE

In addition to information on the labor supply response of NIT recipients, the experiment yielded a number of lessons about the use and possible misuse of experimentation as a policy analysis technique.

First, the Watts-Conlisk model approach to the design of efficient sample allocations has been adopted by virtually all subsequent income maintenance experiments and has clearly contributed to sorting out the important determinants and assumptions of an optimal design. The value of obtaining efficient designs is apparent when the total cost of such large-scale survey work is considered.

Second, the NIT was undoubtedly a vehicle for training a rather large group of scholars and policy analysts in experimental techniques as well as producing a valuable pool of researchers with much empirical and analytical expertise in the field of poverty, welfare reform, and the construction of income-conditioned transfer programs. Alumni of the NIT are to be found in all major experiments mounted since 1968, as well as in the Office of Policy Analysis in HEW, HUD, and the new Congressional Budget Committee. In this respect the "level of policy debate" on welfare reform, at least among these individuals, was raised substantially.

Third, the relative expensiveness, in both time and money, of experimentation underscores the importance of reserving this technique for instances where there is a precisely defined hypothesis to be tested that cannot be examined satisfactorily with existing survey data. It follows that the behavioral response to be tested must be a complex function of several treatment parameters in which the *magnitude* and not just the direction of response is important to the policy decision.

Fourth, the NIT experience underlines the potential for experimentation with alternative *administrative* techniques as well as with responses to other dimensions of transfer programs. We have noted that one of the more persuasive results of the NIT to congressional opponents was the simple evidence that an NIT could, in fact, be administered without intruding excessively in recipients' lives or requiring an army of bureaucrats for the purpose. Robert Levine has suggested that "administrative experiments" related to existing programs may be more useful than tests of other characteristics of new programs.

Fifth, we can see in the policy history of the NIT the importance of *timing* experimentation to produce results before serious political debate begins and of having an interim product to sustain the interest of policymakers attempting to construct a defensible legislative position. This feature alone suggests that experimentation is not likely to be a promising technique for approaching short-term or cyclical issues; by the same token, the half-dozen areas likely to be of national policy concern three to five years ahead *are* generally distinguishable and can, with enough foresight, be amenable to experimental techniques.

Sixth, a corollary of the previous observation, is the potential for use of experimentation as a *delaying tactic* as one suspects was the case in Congress' "resolving" the FAP issue by authorizing an additional $400 million for further income maintenance experiments to run for at least five more years. This strategy appears destined to produce a repeat of the NIT experience in which the political issue becomes active well before experimental results are available or policymakers adopt some alternative transfer program under pressure to act more quickly.

Seventh, a notable effect of the NIT, especially among economists, has been to focus attention on the inadequacies of much non-experimental (secondary source) data in the fields of income, work, and wage statistics as well as other data series measuring consumption, assets, and savings necessary for the testing of microtheory hypotheses.[6] It is interesting to note that the adoption of poverty as an issue of national policy concern in the 1960s went far to elevate microeconomic issues to a status formerly reserved for the macro issues of unemployment and monetary policy. The care with which the NIT was formulated to test a well-specified aspect of microtheory and the attention it focused on gaps in panel data on individual and household behavior have made economists generally more sensitive to the need for improved survey techniques and primary data collection.

Finally, the NIT experience provides a valuable demonstration of the many and frequently subtle ways in which experimentation must be fitted

---

[6] For the first time, a panel devoted entirely to discussion of survey research techniques was on the program of the American Economic Association's Annual Meeting in December 1973.

to the political policy process on the one hand and to the scholarly process of research on the other in order to ensure the integrity of the research results themselves as well as their usefulness in policy debate. Further, the NIT confirms the suspicion that while experimentation can detect individuals' responses to changes in price and income incentives, these adjustments are much smaller and more complex than researchers are generally inclined to think, a finding which suggests that future experimental treatments will have to be much larger and, by implication, more costly to avoid being swamped by the great variety of exogenous influences on individual behavior.

CONCERNING WORK RESPONSE MEASUREMENT

A consistent theme running through earlier chapters has been a plaintive regret that the important variables relating to work response were not measured more adequately.[7] In designing an experiment as complex as an NIT it is tempting to want to use familiar measures and variables wherever possible, particularly measures that are well established and accepted in the research and policy communities. This saves time and intellectual energy needed for other aspects of the experiment and presumably forestalls any debate that might arise over the role of special measures in the final analyses.

The NIT researchers adopted, apparently without sufficient scrutiny, interviewing instruments of the Current Population Survey and the decennial Census as measures of initial labor force effort for the sample. The individual and household income measures generated by these sources have been extensively criticized in previous literature with general agreement that they are of proximate utility only when used in aggregated form. The researchers began to discover the inadequacy of these standard instruments for measuring the individual responses they were interested in as the data collection progressed and made some subsequent changes in the phrasing of questions on the report forms; in other instances the faultiness of a measure was not discovered until analytical work began on the data, too late to retrieve the entire series for use.

---

[7] This is one point at which the lack of survey experience on the part of the NIT staff shows up most strongly. Anyone with previous experience with household surveys in which income and/or expenditures were critical variables would have proceeded much more cautiously in arriving at operational measures. Certainly this would have been the point to call upon consultation with members of the psychological economics group at the Survey Research Center of the University of Michigan or the medical expenditures group at the Health Information Foundation at the University of Chicago.

In particular, more care and forethought should have gone into measurement of

1. *Pre-experimental earnings, income, wage rates, and hours worked.* It might have been worthwhile to postpone the payment of NIT benefits for a period of some months in order to get base line measures of these variables that would be consistent with those collected throughout the experiment.

2. *Earnings of household members.* The difficulties involved in this measure are not trivial. In addition to the confusion between gross and net income, more attention should have been paid to the problems of capturing earnings from casual labor, wages paid in cash, and other easily forgotten or ignored income in the respondents' reports. This problem of fugitive or forgotten income is important not simply to the NIT research results but also to the practicality of a national NIT administration if one does not wish to replace "armies of intrusive social workers" with armies of intrusive IRS agents.

3. *Wage rates of employed persons.* The labor supply model that lay behind the NIT Experiment is couched in terms of changes in the wage rates of persons subject to NIT payments. Wage rates do vary within the same job depending on differentials between shifts, overtime versus straight time, and so on. The wage rates calculable in the NIT Experiment are derivatives of earnings and reported hours of work and hence are some sort of weighted average of actual wage rates, the exact weighting being unrecoverable in the present series.

4. *Hours worked.* This became the main dependent variable used in tests of labor supply response largely by default and is also subject to reporting ambiguities. The fact that its reliability was not testable from the data collected does not guarantee that it was properly measured or that it contains no bias in experimental versus control comparisons.

5. *Other income.* It is clear from the tests of the NIT income series that this component of reported total family income is the most variable but least identifiable by source or type. It was the source of much of the trouble encountered in auditing monthly reports and the overlapping of NIT benefits with welfare payments. In many respects this is the most interesting source of differences among households since it says something about the ability of units to manipulate their incomes from non-wage sources, a major element in the creation of horizontal inequities in formula transfers.

This loss of information from poor measurement had several consequences: 1) It substantially reduced the amount of analysis and testing that could be done of various response hypotheses, including the main labor supply question, thereby raising the real cost of usable information after the fact well above the cost of designing and administering a single response survey in the first place. 2) In the case of earnings it is known to have biased the labor response of experimental families relative to control families, thereby creating a similar, though untestable, suspicion of the other measures. 3) It eliminated the possibility of cross-checking the labor response results obtained using hours with the alternate indices of earnings and wage rates, thereby also forfeiting a chance to see to what extent NIT payments are used as wage supplements by employers. 4) It made the data bank constructed from the NIT panel data much less useful for integration and use in other studies than originally intended. (The construction of a cross-section panel of micro unit data on the poverty population was an important planned by-product of the experiment, one for which OEO and HEW have supplied substantial funding.)

No doubt, a more careful construction and pretesting of dependent variable measures would have required a delay in getting the experiment into the field, but a delay that would have added significantly to the utility of the final results. Had as much effort gone into testing alternative ways of measuring these variables as into working out the design controversy the final analyses would have been much more convincing. In retrospect, the design controversy, itself the cause of considerable time delay, appears to be a mountain shrunk to mole hill size,[8] while the known and suspected deficiencies in the income, earnings, and hours worked series are defects that increasingly undermine the credibility of the research findings.

CONCERNING OTHER TYPES OF MEASUREMENT

The inattention shown to the details of obtaining accurate measurements of the basic labor supply variables was surpassed by an even greater casualness in the specification of other series of interest. Housing costs, medical care, clothing, entertainment expenditures are particularly poorly measured to the extent that analyses of consumption effects attempted as part of the final analyses rest on faith in the analysts' abilities to patch things up with ingenuity and intuition.

At the least, benign neglect also characterizes the measurement of the non-economic variables. It is clear that the main method of developing measures exercised by the sociologists and social psychologists was the wholesale borrowing of instruments, good and bad, from previous studies that had enough notoriety to come to the attention of the researchers. We have previously noted the absence of any "intervening variables" hypothesis to guide the selection of non-economic measures; under these circumstances it would have been surprising to find detailed attention to the quality of the particular measures collected.

Because the interest in consumption patterns as affected by NIT pay-

---

[8] Especially since cost overruns make the payments to NIT families a minor rather than a major component in total NIT costs.

ments was undoubtedly larger than interest in social psychological effects, the defects in the measurement of the former are more serious than for the latter.

CONCERNING FIELD OPERATIONS

A major achievement of the NIT Experiment was to demonstrate that it was possible to carry out a complicated field experiment over a moderately long period of time. This accomplishment excites admiration.

It is also clear that this accomplishment was one that was achieved by rapid learning in the field. The initial screening operation that located eligible households was less successful than later attempts to enroll families. Similarly, initial attrition rates in Trenton, the first site, were considerably higher than the attrition rates experienced by the last group of families recruited in Scranton. Language difficulties in the questionnaires for the Puerto Rican families were discovered and questionnaires revised accordingly. Field offices learned to check and follow up promptly omitted items on the respondents' reports, and cross-check procedures for welfare fraud were incorporated without serious disruption of the "minimum intrusion" strategy. After a disastrous start, final attrition proportions for the total sample were reduced below those for comparable samples used in other studies[9] demonstrating that by providing appropriate incentives it is possible to remain in relatively close and enduring contact with poor families for an extended period of time. In short, the field operations proved to be flexible, humane, and operable within the confines of budget and time allowances.

CONCERNING THE ANALYSIS OF RESULTING DATA

Reading the volumes of the final report, one cannot avoid being impressed by the sophistication and skill with which the data of the NIT Experiment have been analyzed. The transformation of the basic data series into normal wages, income, and hours (as described in Chapter 5) was accomplished with great skill and the introduction of splines contributed to the advanced analytical education of policymakers and researchers alike. Indeed, the worst that can be said about the analyses performed is that

---

[9] For example, the 5,000 families studied in James Morgan, et al., *Five Thousand Families—Patterns of Economic Progress* (Ann Arbor: Institute for Social Research, 1974), apparently suffered an attrition rate in an annual survey extending over five years of around 67 percent, several magnitudes larger than the 23 percent experienced over a three-year period by the NIT families.

more talent and skill was devoted to this aspect of the study than was warranted by the quality of the basic data series. In addition, the separate analyses comprising the final report of the experiment were conducted in a variety of ways on a series of differently defined subsamples of the full data base, a situation that makes it difficult to get a consistent picture of the full findings. The latter is somewhat frustrating for the reader but not material to interpretation of the findings.

It should also be noted that it is the extremely high quality of the analyses that make this evaluation possible. The NIT researchers were extraordinarily clear and frank about the conduct of the experiment, carefully investigated (when they could) the quality of the data series, explored alternative interpretations, and so forth. The main task of the present authors was to gather together and evaluate findings that are presented in a very open fashion in the volumes of the *Final Report.* This candor and openness makes this study possible.

DRAWING A BALANCE

It should be evident from the preceding that we are most critical of certain design features of the NIT Experiment and of the consequences for failures to feed into the political policy process. The design is flawed in ways that make it impossible to extrapolate from findings to any reasonable universe of the poor who might be the object of welfare reform. The basic variables measuring work response are defective in quality so that we cannot be sure that measurement defects have not swamped (or perhaps exaggerated) whatever NIT payment effects "really exist." And the findings themselves, ignoring the design defects, are frustratingly inconclusive, even for the restricted sample examined.

At the same time, it should be clear that we regard the experiment as a great success administratively and that the analyses were carried out in an excellent fashion. Virtually all the evidence the data can yield on the main labor supply question has been extracted.

What we *did* learn from the experiment was that for that small portion of the poverty population in male-headed, eastern, urban industrial families 1) there is no evidence of massive reductions in work effort attributable to an NIT although 2) the modest responses that do occur are differentiated in both direction and magnitude by race and sex, and 3) there appears to be no sensitivity to the program parameters, g and r. Further, we learned that experimentation is an administratively feasible technique although we suspect that design of administrative features, such as the reporting period, means tests, fraud checks, and data processing arrangements, can have as much effect on the outcome and be of as much use to policymakers as the design and allocation of treatments and the sample itself.

The persuasiveness of these results and what they imply for the construction of a national welfare program have been the subject of knowledgeable debate. Boeckmann[10] has documented the mixed congressional reaction to the experimental results, both preliminary and final, noting that most participants in the FAP debate regarded the findings as "inconclusive," biased by the interests of the researchers, or failing to speak to the active issues of political concern about the FAP. Virtually no interest was shown in designing or fine-tuning a national program using the tax and guarantee rates examined by the NIT. By contrast, Barth et al.[11] have indicated that the results were extensively discussed within HEW and that a number of HEW officials "were willing to revise substantially this belief (in large disincentive effects) in the face of the experimental results and other relevant scientific evidence on labor supply." The academic community has been fascinated by the technical design contributions of the experiment and the demonstration that experimentation is an administratively feasible empirical research technique but has been correspondingly skeptical of the results in light of the kinds of design flaws discussed.

Particular disagreement has evolved around the meaning of non-response to the marginal tax rate with some arguing that this implies that an optimal national NIT program should incorporate very high tax rates in order to maximize the guarantee level for any specified welfare budget allotment while others argue that insensitivity to the tax rate merely means that policymakers are free to design transfer programs on the basis of other than strict efficiency and labor supply criteria.[12] Browning[13] has explored some of the redistributive effects between positive taxpayers and negative tax receivers, while Townsend and Lerman[14] have drawn attention to the politically potent fact that in-kind welfare programs are likely to survive in part because they embody greater inequities in benefits than could be either tolerated or afforded under a simple cash transfer program. The beneficiaries of current transfer programs constitute a client group with political

[10] Margaret Boeckmann, "Policy Impacts of the New Jersey Income Maintenance Experiment" (mimeo, n.d.).

[11] Michael C. Barth, Larry L. Orr, and John H. Palmer, "Policy Implications: A Positive View," in *Work Incentives and Income Guarantee,* eds. Joseph A. Pechman and P. Michael Timpane (Washington, D.C.: The Brookings Institution, 1975).

[12] Bette S. Mahoney and W. Michael Mahoney, "Policy Implications: A Skeptical View," ibid.

[13] Edgar K. Browning, "Income Redistribution and the Negative Income Tax: A Theoretical Analysis" (Ph.D. diss., Princeton University, 1971).

[14] Arthur A. Townsend and Robert I. Lerman, "Conflicting Objectives in Income Maintenance Programs," mimeo (Paper prepared for the Eighty-Sixth Annual Meeting of the American Economic Association, December 30, 1973).

influence that will be used to resist the replacement of current programs, and the NIT results are unable to tell us anything about the effects of pyramiding a cash transfer on top of in-kind programs.

In sum, then, we regard the New Jersey Experiment as setting an important precedent in illustrating the feasibility, and some of the pitfalls, of field experiments as research operations that can cast some light on important policy issues. In our view, however, it would be a mistake to regard the experiment as having provided definitive estimates of what work responses or other responses would be to a national NIT program. We have argued that experimentation is too complex, extended, and expensive a mode of research to be devoted solely to hypothesis-testing without equal weight being given to the evidence it can contribute to active policy issues and that sometimes apparently "technical" design decisions can have profound effects on the policy applicability of experimental findings.

INDEX

Aaron, Henry, 63, 77, 83, 98, 100, 119
Administrative costs, assumed by model, 37
Aid to Families with Dependent Children (AFDC), 4, 134
    AFDC-UP, 9, 69, 75, 134, 181
        absence of, 179
    Aid to Dependent Children (ADC), 141–142
    vs. NIT, 53–54, 165–166
Allen, Vernon, 136, 153
ANOVA, 36, 43
Applied social research
    Field experiments in, 4–5
    NIT as, 4–5
    origins of, 3
Attrition, 188
    rate, maximum, 37
    "survival rate" (u_i), 32
        graph of, 33
    table, 60
Audit Review Panel, 70–71
Audits. *See* Audit Review Panel; Review Board
Avery, Robert, 79

Barth, Michael C., 190
Baumol, William, 14, 36, 39, 169
Bawden, Lee, 160
Blau, Peter M., 180
Blum, Zahava D., 146
Boeckmann, Margaret, 14, 158, 163, 190
Branson, W., 40, 41, 42, 43
Browning, Edgar, 128–129, 190
Burns, Arthur, 159

Cain, Glen, 10, 119, 122, 123, 144
Campbell, Donald T., 42
Community Action Program (CAP), 4, 8
Confidentiality, 162–168
Conlisk, John, 14, 17, 36, 38, 41, 42, 43
Constraints
    budget, 37
    sample size (N), 37
Controls. *See* Sample
Council for Grants to Families (CGF), 46, 57, 65, 70, 71, 74
Current Population Survey, 185

Dependent variables
    hours worked, 87–91
    labor force participation, 87–91
    measures of, 88–104
    See also Wage Rate; Income
Duncan, Otis Dudley, 52, 149, 180
Duncan occupational status scores, 149

Elesh, David, 151
Error variance, assumed, 37
Ethnicity
    effect on labor supply response, 95, 103, 109, 113, 116–117
        females, 121–123
        males, 118, 121–123
    eligibility, 80–81
    national generalization, 127
    in sample design, 55
    by site, 110–111, 180
    See also Race; Sex
Evaluation of experiment, 175–191
    measurement issues, 185–188

Evaluation of experiment (*cont.*)
  NIT design, 177–183
  technique, 183–185

Fair, Jerilyn, 51, 57, 70, 73
Family Assistance Plan (FAP), 64, 102, 158–164, 176
Final Report
  description of, 12, 61
  labor response, 87–88
Friedman, Milton, 63

Garfinkel, Irv, 63, 76, 77
General Accounting Office (GAO), 161–164
Green, Christopher, 15
Guarantee levels, 15–24, 85
GWIE, 42, 43

Hall, Robert, 41–42
Handler, Joel F., 73
Hatt, Paul K., 149
Hawthorne effects, 129
Hollingsworth, Ellen J., 73
Hollister, Robinson, 10, 88, 116, 119, 123, 125
Horner, David, 88, 112
Howell, Joseph, 73
Husby, Ralph, 129

Income
  as dependent variable, 88–104
  normal (*Y*), 100–104
  reliability and reporting error, 93–95
  reporting, 92, 95
Income Report Form (IRF), 65, 67, 68, 69, 92, 123
  overtime on, 72, 73, 89
Income supplements, 92
Institute for Research on Poverty (IRP)
  Final Report, 12, 157–158
  interorganization with Mathematica, 168–173
  staff of, 10, 133

Internal Revenue Service (IRS), 7
  reports, 94

Jersey City (N.J.). *See* Sites
Johnson, Lyndon B., 1, 159

Kershaw, David, 10, 11, 42, 51, 57, 64, 66, 69, 70–71, 73, 102, 158, 160, 165, 168, 169
Knudsen, Jon Helge, 119, 144–145

Labor supply response, 15, 85
  data, 87
  effects of children on, 123–126, 141–148
  families, 123–126, 132
  findings on, 107–131
  hours worked, errors in, 90–91
  married men, 112–118, 132
  measures of, 88–89, 95
  national generalization, 126–129
  summary tables, 130–132
  theoretical models of, 16, 108–110
  underreporting, 93–95
  wives, 99, 119–123, 132
  See also Race; Sex; Ethnicity
Ladinsky, Jack, 144–145, 153, 155
Lefcowitz, Myron J., 151
Lerman, Robert I., 190
Levine, Robert, 33, 184
Lewis, Oscar, 135
Lydey, James, 33

Mahoney, Bette, 102, 190
Mahoney, Michael, 102, 190
Mallar, Charles, 91, 93, 101, 103, 110, 111, 119, 122, 123, 126, 147
Mamer, John, 95, 119
Markov chain analysis, 144–145
Mathematica, 8
  Final Report, 12, 157–158
  interorganization with IRP, 168–173
  vs. Mercer County Prosecutor, 164–166

Mathematica (*cont.*)
staff, 10, 133
Memos, internal, 17, 25, 36, 38, 39, 40, 41
design controversy, by date, 42–43
Mercer County Prosecutor, 54, 62, 164–166
Metcalf, Charles, 10, 128, 138–141
Middleton, Russell, 153, 154, 155
Morris, Carl, 41
Moynihan, Daniel P., 136–142, 159, 160
Multiple constraints allocation, 36

National Health Survey, 151
National Opinion Research Center, 46
National Research Council, 166
Negative Income Tax (NIT)
administration of, 45–60
analytical structure, 15–42
effects, 16
experimental design, 14
explanation of, 6–12
history of (as applied social research), 4–5, 10
"New Jersey Graduated Work Incentive Experiment," 6–10
evaluation of, 175–191
overall assessment, 6, 7
picking, NIT, 175–191
politics of, 157–173
relationship to FAP, 161
testimony on, 160–164
total cost of, 11
Nicholson, Walter, 89, 93, 98, 119, 122, 138–141
Non-labor supply response
conclusions, 137–138
consumption behavior, 138–141
education of adolescents, 146–148
family composition and relationships, 141–145
health, 150–152
Non-labor supply response (*cont.*)
job turnover, unemployment, and job characteristics, 148–150
social/psychological variables, 152–155

Office of Economic Opportunity (OEO), 1, 3–5, 6, 8, 9, 33, 40, 133, 157–164, 165
O'Hare Allocation, 35, 37
Opinion Research Corporation, 46
Orcutt, Alice, 41, 168
Orcutt, Guy, 41, 168
Orr, Larry L., 190

Palmer, John H., 190
Passaic (N.J.). *See* Sites
Paterson (N.J.). *See* Sites
Patterson, Geoffrey, 163
Payments
experimental vs. welfare, 75–85
system of, 64–68
Pechman, Joseph A., 74, 190
Peck, Jon, 61
Perlman, Richard, 17
Poirier, Dale, 91, 93, 97, 101, 103, 104, 110, 111
Policy space, 18–21
diagram of, 19
explanation of, 18–21
Policy weights, 32–34
table, 37
Politics, 157–173
early disclosure, 158–164
external, 166–168
internal, 168–172
Population frequency, 37
Princeton University. *See* Mathematica

Quarterly interviews, 69

Race, effects on response, 98, 99, 101, 103, 113, 114, 115, 116–118, 122–127, 131–132
in employment rates, 116–118
by sample, 110–111

Race, effects on response (*cont.*)
  See also Ethnicity; Sex
Rand Health Insurance Experiment, 41, 82
Rees, Albert, 8, 30, 91, 169, 171
Reiss, Albert, 149
Review Board, 71
Ribicoff, Abraham, 163
Ross, Heather, 8, 23, 25, 34, 38, 39, 168, 169
Rossi, Peter H., 136–137, 146
Rural Income Maintenance Experiment, 160

Sample
  allocation, alternatives, 34–36
  allocation, by income stratum, 23
  allocation, by plan, 23–24, 111
  allocation, by race, 54–55, 111
  allocation, by site, 23, 54–55, 111
  allocation, final, 23–24, 111
  allocation, theory of, 19–21
  attrition of, 59–61
  characteristics of, 51–52
  selection of, 47–51
  size, 47, 110–112
  See also ANOVA; Multiple Constraints Allocation; O'Hare; Tobin solution; Watts-Conlisk model
Schultz, George, 159
Scott, Robert, 119, 144
Scranton (Pa.). *See* Sites
Sex
  effects on response, 99, 107, 112, 119–127, 131–132
  head of household, 112–118
  wives, 119–123
  See also Ethnicity; Race
Shore, Arnold A., 119, 144
Sites
  consequences of, 53–55
  distribution of sample by, 110–112
  interviews by, 57
  Jersey City, N.J., 39, 54

Sites (*cont.*)
  labor market differential, 149
  Passaic, N.J., 95
  Paterson, N.J., 95
  Scranton, Pa., 39, 95, 99, 103
  selection of, 9, 75–77, 179–181
  Trenton, N.J., 97, 99
Social Security
  Act, 1967, 7
  measures of validity, reports as, 72–73, 92, 94–95
Spilerman, Seymour, 51, 148–150, 155, 172
Spline technique, 97, 101, 109, 110
  explanation of, 104–106
Stanley, Julian, 42
Storey, James, 102
Survey Research Center, 4, 46

Taussig, Michael, 51, 111
Tax rates, 85
  marginal, 15–24
  nominal vs. actual, 74, 78
"Test bore" strategy, 53, 62, 179
Timpane, P. Michael, 74, 190
Tobin, James, 14, 21–24, 32, 36, 38–42
  compromise, 169–170
Tobin solution, 14, 36–37, 38–42, 111
Townsend, Alair, 102
Townsend, Arthur A., 190
Treatments, experimental, 63–68
Trenton (Mercer County, N.J.). *See* Sites

U.S. Department of Health, Education, and Welfare (HEW), 5, 108, 190
Urban Opinion Surveys, 46. *See also* Mathematica

Wage rate, 16
  ethnicity, 98–99
  females, 99
  normal ($\hat{w}$), 95–100, 103–104
  See also Labor supply response
War on Poverty, 1, 3

Watts, Harold, 10, 14, 17, 25, 33, 36, 42, 43, 64, 88, 92, 93, 95, 97, 101, 103, 104, 110, 111, 112, 113, 114, 115, 116, 117, 125, 160, 181
  on confidentiality, 64
Watts-Conlisk model, 14, 25–38
  budget constraint, 28, 37
  objective function (Q), 27, 36
  policy weights, 32–34, 37
  response cost (C_i), 26–27, 37
  response function (Z), 25, 37
  "vanishing point" (M), 30–31, 37
Ways and Means Committee, hearings on FAP, 160–164
Welfare,
  differences with experimental treatment, 66–69, 72, 75–83, 85
  eligibility levels, 68, 83
  fraud, 164
  See also AFDC
Wells, Anna, 144–145, 153, 155
Williams, John J., 162–163, 164
Wisconsin, University of. *See* Institute for Research on Poverty
Wooldridge, Judith, 52, 119, 122, 138–141
Wright, Sonia, 153, 154